A HISTORICAL GUIDE TO
Nathaniel Hawthorne

HISTORICAL GUIDES
TO AMERICAN AUTHORS

The Historical Guides to American authors is an interdisciplinary, historically sensitive series that combines close attention to the United States' most widely read and studied authors with a strong sense of time, place, and history. Placing each writer in the context of the vibrant relationship between literature and society, volumes in this series contain historical essays written on subjects of contemporary social, political, and cultural relevance. Each volume also includes a capsule biography and illustrated chronology detailing important cultural events as they coincided with the author's life and works, while photographs and illustrations dating from the period capture the flavor of the author's time and social milieu. Equally accessible to students of literature and of life, the volumes offer a complete and rounded picture of each author in his or her America.

A Historical Guide to Ernest Hemingway
Edited by Linda Wagner-Martin

A Historical Guide to Walt Whitman
Edited by David S. Reynolds

A Historical Guide to Ralph Waldo Emerson
Edited by Joel Myerson

A Historical Guide to Henry David Thoreau
Edited by William E. Cain

A Historical Guide to Edgar Allan Poe
Edited by J. Gerald Kennedy

A Historical Guide to Nathaniel Hawthorne
Edited by Larry J. Reynolds

A
Historical Guide
to Nathaniel Hawthorne

EDITED BY
LARRY J. REYNOLDS

OXFORD
UNIVERSITY PRESS

2001

OXFORD
UNIVERSITY PRESS

Oxford   New York

Athens   Auckland   Bangkok   Bogotá   Buenos Aires   Cape Town
Chennai   Dar es Salaam   Delhi   Florence   Hong Kong   Istanbul   Karachi
Kolkata   Kuala Lumpur   Madrid   Melbourne   Mexico City   Mumbai   Nairobi
Paris   São Paulo   Shanghai   Singapore   Taipei   Tokyo   Toronto   Warsaw

and associated companies in
Berlin   Ibadan

Copyright © 2001 by Oxford University Press, Inc.

Published by Oxford University Press, Inc.
198 Madison Avenue, New York, New York 10016

Oxford is a registered trademark of Oxford University Press.

Library of Congress Cataloging-in-Publication Data
A historical guide to Nathaniel Hawthorne / edited by Larry J. Reynolds.
p.   cm. — (Historical guides to American authors)
Includes bibliographical references and index.
ISBN 0-19-512413-8; — ISBN 0-19-512414-6 (pbk.)
1. Hawthorne, Nathaniel, 1804–1864—Criticism and interpretation.
2. Literature and history—United States—History—19th century.
3. Literature and society—United States—History—19th century.
I. Reynolds, Larry J. (Larry John), 1942– .   II. Series.
PS1838.H57   2001
811'.3—dc21   00-058917

1 3 5 7 9 8 6 4 2

Printed in the United States of America
on acid-free paper

For Susan

"Content to linger just beyond history."

Contents

A HISTORICAL GUIDE TO
Nathaniel Hawthorne

Introduction

Larry J. Reynolds

With the publication of *Twice-Told Tales* in 1837, Nathaniel Hawthorne gained recognition as an important American author; "a new star rises in the heavens," declared his friend Henry Wadsworth Longfellow in a review of the book.[1] Some thirteen years later, with the publication of *The Scarlet Letter* (1850), Hawthorne joined the ranks of America's greatest writers. "None but a man of true genius and a highly cultivated mind could have written it," declared a typical contemporary review. "It is a work of rare, we may say of fearful power."[2] During the 150 years since the publication of his masterpiece, Hawthorne has continued to occupy a central place in the American literary canon despite major shifts in critical fashions and reading tastes. Although recent scholarship has revealed the ways that influential friends, editors, and publishers assisted in the construction of Hawthorne's literary reputation,[3] his short stories and novels continue to speak to a reading public fascinated by stories of sin and guilt and by exceptional individuals struggling with themselves and repressive institutions. Hawthorne's famous moral ambiguity, his rich visual imagination, his deep exploration of the dreamscapes of individuals, communities, and the nation, and especially his "power of blackness," as Melville called it, are distinguishing features of his achievement and help explain his durability as an American classic author.

The vast critical commentary devoted to Hawthorne's writings throughout the twentieth century provides ample evidence of the strength and diversity of his appeal. In *Our Old Home* (1863), Hawthorne relates the effect of gazing upon the Cathedral of Lichfield, which becomes "a kind of kaleidoscopic mystery, so rich a variety of aspects did it assume from each altered point of view," and the same can be said about many of his works.[4] With each new critical perspective, a new aspect of his writings has come into view. Psychoanalytic critics, for example, long ago noticed and praised the depth and acuity of his studies of hidden sin. Countless New Critics have discussed the artfulness of his structural patterns and the brilliance of his symbolism, irony, and narrative techniques. Literary historians have traced his major contributions to the genres of the short story and the American romance. And feminists have observed and continue to debate the implications of his treatments of victimized women.

In the last fifteen years of the twentieth century, as Leland S. Person points out in his chapter, "Hawthorne and History," an abundance of New Historicist scholarship has focused attention on Hawthorne's engagement with contemporary social and political contexts, and the result has been a more worldly Hawthorne than the Great Artist admired and explicated so well by the New Critics. Readers have been made aware of the subtle ways in which Hawthorne's writings respond to his own times as they draw upon the past. *The Scarlet Letter*, for example, though set within the Puritan world of seventeenth-century Boston, reacts to a number of mid–nineteenth-century developments, such as the European revolutions of 1848, the Women's Rights Movement, and the growing controversy over slavery in the United States.[5] The novel, in other words, is product and producer of the culture surrounding it.

A Historical Guide to Nathaniel Hawthorne recognizes and extends this historical approach to Hawthorne by placing his works within specific contexts to help illuminate original meanings often hidden from us by the passage of time and the changes in our circumstances and values. Hawthorne represented himself in his letters and prefaces as a shy, reclusive artist, yet the chapters in this volume show his interest in and responses to a number of key concerns of his day, including the mysteries of mesmerism, changing concepts of childhood and childrearing, the development of the visual arts, and the question of slavery. The Hawthorne who emerges here displays a number of traits and attitudes that may seem unattractive today, yet to his credit hypocrisy is one he tried hard to avoid. He well understood the darker side of human nature, especially his own, and self-criticism was a dominant, if submerged, feature of his life and his art.

Brenda Wineapple, in her brief biographical sketch, points out that Hawthorne's life was marked by opacity and ambivalence, which are also key features of his writings. He was a wily man, prone to concealment, duplicity, and flight, yet he could also be openly aggressive, hostile, and contentious, especially when responding to threats to his livelihood or the well-being of his family and friends. His wife, Sophia, long considered the ideal Victorian "angel in the house," was also "a mighty woman," as Wineapple shows, often critical of others and adept at asserting her will. Although Hawthorne was attracted to and identified with strong women, his fiction often subjects them to humiliation, suffering, and death, and, as Wineapple explains, here, too, ambivalence is the key: he "wrote compellingly of a feminism that attracted and repelled him." Not coincidentally, the woman with whom Hawthorne experienced the most conflicted relationship of his life, Margaret Fuller, was the leading feminist of the age.[6]

Women's rights, however, was but one of many reform movements, known collectively as the "Newness," that surrounded and stimulated Hawthorne in antebellum America. During his lifetime (1804–1864), which spanned the first half of the nineteenth century, the United States transformed from a small, slow-paced agricultural nation into a rapidly growing, competitive, urban, industrialized one, and these changes were accompanied and challenged by a host of religious and social reform movements, including millennialism, transcendentalism, associationism, mesmerism, spiritualism, vegetarianism, temperance, and abolitionism. Hawthorne studied many of these movements closely and discerned their weaknesses, which he most often attributed to fallible human nature—as in "Earth's Holocaust" (1844)—yet he was often appreciative of the spirit that impelled them, sometimes sharing it himself. As a young man, he thought for a time about joining the Shakers (a utopian religious sect known for its emphasis on celibacy and chastity); he subscribed to many of the tenets of transcendentalism (especially the belief that nature is the symbol of spirit); and he joined the utopian Brook Farm community at West Roxbury, Massachusetts, devoting himself for a time to the success of the project, though he was certain it would fail. Later, in works such as "The Celestial Railroad" (1843), "The Hall of Fantasy" (1843), and *The Blithedale Romance* (1852), he satirized reformers and reform movements, including a utopian commune based on Brook Farm.

Hawthorne's world was distinguished from ours not only by the "Newness" but also by its relatively small size and rural character. Although the United States would establish itself as a powerful, industrial nation during the course of the nineteenth century, when Hawthorne was born in 1804, its total population was only some 6 million (compared to 281 million in 2000), and 90 percent of Americans lived on farms (compared to 25 percent in 2000). His college class at Bowdoin had only 38 students; his entire college 108. Most of the population of the young nation was concentrated on the eastern seaboard, looked across the Atlantic for models in literature and art, and considered the "West," which was Ohio, Illinois, and the Great Lakes region, a primitive, uncivilized place.

Like a number of his artistic contemporaries, such as James Fenimore Cooper, Longfellow, and Melville, Hawthorne felt the need to achieve American literary independence from England and to establish an indigenous literature worthy of comparison with the tradition of Shakespeare, Milton, and the immensely popular Sir Walter Scott. Soon after the War of 1812, editors and authors began to urge the use of American history and legend as a means of establishing a national literature, and Hawthorne, responding to this suggestion, read widely in New England history during his years of literary apprenticeship. His interest in this history was enhanced by the roles his ancestors had played in it. His great-grandfather John Hathorne, for example, had been one of the judges in the infamous Salem witchcraft trials, and Hawthorne's treatment of the complexities of witchcraft in stories such as "Young Goodman Brown" (1835) thus combines national and familial regard.

While living in Salem after graduating from college in 1825, Hawthorne occasionally walked to a particular barren elevation on the western side of town known as Gallows Hill, where nineteen persons had been executed as a result of the witchcraft trials in 1692. Although a sense of Satan's presence had receded into the past by the 1820s and '30s, belief in the power of the supernatural had not. The eighteenth-century enlightenment (best represented in America by Benjamin Franklin, Thomas Jefferson, and Thomas Paine), had ushered in the secularization of American culture, but superstitions persisted, even for college-educated men such as Hawthorne. Ghosts, specters, and haunted houses still constituted a very real feature of American life, and in April 1842, Hawthorne himself saw a ghost in the Boston Athenaeum for several days, an apparition of Dr. Thaddeus Harris. Later, during 1842–46, when he lived at the "Old Manse" in Concord with his new wife, Sophia, they felt the presence of a ghost in the house. One night, it even touched Sophia as she lay in bed with her husband.[7] "I am still incredulous," he wrote in September 1858, while in Florence, "both as to the Doctor's ghostly identity and as to the reality of the mysterious touch."[8]

Many of the pseudosciences, such as mesmerism, spiritualism, physiognomy, phrenology, and homeopathy, which rose to popularity in the antebellum period, captivated Hawthorne's interest and shaped his fiction. As Samuel Chase Coale points out in his chapter, "Mysteries of Mesmerism: Hawthorne's Haunted House," mesmerism affected not only the content but also the method of Hawthorne's writings. Coale traces the history of mesmerism from its beginnings in eighteenth-century France through its popularization in the United States in the 1830s to its metamorphosis into spiritualism in the 1850s. For Hawthorne, mesmerism was a dangerous practice, which allowed one person to violate the soul of another, and he gave a number of the villains in his works the ability to induce mesmeric trances. Matthew Maule's powers as a mesmerist, for example, are central to *The House of the Seven Gables* (1851), and Coale argues that Hawthorne himself sought through his own narrative techniques to mimic the mesmerist and ensnare the reader in "a kind of dark trance," knowing full well this made him, too, "a kind of spiritual villain."

Perhaps the one institution that changed the most in antebellum America, even more than religion and science, was the middle-class family. The emerging market-centered economy, characterized by booms and busts, had transformed the family, creating new divisions of labor and the belief that men and women had been assigned, by God, to separate spheres: the masculine marketplace and the femininized home, respectively. In prerevolutionary America, the family had been a public institution engaged for the most part in farming and home manufacturing, but during the first decades of the nineteenth century, it became a private institution centered upon marital companionship and the care of children.

The fragility and brevity of life focused considerable attention on death and mourning, particularly when children were stricken. In 1804, when Hawthorne was born, life expectancy was only thirty-eight years for men, forty for women, compared to seventy-three and eighty in 2000, and one out of every eight infants died during birth. Families became increasingly smaller throughout the nineteenth century; family size, which averaged more than seven in 1800, dropped to about five by 1850, in part because children had become economic burdens rather than assets. As the nature and size of the family altered, the value it placed on individual children increased, stimulated by a new romantic sensibility. The child, Wordsworth wrote, came into the world "trailing clouds of glory," and many Americans acted upon this belief.

Images of the new middle-class family in antebellum America were drenched in sentiment, and educational reformers debated the best way to raise healthy, talented, pious children. The Hawthornes, skeptical of the abilities of anyone else to teach their precious Una, Julian, and Rose, chose to home-school their son and two daughters. Nevertheless, during the 1840s, the United States experienced a revolution in education, which was led by Hawthorne's brother-in-law Horace Mann, who pioneered the Common School movement. As the public schools proliferated, so, too, did related means of education, such as academies, colleges, libraries, lyceums, manuals, tracts, journals, books, and newspapers. The invention of the steam-powered cylindrical press brought about a drop in the price of printed material and a surge in its volume, which helped create a mass reading audience. Hawthorne had taken little interest in his own formal education due to a "natural repugnance" toward it, but at the beginning of his writing career, he participated in and sought to profit from this revolution in education, first by compiling the mass-produced children's book *Peter Parley's Universal History* (1837) for Samuel Goodrich's series of textbooks and then through his own books of histories and biographies for children, including *Grandfather's Chair* (1841), *Famous Old People* (1841), *Liberty Tree* (1841), and *A Wonder-Book for Girls and Boys* (1852).

Gillian Brown, in her chapter, "Hawthorne and Children in the Nineteenth Century: Daughters, Flowers, Stories," addresses Hawthorne's innovative approaches to writing about children and childrearing. She traces changing conceptions of the child from Puritan colonial times to Hawthorne's present, focusing on the importance of the figure of the salvific child featured in abolitionist and temperance literature, such as Little Eva of *Uncle Tom's Cabin* (1852) and Mary Morgan of *Ten Nights in a Bar-Room* (1852). Hawthorne, Brown shows, both exemplified and criticized the nineteenth-century American imaginative practice of using children as agents of moral reform, and in works such as "The Gentle Boy" (1831), "Rappaccini's Daughter" (1844), and "The Golden Touch" (1852), he explores the abuse of children by bad parenting and the ways children could resist this abuse through their own agency. Although Brown does not discuss Hawthorne's life, she does note the difficulties he faced with his own children, especially Una, whose psychic disorders have been attributed to the Hawthornes' intense parenting.[9] Long after Hawthorne's death, his son, Julian, was convicted of mail fraud and spent a year in a federal penitentiary, while daughter Rose founded an order of nuns devoted to caring for incurable cancer patients.

For young people or, rather, young men of means in antebellum American society, travel abroad—preferably a Grand Tour of England, France, Germany, and Italy lasting a year or more—was regarded as a necessary conclusion to a complete education. Historians George Ticknor and George Bancroft, artists Thomas Cole and Washington Allston, sculptors Horatio Greenough and Thomas Crawford, as well as such authors as Irving and Cooper all traveled and lived in Europe to round out their educations and satisfy their romantic yearnings for the past, especially the grandeurs of ancient Greece and Rome and the antiquities of the Middle Ages. Hawthorne shared his predecessors' interest in the Old World, not least because he thought it congenial to the kind of romance writing he did. "Romance and poetry, ivy, lichens, and wallflowers," he declared in his often-quoted preface to *The Marble Faun* (1860), "need ruin to make them grow."[10]

Though drawn to the Old World, Hawthorne did not have the opportunity to go abroad until fairly late in his career; nevertheless, the experience proved nourishing. As Rita K. Gollin shows in her chapter, "Hawthorne and the Visual Arts," during seven years abroad (1853–60), Hawthorne expanded and enhanced his understanding of the visual arts, becoming fascinated by the interrelations among the artist, the art, and the spectator. Early in his career, Gollin points out, he had paid close attention to American painters and their methods for achieving certain effects in their works. The techniques they used to capture inner realities intrigued him, especially in portrait painting, the dominant genre of the time. For Hawthorne, the portrait often served as a means of Gothic effects, connecting this world to the ghostly past, as in his stories "The Prophetic Pictures" (1837) and "Edward Randolph's Portrait" (1838). As Gollin points out, while abroad, his understanding of art as a locus of moral perception and self-perception acquired new depth and sophistication. His last complete romance, *The Marble Faun*, benefited as a result, and in it, one sees a new emphasis on "the spectator's own character and prior experience."

Recently, Nancy Bentley has shown that this novel also engages the contemporary issue of racialism through its association of Miriam with the figure of the southern mulatta and Donatello with a politics of primitivism.[11] In an 1862 essay, Hawthorne compared a group of escaped slaves he had observed to "fauns and rustic deities of olden times," thus revealing how he and his conservative contemporaries could use the discourse of primitivism to displace an anxious social reality into the pleasing fabulous past.[12] Though willfully detached from the slavery controversy, Hawthorne, as Jean Fagan Yellin shows in her chapter, "Nathaniel Hawthorne and the Slavery Question," had ample opportunity to learn about chattel slavery, to encounter enslaved Africans, and to ponder their character and fate. Yellin marshals compelling evidence from Hawthorne's *Notebooks*, from the social history of Salem, and from books he read and wrote to show that, although he was familiar with Africans (even employing one free black as a servant to care for his house and children), he was still uncertain about their full humanity and was willing to imply in writing that black skin denoted a blackened soul. The Black Man of *The Scarlet Letter*, Yellin suggests, reveals Hawthorne's—and his readers'—repressed anxiety about black sexuality and the presence of "a dangerous dark group within society's midst."

By placing Hawthorne within specific contexts of antebellum America, this volume helps to reveal the extent to which this reserved, taciturn individual addressed the times as well as the eternities as he wrote. The chronologies and illustrations included here are meant to provide additional understanding of the texture of his world. While Hawthorne clearly preferred to be known as the daydreaming recluse of his own self-fashioning, the grounding of his writings in his own social reality yields a far more interesting and artful author, one who struggled with issues that still haunt us today.

NOTES

1. *North American Review* 45 (July 1837), rpt. *Nathaniel Hawthorne: Critical Assessments*, ed. Brian Harding, 4 vols. (Mountfield, England: Helm Information, 1998), 1:64.

2. *Brownson's Quarterly Review* 4 n.s. (Oct. 1850), rpt. *ibid.*, 1:266.

3. See, especially, Jane Tompkins, *Sensational Designs: The Cultural*

Work of American Fiction, 1790–1860 (New York: Oxford University Press, 1985), and Richard Brodhead, *The School of Hawthorne* (New York: Oxford University Press, 1986).

4. Nathaniel Hawthorne, *Our Old Home: A Series of English Sketches* (1863), rpt. *The Centenary Edition of the Works of Nathaniel Hawthorne* (Columbus: Ohio State University Press, 1970), 5:124–25.

5. See, for example, Larry J. Reynolds, "*The Scarlet Letter* and Revolutions Abroad," *American Literature* 57 (1985): 44–67; Jonathan Arac, "The Politics of *The Scarlet Letter,*" in *Ideology and Classic American Literature,* ed. Sacvan Bercovitch and Myra Jehlen (Cambridge, Mass.: Harvard University Press, 1986), 247–66; and Sacvan Bercovitch, "Hawthorne's A-Morality of Compromise," *Representations* 24 (1988): 1–27.

6. For the most substantial study of this relationship, see Thomas R. Mitchell, *Hawthorne's Fuller Mystery* (Amherst: University of Massachusetts Press, 1998).

7. For an account of Hawthorne's encounter with Harris, see "The Ghost of Doctor Harris," in *Centenary* 23:382–89.

8. *Centenary* 14:419.

9. See T. Walter Herbert, *Dearest Beloved: The Hawthornes and the Making of the Middle-Class Family* (Berkeley: University of California Press, 1993).

10. *Centenary* 4:3.

11. Nancy Bentley, "Slaves and Fauns: Hawthorne and the Uses of Primitivism," *ELH* 57 (1990): 901–37.

12. *Centenary* 23:420.

Nathaniel Hawthorne
1804–1864

A Brief Biography

Brenda Wineapple

> It is remarkable that persons who
> speculate the most boldly often con-
> form with the most perfect quietude to
> the external regulations of society.
>> Nathaniel Hawthorne,
>> *The Scarlet Letter*

> Life is made up of marble and mud.
>> Nathaniel Hawthorne,
>> *The House of the Seven Gables*

Since the publication of *The Scarlet Letter* in 1850 and certainly after his death in 1864, Hawthorne has become a national prodigy routing skeletons out of New England closets long before Stephen King. And, like one of his own—or King's—characters, Nathaniel Hawthorne of Salem, Massachusetts, born on the Fourth of July 1804, often seems enigmatic and impenetrable. Searched and seized and, more frequently than not, diagnosed, even by contemporaries, he has nonetheless kept what he called the "Inmost Me" behind the veil.

Partly, the problem of his inscrutability lies with Hawthorne himself. He was a wily, watchful man who gave little away. He evidently burned his manuscripts periodically as well as letters sent to him, and he entreated friends to destroy all correspondence. He tried to suppress information about his first novel, *Fanshawe*, shortly after its anonymous publication in 1828. Indeed, the man who coveted fame as a writer often published his first tales on the condition of anonymity or used a pseudonym. Even as late as 1840, he occasionally hid his identity by choice, employing fictional names like Ashley Allen Royce.

If concealment was Hawthorne's keynote, so was ambivalence. Wary of his patrician cognomen—originally Hathorne, it was he who changed it to Hawthorne—and abashed by its blood-soaked past (his ancestors participated, in no small way, in the witchcraft trials, his great-grandfather, John Hathorne [1641–1717] being one of the judges), he nonetheless prized the antique pedigree so dear to New Englanders. To a certain extent, he was like one of his most colorful creations. He savored the exquisite elegance of a tea service from China but was a lifelong, cigar-smoking Democrat who profited from and dispensed party favors. He would not abide a cracked or broken dish on the table, and he detested anything, or anyone, he deemed ugly, particularly women. He was something of an aristocratic huckster, as he described his character Hepzibah Pyncheon, simultaneously proud of and shamed by his delicate sensibility, which he regarded as both elitist and feminine—as was the profession of author. "What is he?" Hawthorne imagined one of his illustrious, hard-bitten forefathers snorting, nothing but "a writer of story-books!"[1]

His father and namesake, Nathaniel Hathorne, was a ship's captain who died in Surinam of yellow fever in 1808, leaving a widow, a son, and two daughters. The son, the only male heir on both sides of the family, was clearly adored, especially by the Mannings, the maternal relatives with whom the bereft Hathornes now lived. Nathaniel grew up in a bustling, busy household. His Manning grandparents and three Manning aunts and five uncles, all unwed, dwelled in the commodious wooden building (then called, perhaps with irony, a mansion) on Salem's Herbert Street, not far from the wharves. Yet, within this large group, Elizabeth Manning Hathorne and her three children were an enclave, tenants in another's home—they paid for their board—living on the third story of the house for ten years.

Ever since he was a young boy, Nathaniel loved to read, according to his doting sister Elizabeth, who recalled her younger brother as a six-year-old sitting in a corner with a fat volume of Bunyan's *Pilgrim's Progress* on his lap. He might not have understood a word, she mischievously added, but he certainly liked to impress the family. Furthermore, he likely took to constant reading after an accident to his foot incapacitated him in the fall of 1813. Afterward, when the injured foot did not develop as fully as the other, he had to wear a heavily lined boot for support and limp about on crutches. His mother was anxious about a deformity in her only son, and conversely, he hated her cloying devotion but was unable, or unwilling, to free himself of it.

Never explaining the nature of the injury, Hawthorne merely remarked that, as a consequence, he did not go to school as much as other boys because of the "delicate health which I made the most of for the purpose."[2] While his ailment seems not to have haunted him as demonstrably as did Henry James's "horrid even if obscure hurt,"[3] Hawthorne nonetheless saw himself early as one apart, marked and wounded, a victim with a special destiny who was, at the same time, as angry as the lame child in the story "The Gentle Boy." In fact, like that child's, Hawthorne's health was a matter of some family concern, for not long after his foot healed, he again fell ill and, at least according to his sister, strangely lost the use of his limbs. The family took out the crutches again, lengthening them to suit Hawthorne's taller frame. The doctors, however, could find nothing physically wrong with the boy.

The Manning family owned extensive land parcels in Maine near Sebago Lake, and shortly after the death of Grandfather Manning in 1813, Nathaniel's eldest Manning uncle, Richard, moved to Raymond, Maine, in anticipation of what he hoped would be the entire Manning-Hathorne clan's eventual departure from Salem. That never occurred, but the Hathornes did spend the summer of 1816 in Raymond. Nathaniel bloomed. He loved the outdoors, the long winding walks around the shore of Sebago Lake; he caught salmon trout in a nearby river; and he liked to hunt so much that one of his aunts chided him about overusing his gun. To her children's delight, two years later, in 1818, the Widow Hathorne decided to move permanently to Maine and to occupy the house that Uncle Richard had expectantly built.

When her health, never robust, began to improve, Elizabeth Hathorne's recovery in Maine resembled her son's, for not only did she and Nathaniel resemble one another physically, with their raven-dark hair and fine gray eyes, their bond transcended appearances.[4] Hawthorne was later to observe that "there has been, ever since my boyhood, a sort of coldness of intercourse between us, such as is apt to come between persons of strong feelings," but their feelings reached deep.[5] Both, for instance, dreaded separations. The first occurred in the winter of 1819 when Nathaniel went to board in Stroudwater, near Portland, and to attend school nearby. Homesick and refusing to go back there, he was instead sent to Salem to live with the Mannings.

This separation from his mother had been Uncle Robert Manning's decision. Though younger than his brother Richard, as Nathaniel's guardian and the paterfamilias, Robert presided over not just investments and business ventures but all matters of Nathaniel's education. A complicated, somewhat narrow man, worldly, ambitious, and pretentious, Robert nonetheless recognized in his nephew both aptitude and talent. Nathaniel, however, sulked. "I am extremely homesick," he wrote his mother in an oft-quoted letter, lamenting, "Why was I not a girl that I might have been pinned all my life to my Mother's apron."[6]

In 1821, Hawthorne left Salem for Bowdoin College in Brunswick, Maine. Nervous about his entrance exams, he was encouraged by Uncle Robert, who, however insensitive, wanted the best for his nephew. Years later, a relative recalled that Nathaniel went to Bowdoin both because it was inexpensive—Robert carefully administered the family purse—and because of the family business connections nearby.[7] But Nathaniel probably chose the sweet pines of Bowdoin at least partly to be close to his mother and sisters, who still lived in Raymond.

Mother, Maine, and the rustic living preferred by Uncle

Richard constitute in Hawthorne's writing an affective connection running counter to the authority of the priggish Parson Thumpcushions of the world, or Hawthorne's caricature of a small-minded, small-town guardian. In addition, narratives of departure and projected or disappointed return also pervade Hawthorne's work, frequently echoing the more undisguised plaints of his earliest writing. In 1820, for example, Hawthorne devised a family newspaper, presumably to link the Maine and Salem branches, to which he contributed short essays. His first subject was separations: "There is no idea more unfounded than the supposition that the pains of a seperation [*sic*] are repaid by the pleasure of a meeting."[8] To Hawthorne, the pains of separation turn one into a stranger, even in one's home town. Thus, Hawthorne, who already conceived of himself as something of an outsider, aptly named his family paper the *Spectator*—reflecting homage to Addison and Steele while inaugurating the metaphor that describes so many of his fictional characters, from Wakefield and Parson Hooper to Clifford Pyncheon and Miles Coverdale.

At college, Hawthorne was averse to committing himself to a conventional profession. With his sense of pride and aristocratic entitlement, he resolutely defined himself in opposition to the bourgeois Uncle Robert, who by then ran a profitable stage coach company. Hawthorne scorned a common fate and declined a predictable profession, explaining in a justly celebrated letter that the

> being of a Minister is of course out of the Question. I should not think that even you could desire me to choose so dull a life. . . . As to Lawyers there are so many of them already that one half of them (upon a moderate calculation) are in a state of actual starvation. A Physician then seems to be "Hobson's Choice," but yet I should not like to live by the diseases and Infirmities of my fellow Creatures.

Rather, he preferred "becoming an Author, and relying for support upon my pen."[9]

If Hawthorne began to consider authorship at Bowdoin, he nonetheless distinguished himself little except in friendship, for at college he met his lifelong confidants, Horatio Bridge and Franklin Pierce, both instrumental in shaping Hawthorne's career. Although neither of these men selected literature as their profession, they obviously respected Hawthorne's gift and his aims. Bridge initially underwrote, without Hawthorne's knowledge, his first published volume of short stories, *Twice-Told Tales* (1837), and Pierce, as the fourteenth president of the United States, sent Hawthorne to Liverpool as consul in 1853, hoping the then-lucrative post would allow Hawthorne to save enough money to write unencumbered by financial anxieties.

But this came later. After college, a twenty-one-year-old Hawthorne returned to Herbert Street in Salem, where his mother again resided, confining herself to her room when "the headache" or another illness (she complained of "debility") incapacitated her, as it often did.[10] The son suffered, too, but from a different source: he endured the ignominy of invisible labor, or authorship. A strong young man, as he now was, should be visibly employed; writing might just as well be woman's work, which in Jacksonian America it mainly was.

Partly because he made no external mark in the world of affairs at this time, a long shadow falls across the first twelve years Hawthorne spent in the Manning house after college. He apparently received money enough from his grandmother's estate to allow him to write at leisure and to travel occasionally, especially to Maine. But, soon after he reached the age of twenty-one in 1825, he changed the spelling of his name from "Hathorne" to "Hawthorne" in what must have been a declaration of independence both from the enterprising, busybody family he knew intimately (the Mannings) and from the more aristocratic family (the puritanic Hathornes) he actively imagined—and with whom he identified. "The spirit of my Puritan ancestors was mighty in me," he declared as late as 1857.[11]

Most often, this long hiatus after college is explained away by critics as an apprenticeship during which the young man honed his style in short tales, torching them (he was passionate) when they displeased. Doubtless, however, an artful Nathaniel circulated this story to justify so many years of unrecognized productivity, to say nothing of unfocused depression, unrealized ambi-

tion, and embarrassing penury. "I had a quick sensitiveness to public opinion," he wrote in "Passages from a Relinquished Work,"
explaining that his apparent indolence "ranked me with the
tavern-haunters and town-paupers,—with the drunken poet, who
hawked his own fourth of July odes,—and the broken soldier, who
had been good for nothing since [the] last war. The consequence
of all this, was a piece of light-hearted desperation."[12]

Hawthorne's first novel, *Fanshawe* (1828), was a deafening failure. Published for $100 by the Boston firm of Marsh and Capen
at Hawthorne's expense, *Fanshawe* is a derivative work, an amal-
gam of Sir Walter Scott and C. R. Maturin in a setting reminis-
cent of Bowdoin College and with a romantic, doomed hero,
who resembles Hawthorne at his most histrionic. (Hawthorne
once said he thought he would not live past the age of twenty-
five; inevitably, his protagonist had to die young.) Loosely antici-
pating the Gothic and thematic structures as well as the symbols
Hawthorne would adapt to better purpose in his subsequent
tales, the novel does suggest some interest in indigenous American material. In college, he had avidly read John Neal, who
populated the American landscape with nightmarish visions and
called for a particularly national literature of "stout, original
power."[13]

According to his sister Elizabeth, before he published this
novel, Hawthorne was already at work on a volume of short stories to be called "Seven Tales of My Native Land" in ostensible
keeping with the literary—and political—nationalism of the day.
But of his proposed seven tales, only part of "Alice Doane's
Appeal" can be indubitably traced to this project. Presumably
(again, the testimony comes from Hawthorne's elder sister,
but many years after the fact), Hawthorne burned most of this
manuscript after recalling it from a publisher who had long delayed in bringing it forward. The story, however, is unauthenti-
cated and may be an instance of Hawthorne's penchant for self-
dramatizing, even though he probably did destroy many early
manuscripts. Yet, whatever the psychological or material circumstances, Hawthorne did keep writing.

About a year after he published *Fanshawe*, he was putting together the collection called "Provincial Tales," quasi-historical

stories, including "The Gentle Boy," "My Kinsman, Major Mo-lineux," "Roger Malvin's Burial," and possibly "The Wives of the Dead." These stories, and others, were all published for a pit-tance in Samuel G. Goodrich's annual, *The Token and Atlantic Sou-venir.* Although it is difficult to determine with absolute certainty what other stories might have been composed for these collec-tions, they do suggest that Hawthorne scavenged the past, draw-ing on tales of his ancestors, those bold cruel Puritans known for stealing land and hanging witches, to compose stories of crime and punishment, of incest, woe, and revenge, of cruelty and vio-lence, of spoiled patrimony and ghostly visions. He served up Dante-esque horrors in visions of melancholy nightmare: ambi-tion realized in dread, wayfarers homeless and lost, mothers who lose their only sons, and sons who slay their fathers.

Not surprisingly, this material invites psychological interpreta-tion: fathers are supplanted, mothers punished, and guilt suffuses an atmosphere already saturated with rivalry, aggression, and de-sire. But, from no less a biographical or psychological point of view, the stories also demonstrate Hawthorne's preoccupation with origins and the extent to which he devoted his time to the imaginative excavation of both place and past. (Rich in New England history and with a strong sense of social caste, Salem was a town obsessed with itself.) Hawthorne knew, however, that found objects—the shards of history, its dry facts and unimag-ined events—mean nothing unless their finder, or narrator, exer-cises a power over them. And this search for power—Hawthorne later dubbed it the "faculty of romance"—characterizes his liter-ary method from his earliest published writings onward. "A li-cense must be assumed," he wrote in the early essay "Sir William Phips," "in brightening the materials which time has rusted, and in tracing out the half-obliterated inscriptions on the columns of antiquity; fancy must throw her reviving light on the faded inci-dents that indicate character when a ray will be reflected, more or less vividly, on the person to be described."[14] Not a mere archivist or historian, Hawthorne wanted to be something of a poet.

The collection did not find a publisher, and Hawthorne kept writing. By 1832, he conceived of a new project, "The Story

Teller," a set of stories based on his travels through New England and linked through the persona of a wandering storyteller, part entertainer and part spectator, who guiltily evades the rigid moral sway of his guardian. Here, too, autobiographical associations that link the guardian to Robert Manning are inevitable. (These associations persist in later stories, such as "Rappaccini's Daughter," where Dr. Rappaccini's obsessive interest in his garden recalls Robert Manning's later career as a pomologist; Manning receives kinder treatment when Hawthorne writes fondly of tending apple trees in "The Old Manse.") Even more significant, though, are the stories in which a young man's overweening ambition is punished. Indeed, many of these self-reflexive tales reveal a profound ambivalence about the incendiary, rebellious act of storytelling, as if the act itself, not the heedlessness of a benighted public, warrants punishment by fire.

Unlike his vagabond storyteller, Hawthorne did not leave Salem, except for short excursions, until 1836, when he was thirty-two years old. He lived in Boston for eight months, first as the editor of the *American Magazine of Useful and Entertaining Knowledge*, a job secured through Samuel Goodrich, and then as editor of the children's book *Peter Parley's Universal History on the Basis of Geography*, a volume for which his clever sister Elizabeth did much of the research and, for the historical pieces, some of the writing. Adored by his two sisters, one older and one younger, he seemed to find in their company both the intellectual rapport and unconditional affection he craved. No wonder pairs of women, much like them, frequently haunt his fiction: the two wives of the dead from the story of the same title or, later, the coupling of Zenobia with Priscilla or Miriam with Hilda. One of the two is usually an exotic beauty, dark-haired, brilliant, and eccentric, like his older sister, Elizabeth; the other, like Marie Louisa, is more overtly conventional, self-effacing, and domestic. When Hawthorne lived in Boston, Elizabeth sent him extracts and abstracts for the magazine, and Louisa sent clean collars.

These unmarried siblings pampered their brother, who as a thirty-two-year-old bachelor had remained safely committed to them. Though Hawthorne had indulged in quite a number of flirtations, the first woman he seriously courted demanded he net $3,000 before she would consider his suit, according to Elizabeth Peabody (later, his sister-in-law).[15] But his prospects and income were poor. A confirmed Jacksonian in politics, he considered working for Frank Blair's *Washington Globe* but declined. Perhaps he thought his future would be made by his first collection of stories, *Twice-Told Tales*, published by the soon-to-be-defunct American Stationers' Company, where Goodrich was a director, and secretly underwritten by the loyal Horatio Bridge. "If anybody is responsible for my being at this day an author, it is yourself," Hawthorne later thanked him publicly in his preface to *The Snow-Image*.[16]

Shrewdly, Hawthorne promoted the book, insofar as he was able, garnering reviews from such respected figures as his Bowdoin acquaintance Henry Wadsworth Longfellow, but the volume netted little in the way of profits. The result was a succès d'estime that, while it ushered Hawthorne into the literary world, earned him no large income or huge following. Yet, if it was fame he coveted, he would in the interim accept love.

Sophia Amelia Peabody was a mighty woman, ruling her family for years with the bitter headaches she wielded with gentle, tyrannical force. Even the clatter of silverware might set her head throbbing, ample weaponry against the intellectual and educational activism of her two older siblings, Mary and Elizabeth, and her mother. Sophia Peabody was also a moderately skilled painter determined to receive public kudos commensurate with the attention she commanded at home—that is, until her eldest sister, Elizabeth, introduced her to Nat Hawthorne, and Sophia became a nineteenth-century Alice Toklas.

According to legend, Hawthorne came to call on the Peabodys with his sisters one evening in the fall of 1837, the year *Twice-Told Tales* appeared, and the romance began. In fact, at the time, Hawthorne was enamored of the blue-blood belle of Salem, Mary Silsbee, and would soon enter into a confused misalliance with Elizabeth Peabody, the talkative, energetic eldest Peabody sister. Bristling with ambition, good will, and a devotion to Hawthorne, Elizabeth Peabody was a galvanizing, passionate advocate involved with all the major reform movements of the nineteenth century. (Henry James satirized her as Miss Birdseye in *The Bostonians*.) She liked to think of herself as an accessory to the early phase of Hawthorne's public career and took credit for having "discovered" him as the author of his early anonymous sketches, though Hawthorne later resented what he understood as an implicit appropriation of his achievements. Soon after they met, Hawthorne and Elizabeth Peabody were often seeing one another and frequently corresponding, with Peabody urging him to collect more of his tales in a second volume. She also encouraged his historical writing for children (*Grandfather's Chair, Famous Old People, Liberty Tree,* and *Biographical Stories*) and helped secure him, in early 1839, a post as weigher and gauger at the Boston Custom House—perhaps to spring Hawthorne from Salem and his proximity to her youngest sister, Sophia, with whom he had fallen in love.

In Boston, Hawthorne measured salt and coal by day and at night wrote love letters to the semi-invalid Sophia, who liked to say she could never marry. By the time a second volume of *Twice-Told Tales* was issued in early 1842, however, Nathaniel and Sophia had been affianced for three years—secretly, of course. "Naughty Sophie Hawthorne," he called his intended, having given her his surname as soon as she accepted his proposal of marriage; he also called her "Dove," as if to recall the sublimer side of physical desire. "By that name, I think, I shall greet you when we meet in Heaven," he told her. "That word will express . . . yearning for you—then to be forever satisfied," he continued, a little less spiritually, "for we will melt into one another, and be close, close together then."[17]

Sophia Peabody Hawthorne was both a lusty woman and the angelic Victorian fiancée of delicate sensibility, whose frequent withdrawal into the bedroom curiously resembled Hawthorne's mother's. But the split was not in Sophia; it was in her lover. Hawthorne could not yet reconcile his bifurcated view of women: independent, defiant, brilliant, on the one hand, and passive, meek, and adoring, on the other. So he delayed his marriage. The ostensible reason was Sophia's health.

In the meantime, Hawthorne enrolled in the transcendental commune, Brook Farm, as a full-fledged member, spending

$1,500 in all (the full amount of his earnings for the previous year). Five hundred dollars went toward the building of a house, and the other $1,000 purchased two shares in the West Roxbury community, located on a 200-acre farm outside of Boston. He took up the rake, began to milk cows, worked in the fields. "What is the use of burning your brains out in the sun when you can do anything better with them?" asked his solicitous sister Louisa.[18] Hawthorne later claimed he was simply trying to find a place for Sophia and himself to live. The truth, however, was more complicated. Hawthorne shared, in part, the socialist dreams of the Brook Farmers, for their notions promised to catapult him above class and release him from the conventions of gender—ideally, so he could write.

"At Brook Farm," said one visitor, "they are all so free and merry."[19] But utopia collided with the grizzly realities of a rough and tumble America, which rewards less starry pursuits. The experiment at West Roxbury lasted only six years, until 1847. By then, Hawthorne was long gone. Just two months after his idyll with rake and pitchfork had begun, Hawthorne wrote his fiancée in exasperation, "A man's soul may be buried and perish under a dung-heap or in a furrow of the field, just as well as under a pile of money."[20]

As for Sophia, she was tired of being cast as patient Griselda and delivered her ultimatum: Hawthorne must tell his mother and sisters of their engagement. No longer could he evade a commitment. As if in retaliation, Hawthorne wrote a new short story just months after his 9 July 1842 wedding. "The Birthmark" tells of a newly married man's fixation on the odd-shaped birthmark that decorates his wife's left cheek. His sexual guilt thinly disguised as cosmetology, the husband insists his bride's deformity be removed. It is, and the procedure kills her.

Sophia Peabody Hawthorne, however, fared better. After her marriage, her headaches miraculously disappeared, at least for a time. And she was delighted to have moved to pastoral Concord, Massachusetts, about twenty miles west of Boston. It had been her idea. For in Concord, Ralph Waldo Emerson held transcendental court, and Henry Thoreau scoured the grassy woods for Indian relics and ancient lore. (Sophia met Emerson, as she met Hawthorne, through her sister Elizabeth.)

Ensconced at the aging gray residence he later memorialized as the "Old Manse," Hawthorne respectfully kept his distance from his Concord neighbors. (Henry James, Senior, would characterize Hawthorne as a "Concord owl" brought "blindfold into the brilliant daylight and expected to wink and be lively like any little dapper Tommy Titmouse or Jenny Wren."[21]) He preferred the snug, magic circle of his new marriage from which he could cheerfully undermine the Concord brethren, both in print ("The Celestial Railroad") and to the star-struck Sophia. For he implicitly competed with Emerson, a former resident of the Manse, which had been built by Emerson's grandfather and in which Emerson began, in the upstairs study Hawthorne now occupied, the declamatory and influential *Nature*.

Of these transcendentalists and intellectuals, Hawthorne was particularly infatuated with, and angry at, the brilliantly prodigious Margaret Fuller, editor, journalist, translator, and charismatic polemicist, who asked why women could not be ship's captains should they so desire. Born before her time, activist and eloquent, Fuller in 1839 began to hold her popular "conversations," or discussion classes for women, in the parlor at 13 West Street in Boston, the new home of the Peabody family. (The next July, Elizabeth Peabody would open an important foreign book shop at the same address.) Sophia revered Fuller, composing a sonnet to her as the "Priestess" before whose shrine she worshipfully stands.[22] More prosaically, when Hawthorne and Sophia decided to rent the Old Manse in Concord, Sophia immediately wrote Fuller to say that when the latter visited Emerson, she could spend part of her time with the Hawthornes.

Fuller did. Visiting Concord in 1842, shortly after the Hawthornes' marriage, Fuller stopped by the Manse and on lazy afternoons strolled along the bank of the Concord River. Hawthorne sat with her one afternoon, talking of "Autumn—and about the pleasures of getting lost in the woods—and about the crows, whose voices Margaret had heard—and about the experience of early childhood, whose influence remains upon the character after the recollection of them has passed away."[23] In addition, Fuller's 1845 *Woman in the Nineteenth Century*, a book detailing the oppressed position of women in American society,

was of incalculable significance to Hawthorne, who unquestion-
ably modeled from it the thirteenth chapter of *The Scarlet Letter*
as well as Hester Prynne's most radical thinking about "the
whole race of womanhood."[24] Yet, Fuller threatened the Hawthornes, particularly Sophia, who insisted that an unmarried
woman could have no inkling about the true position of women
and definitely knew nothing about men.[25]

Not surprisingly, the twenty-one tales Hawthorne wrote
during the Manse period explore the subtle psychological ac-
commodations at stake in sexual relations; one thinks of tales
such as "The Birthmark," "The Artist of the Beautiful," "Rappaccini's Daughter," "Egotism, or the Bosom Serpent," and even
"Drowne's Wooden Image." Interestingly, though Hawthorne
would later claim to have been happiest at this period, and doubtless he was, many of these stories also betray his sense of isolation in personal affairs as well as from the Concord community.
For example, "The Artist of the Beautiful" reveals, biographically,
a father's nascent anxiety about the birth of a child, who threatens to destroy the man's other progeny, his work.

Soon after the 3 March 1844 birth of their daughter Una
(named for a character in Spenser's *Faerie Queen*), Hawthorne suffered a mortifying blow: he was to be driven from the sheltered
community that counted thoughts more golden than coin. Even
in transcendental arcadia, it seemed, the piper had to be paid.
The payments of rent on the Old Manse were overdue, and the
landlord nudged out the indigent Hawthornes. (Emerson, who
had never known poverty, offered small comfort; everybody's in
debt, he transcendentally declared.[26])

Desperate, the Hawthornes sought shelter in Nathaniel's
mother's house, back in Salem, in October 1845. Hawthorne in-
stalled Sophia and Una as paying boarders in the old kitchen beneath the parlor, and he retired upstairs to his former study,
where he worked on the piece that would become "The Old
Manse," the essay introducing a new volume of stories. Published by editor Evert Duyckinck as one of Wiley and Putnam's
Library of American Books—an attempt to create a "classic"
American literature that, significantly, included Hawthorne—
Mosses from an Old Manse contained much of Hawthorne's recent

work as well as older tales, such as "Young Goodman Brown" and "Roger Malvin's Burial." But the real innovation was the essay "The Old Manse" in which Hawthorne affected to lift the veil by speaking directly to the reader of his home and his thoughts, even of his wish to "achieve a novel" of "physical substance." Then, as if to retract such naked statements, he disclaimed them, tartly reminding his reader he positively was not "one of those supremely hospitable people, who serve up their own hearts delicately fried, with brain-sauce, as a tidbit for their beloved public."[27]

In all, though, the elegaic and plangent tone of "The Old Manse" reflects the burden of care Hawthorne now confronted, in terms both of his literary career and of his financial situation. Apprehensively seeking a political appointment to fill his purse and inflate his depressed self-image, he was rewarded by local Democrats working in concert with the party leader, historian George Bancroft; Hawthorne was named surveyor of the Salem Custom House on 3 April 1846. But political favors dispensed can be easily withdrawn, and Hawthorne became the controversial center of a bipartisan maelstrom three years later when the Whigs unseated the Democrats. He was removed from his position in early June 1849—"decapitated," he provocatively and furiously called his firing.

Yet, it was also the release he sought, not just because he now would have time to write but because he could do so in the full tide of anger, which temporarily overcame his ongoing ambivalence about his work. He was no longer a scribbler; he was avenger, judge, and adjudicator primed by the force of rage unleashed. All this, just months after his mother died.

The death of his mother that July was also a decapitation of sorts, ironically liberating Hawthorne to create Hester Prynne, whom he loved and hated, branded, redeemed, and left quite as bereft, at the end of The Scarlet Letter, as he felt he had been. "There was wild and ghastly scenery all around her, and a home and comfort nowhere." (Although the germ of the book lay undeveloped in Hawthorne's very early tale "Mrs. Hutchinson" and his somewhat later story "Endicott and the Red Cross," the full-blown idea was developed, not coincidentally, while Hawthorne lived with four women: his two sisters, his wife, and his firstborn daughter.) The sturdiest of his heroines, Hester is the most ably imagined and the one who most sadly endures homelessness, exclusion, and the forfeiture of her sexuality. Like her creator, Hester Prynne knows herself to be different. Like him, she conforms. She resumes wearing the scarlet letter "of her own free will," Hawthorne writes, although Boston no longer demands it.[28] He too took up the mantle of respectability in order to survive, returned to his natal home, and suffered once again the perceived shame of failed ambition.

But not for long. Now, he was buoyed by the genial publisher-poet James T. Fields in whom Hawthorne found at last a shrewd ally who offered what Sophia herself provided, unconditional support.[29] Evidently enlisted by mutual friends in the effort to keep Hawthorne from being ejected from the Salem Custom House, Fields visited the depressed author in Salem and, according to his later account, returned to Boston with the manuscript of *The Scarlet Letter*, having pried it from a reluctant Hawthorne. While dramatic, Fields's story does not include the pedestrian fact that Hawthorne had been working on a new volume of stories since at least late 1848, before he was expelled from the custom house; these tales would at least include "Ethan Brand" and "Main Street" (initially written for Elizabeth Peabody's *Aesthetic Papers*).[30] As he continued to meditate on his volume through the spring and summer, he composed two long stories—and was clearly aware of the women's rights convention in Seneca Falls in July 1848, which no doubt also helped to produce Hester Prynne.

But Fields's perspicacity did detach the story "The Scarlet Letter" from the rest of the proposed collection, and his encouragement did lift Hawthorne's spirits. Moreover, Fields's publishing house (then Ticknor, Reed, and Fields) commanded respect and prestige, which, in turn, the huge critical success of *The Scarlet Letter* would augment. Thus, the Fields-Hawthorne connection was mutually satisfying—and absolutely essential to Hawthorne's sense of himself, which is to say his literary future. And his self-esteem.

On the heels of the custom house debacle, Hawthorne banished himself from Salem. By this time, the Hawthornes had occupied three different houses in Salem in the course of three years, and now, after considering his prospects in Boston, Hawthorne took flight to western Massachusetts. Having considered a move to Portsmouth, New Hampshire (near his friend Bridge), and Kittery, Maine, the Hawthornes settled on Lenox, Massachusetts, in the Berkshire Mountains—Sophia's choice, again. They were by now four, a son, Julian, having been born in 1846. At Sophia's insistence, Hawthorne consented to lease the small red-stained cottage in Lenox owned by the vivacious and wealthy Caroline Sturgis Tappan, who occupied a more manorial home nearby. (This property eventually became the site known today as Tanglewood.) "My house is an old red farm house, (as red as the Scarlet Letter)," Hawthorne wrote a friend about the new dwelling.[31] He might as well be living on the moon, he continued, jesting only by half. He was still a tenant.

An eager Fields pressed for more of Hawthorne's work and in fairly short order received the manuscript of *The House of the Seven Gables*. With its minute dissection of class, heredity, and the almost incestuous domesticity implied by living in one spot for generations, it is, in many ways, Hawthorne's nostalgic farewell to a boyhood, prelapsarian Salem despoiled by the age of telegrams and anger. In a sense, it is also Hawthorne's first novel, conceived and executed as such; this accounts in part for its tableau-like nature. In the book, Hawthorne seems uncomfortable sustaining an action-based narrative, electing instead to craft stationary scenes with characters set in relief: Hepzibah opening her shop, Jaffrey Pyncheon sitting in his chair. At the same time, he brings to the meticulous detail of these psychologically nuanced portraits a humor, a pathos, and a cynicism that showcase his penchant for almost naturalist writing, similar visually to that of the Dutch realists he admired. Of course, he abjures conventional realism per se, preferring to redefine his form of naturalism as romance, the alchemical mingling of the "marvellous" with the "actual."[32]

Hawthorne was coining a psychological vocabulary in literary terms, just decades before Freud embarked on a similar project. Interestingly, Hawthorne offered something of a psychological rather than a critical judgment of his own book, calling it "a more natural and healthy product of my mind" than *The Scarlet Letter*. Writing implied psychic exorcism.[33] But this book's accommodation of inner and outer with past and present also augurs Hawthorne's turn toward current events for subsequent material.

In April 1851, *The House of the Seven Gables* appeared to largely favorable reviews. With Fields urging Hawthorne to "keep the pot boiling," Hawthorne continued to work, publishing in the next year a book of myths rewritten for children, *A Wonder-Book for Girls and Boys*, and another collection of stories, *The Snow-Image and Other Twice-Told Tales*. But as he wrote to his longtime confidant Horatio Bridge, "How slowly I have made my way in life!"[34] Hawthorne's output was actually quite small. He wrote in spurts. "A life of much smoulder, but scanty fire," he characterized his career with a modicum of truth.[35] Of his four novels, all written after he turned forty-five, only *The Scarlet Letter* and *The House of the Seven Gables*, finished within a year of one another, achieved the same critical stature as his earliest stories.

Yet, for a while, the period in Lenox proved productive. Remote though it was, the rural Lenox enclave was not without its celebrated literary and artistic personages. Popular novelist Catharine Maria Sedgwick and notorious actress Fanny Kemble, who astonished Hawthorne with unladylike feats on horseback, both lived in Lenox; Harriet Hosmer, the American sculptor, whom the Hawthornes would meet in Rome, studied at the nearby Sedgwick school. Oliver Wendell Holmes summered in the area, and Herman Melville, travel writer renowned for his exotic South Sea tales, had settled in nearby Pittsfield. (He had not yet spoiled his reputation entirely by writing *Moby-Dick*.)

The hasty and fervent friendship, at least on Melville's part, that developed between Hawthorne and Melville has become a barometer of the times. No longer regarded as simply platonic, or the meeting of two hungry, curious minds in the lush Massachusetts hills, it now seethes with all the unruly passion of Melville's evident bisexuality. But that is not all: Hawthorne, the man of masks, is regarded these days as a repressed homosexual averse to Melville's large, amatory gestures of friendship. Valid as this various interpretation is—who would deny a polymorphous perversity at the heart of all human endeavor?—it somewhat oversimplifies Hawthorne.

Hawthorne and Melville were each lonely, depressed, agnostic men troubled by the irrational opacity of the world and of themselves. Each found in the other a like-minded wayfarer with whom he could miraculously and freely speak. "There is the grand truth about Nathaniel Hawthorne," said the younger Melville in his justly famous formulation, "He says NO! in thunder; but the devil himself cannot make him say *yes*."[36] Clearly, their common estate was pride, ambition, and those deep hypos that set Ishmael on his journey; certainly, in regard to publishing, they knew, or suspected, the ways in which Melville was right when he declared to Hawthorne, "All Fame is patronage."[37] And when Hawthorne confided to his journal, after seeing Melville in 1856, that Melville "can neither believe, nor be comfortable in his unbelief; and he is too honest and courageous not to try to do one or the other," surely Hawthorne spoke of himself.[38]

Hawthorne not only inspired Melville in the writing of *Moby-Dick* but to one of the most heartfelt and compelling gestures in American literature: Melville dedicated the book to his new friend, "Nathaniel Hawthorne, in token of my admiration for his genius." But often Hawthorne, whose sense of masculinity was indeed unstable, balked at the affections he inspired, as if their warmth kindled feelings best left to literature or to the fraternal badinage at the Salem docks and custom house, where Hawthorne played cards, told stories, and smoked cigars safe in the rough and tumble world of coded male intimacy. For such a man, Melville's beseeching and delirious letters lay too unveiled, exposed, needy.

In the spring of 1851, a third child, Rose, was born to the Hawthornes, inspiring a curious outburst from the new father, who, depressed, coldly wrote his sister-in-law that "I think I never had any partiality for my children. I love them according to their deserts [*sic*]; they have to prove their claim to all the affection they get; and I believe I could love other people's children better than mine, if I felt they deserved it more." But, he acknowledged, he was drawn to this new baby as "my last and latest, my autumnal flower."[39] Approaching his forty-seventh birthday,

Hawthorne grew restive; he began to think of the sea and of leaving Berkshire for some seaside dwelling (though not in Salem, but perhaps nearby); he read Fourier to help him outline a new novel about socialism, spiritualism—the vogue in reform that year—and women's rights, but he complained of languor. Even though he had rented Fanny Kemble's house for the following year, in the fall Hawthorne resolved to leave the Berkshires, where he felt he could no longer write.

Flight suited him. Friends sensed Hawthorne's deep-rooted restlessness. He would grow critical of those venturing too close—all except Sophia, who made their home an inviolate kingdom, her husband its titular head. ("He is fast becoming Crowned King in the realm of Letters & Genius," she exclaimed.[40]) She even insisted the children not learn to read until they were seven—odd injunction for the wife of an author—as if to perpetuate their romanticized innocence. But she could not protect Hawthorne from himself or from the fast-changing, volatile political world about him. After 1850, the taste of the Fugitive Slave Law had soured Massachusetts voters, who put Hawthorne's acquaintance Charles Sumner into the U.S. Senate on a Free Soil, antislavery platform. Even Hawthorne momentarily stirred, acting against his own class-based political instincts, which were definitely not abolitionist. Or, as he explained to a friend in 1851:

> I have not, as you suggest, the slightest sympathy for the slaves; or, at least, not half so much as for the laboring whites, who, I believe, as a general thing, are ten times worse off than the Southern negros. Still, whenever I am absolutely cornered, I shall go for New England rather than the South;—and this Fugitive Law cornered me. I knew what I was doing when I signed that Free-Soil document.[41]

Having fled Lenox, the Hawthornes soon resettled in Concord and, as if to make good this time among the ethereal elect, Hawthorne bought a homestead from Bronson Alcott in the spring of 1852, which he fittingly called "The Wayside." By this time, he had finished *The Blithedale Romance*, based on his experiences at Brook Farm. Acclaimed less frequently than his other novels, this underrated satire of philanthropic socialism is decidedly one of Hawthorne's most peculiar books and certainly one of the most striking novels written in America, blending male friendship and mesmerism, utopian idealism and erotic, articulate, writing women. Its doomed protofeminist heroine, the magazine writer Zenobia—again, based partly on Margaret Fuller—emerges as a vibrant woman too advanced, too overwhelming, too modern for the Prufrockish narrator, who can neither comprehend nor compete with her. A voyeur fundamentally incapable of love, this narrator is Hawthorne's self-satirizing double.

So, too, is Zenobia, who each day plaited an exotic white flower into her hair and asked, "Did you ever see a happy woman in your life?" Hester Prynne recast as the subversive advocate of women's rights, she presents a Hawthorne aware of the dire effects of difference—chiefly, his own. Like Hester Prynne before her, Zenobia is Hawthorne's homage to and rebellion against strong, sexual women; she is the mirror of himself, a writer, a scribbler, an outsider, and a nonconforming conformist. As these portraits suggest, Hawthorne could identify with women, and he constructed vibrant female characters whom he punishes, humiliates, and kills, as if exorcising that which enthralls. Hawthorne censured and scolded those women who, he felt, threatened to rob him of his income, his professional stature, his masculinity: that "d—d mob of scribbling women," he called the female competitors, who, he feared, sold more books than he. (They wrote more.) "*All* women, as authors, are feeble and tiresome," he wrote his publisher, William D. Ticknor, in a fit of cruel pique. "I wish they were forbidden to write," he wrote Fields, "on pain of having their faces deeply scarified with an oyster-shell."[42] Later, when Fields naively suggested that Sophia write travel essays for his magazine, the *Atlantic Monthly*, Hawthorne was furious. When his youngest daughter began to write tales, he stood over the girl, "dark as a prophetic flight of birds," she recalled. "Never let me hear of your writing stories!" he boomed.[43]

Nevertheless, Hawthorne wrote compellingly of a feminism

that attracted and repelled him. And in the fate of Hester or Zenobia, we can read the components of Hawthorne's life: his preoccupation with women, women's bodies, women's writing; with reform and reformers; with transcendentalism and its costs; and with being the good husband and responsible neighbor no one really knew, the man who watchfully brooded over the ambiguous meaning of experience.

Yet, as if to counteract the radical subtext of *Blithedale*, Hawthorne indecorously drowns Zenobia, dismissing his attraction to and identification with her, and immediately turns his attention, as if in relief, to the campaign biography of his old friend Franklin Pierce—which would earn him, he knew, a political office. Although the Pierce biography has been dismissed as the political puffery it was, it also reveals much about Hawthorne's preoccupation with social life—as well as his inveterate fear of his own unsocialized impulses. Taken together, *The Blithedale Romance* and *The Life of Franklin Pierce* also signal the end of something. Hawthorne will not write again for publication for seven years, as if his recent achievement contained within it the seeds of its own demise—just as his revolutionary thinking contained, at its core, a basic conservatism. The matter of history, his own or the nation's, would no longer stir him to produce tales that link historical verisimilitude to psychological inquiry, stories like "My Kinsman, Major Molineux," "The Maypole of Merry Mount," or even *The Scarlet Letter* itself. Nor did the contemporary world move him to fiction, even though he could easily blend naturalistic precision and gentle satire in his so-called romances. (The machine age and technology are the embedded subjects of the Gothic-seeming *The House of Seven Gables*; rural Brook Farm and an industrializing Boston are essential to *Blithedale*.) His children inspired no more productions like *A Wonder-Book* or *Tanglewood Tales*. And he had long since written the sketches charting such ephemeral states as waking from sleep or the desultory thoughts of a lonely Sunday afternoon. Regardless, he stayed an adroit manipulator of his reputation as an exemplary American writer; such skill served him well whenever he sought asylum from what he conceived as the female world of scribbling, as he often did, in the male world of politics.

Not surprisingly, Hawthorne's continual retreat from literature into politics was also fraught with conflict. Despite his well-advertised talent for empathy, he was a rivalrous, contentious man, a political contrarian comfortable with the humble and uncelebrated as long as they made no demands on him. Contemptuous of the abolitionists, he considered them fanatics and slavery a repugnant system that, if left alone, would perish in its own good time, a view hardly credible for a man cynical about humanity and its enlightenment. In his biography of Pierce, he named slavery as "one of those evils which divine Providence does not leave to be remedied by human contrivances, but which, in its own good time, by some means impossible to be anticipated, but of the simplest and easiest operation, when all its uses shall have been fulfilled, it causes to vanish like a dream."[44] But while neither the literary men nor the women of his acquaintance shared Hawthorne's optimistic fatalism, rather than denounce it publicly, they dismissed Hawthorne's position as something of an enigma, preferring to rationalize his reactionary statements as evidence of his being too dreamy to fathom politics.

Hawthorne's work on Pierce's campaign biography was interrupted by a horrible accident during the summer of 1852, which claimed the life of his sister Louisa. She had been on her way to see the Hawthornes in Concord after a trip to Saratoga Springs and New York City, but as the steamer *Henry Clay* headed south from Saratoga and into New York harbor, it caught on fire. People panicked. Several jumped overboard to avoid the flames, Louisa among them. When Hawthorne heard the news from a friend, he listened quietly and then abruptly left the room to shut himself in his study. That afternoon, one could glimpse him walking slowly on the hill to the rear of the house, hands clasped behind his back, head sunk on his chest.

He managed to finish the biography and then left home for three weeks, to recover in Maine and on the Isle of Shoals, where he visited with Pierce. Hawthorne's friendship with Pierce seems an unlikely pairing, and by and large, it has gone unremarked. The author who by now was renowned in America and abroad, who more or less kept to himself, and who cultivated the romantic image of shy recluse found in the unimpressive politician from New Hampshire the companionship and rectitude he questioned in other men and women. To many, Pierce was at best just an average man, congenial enough but gifted neither in oratory, legal acumen, political savvy, nor compassion. (Emerson would call him paltry.) His presidency leaned precipitously toward the South, which meant toward slavery; he read the Constitution unimaginatively; he sent federal troops to Boston to recapture a fugitive slave; and he presided over the bleeding debacle of the Kansas-Nebraska Act. Even Hawthorne said of him that he was "not far-seeing, nor possessed of vast stores of political wisdom in advance of occasions," but Hawthorne also thought Pierce "endowed with miraculous intuition of what ought to be done, just at the time for action."[45] History would disagree.

Hawthorne's campaign biography earned him the coveted consulship in Liverpool to which the Hawthornes sailed on 6 July 1853. Keeping the appointment until 1857, Hawthorne during these years wrote extensively in his journals but completed no fiction, even though he tried to write of an American claimant, psychologically like himself, who uncovers in the mother country of England a rich patrimony unconsciously sought. But Hawthorne found no such patrimony, real or imagined; his attitudes toward England predictably ambivalent, he waxed cool and warm, wishing to leave England and, as soon as he left, longing to return.

He constantly fretted over money, particularly when Congress passed a new consular bill establishing a fixed salary to replace the one currently used, based on fees. Yet, Hawthorne's concern over his income, however justified, was also inspired by paranoia. His dread of the poorhouse masked and fueled an underlying terror that he could no longer write. As it was, he could count his income and assets at more than $20,000 a year. Regardless, Hawthorne moved the family again, to save on rent. He dismissed servants. But his fear of impoverishment inevitably persisted. His temper was short. Hawthorne complained of age and lost physical vitality. His formerly abundant hair was thinner, grayer. He was tired, could not concentrate, could not sleep, and felt lonely without Sophia, who had sailed to Lisbon with Una and Rose in

October 1855. For her, Liverpool had been a terrible disappointment. Exasperated by its grime and the dreariness of its climate, she so despaired of a persistent cough that she decided to leave, not returning to England until June 1856. Then came disturbing reports of violence in America. (Hawthorne was, after all, presiding over a British port closely allied with the cotton trade of the American South.) Free Soil agitation, John Brown, the news that Charles Sumner was beaten insensible at his desk in the Senate, and the moral outrage of the abolitionists—the larger world of coming war mirrored Hawthorne's private unrest.

In June 1856, Franklin Pierce lost the Democratic nomination for the presidency. The following February, Hawthorne resigned his Liverpool post and applied for an Italian passport. On the application, he lied about his and Sophia's ages, as if to recapture the past or find some elixir for the present. ("I have had enough of progress" he once wrote Longfellow, "—now I want to stand stock still; or rather, to go back twenty years."[46]) Hawthorne was fifty-two.

In the wintry rain of January 1858, the Hawthornes arrived in the Eternal City, which Nathaniel and Sophia had long dreamed of visiting. A small cadre of American artists lived there, and soon the Hawthornes were visiting their studios and becoming part of the band that included Cephas Thompson, Benjamin Akers, Emma Stebbins, William Wetmore Story, Louise Lander, and Harriet Hosmer. Inspired, Hawthorne was writing. By spring, the Hawthornes understood Italian life well enough to escape the heat of Rome in a secluded hilltop villa overlooking Florence in the cool, green suburb of Bellosguardo—"a very good air to dream in."[47] Here, Hawthorne continued to sketch a new romance inspired by a copy of the *Faun* of Praxiteles, on view in the sculpture galleries of the Roman capitol. This was to be his last completed novel.

The Marble Faun took more than a year to finish, much longer than his other books, perhaps because its role reversals, gender anxiety, and desirous, murderous sexuality all percolate near the book's surface. Also permeating the book is Hawthorne's shifting views of Italy, that magically seductive country where the "ponderous gloom of the Roman Past" will "crush you down as with the heaped-up marble and granite, the earth-mounds, and multi-tudinous bricks, of its material decay."[48] Within this waste of broken images, one frantically searches for some emblem of redemption—in art, in religion, perhaps even in love. To Hawthorne, the story of Italy is the story of the Fall, told through the experiences of four characters who encounter the crushing pain of tragic experience.

A personal story told in a somewhat vague, somewhat philo-sophical, somewhat allegorical way, *The Marble Faun* is in many ways unlike anything Hawthorne had ever written. Moreover, one can even retrospectively interpret from its most doleful pas-sages a Hawthorne forecasting the end of his writing career. But to do so specifically ignores the personal anguish that interrupted its completion. Una had contracted malaria in the Coliseum shortly after the family had returned from Florence to Rome. Her health entrusted to a physician who decided Una would die on 17 November, Nathaniel and Sophia, oddly passive, counted down the days. Una survived, but some said Hawthorne never recovered from those anguished months watching by Una's bedside.

Hawthorne did not finish *The Marble Faun*, called *Transforma-tion* in Great Britain, where it was first published, until the fall of 1859. The Hawthornes tarried in England, presumably so Sophia could regain her health after the long months at Una's side. Returning to America, however, swallowed much of his equa-nimity. Still an expatriate of sorts, Hawthorne had come back to Concord mainly for the sake of the children, he said. But Una re-fused to stay at home and took so violently ill that her parents strapped her to the bed and called, in desperation, on the minis-trations of what Hawthorne dubbed an "electrical witch."[49] Grievously depressed, he decided to submit to the galvanic bat-tery himself.

He tried his hand at fiction again, unsuccessfully, first return-ing to the romance of the American claimant, soon abandoned, and then experimenting with a tale about eternal life. Haw-thorne's was a long-standing fascination with elixirs of immort-ality, but at this time, his renewed interest in the subject reveals a preoccupation with his pervasive sense of physical, mental, literary failure. Despite his burgeoning fame, notoriety and adulation created an anxiety of expectation—his own. He turned to a series of essays, more easily completed, on his experiences in England, publishing "Some of the Haunts of Burns" in the October 1860 issue of the *Atlantic Monthly*, now edited by James T. Fields, and "Near Oxford" the following fall.

By then, however, the attack on Fort Sumter had lit the conflagration of the Civil War. Soon, Brook Farm was an army trading post, renamed Camp Andrew, after the abolitionist Massachusetts governor, John Albion Andrew, and Hawthorne did not attend a dinner held in Andrew's honor. "What are we coming to?" he asked Charles Sumner, whom he liked but whose commitment to abolition and war he deplored.[50] Lowell, Longfellow, Emerson, Whittier—men generally sedate, rational, and genteel—were all stirred by the frenzy, the madness, of war, and all of them, each in his way, added to it. The world was crumbling about him. The era of the Jacksonian Democrat had resoundingly ended.

Hawthorne's March 1862 trip to Washington, D.C., and Virginia with the publisher William D. Ticknor prompted "Chiefly about War-Matters. By a Peaceable Man," which was printed in the subsequent July issue of the *Atlantic Monthly*. In the essay, Hawthorne sustains a cool ironic voice in the face of history's cataclysm. "There is no remoteness of life and thought," he writes, "no hermetically sealed seclusion, except, possibly, that of the grave, into which the disturbing influences of this war do not penetrate."[51] Indeed, the man who obsessed with history discovers that history has caught up with him; the discovery is disconcerting. Taking refuge in his distrust of heroes and heroism, his iconoclasm, and his generally pacifistic feelings, Hawthorne produces a tour de force chilling in its wit, distressing in its racism, and poignant for its cynicism. Even the faithful James T. Fields was unnerved and asked Hawthorne at least to omit his description of Abraham Lincoln.

But if the war, as well as Una's precarious health, strained Hawthorne to the limit, it was not the only cause of a protracted breakdown of his spirits. Una seemed to improve; her father did not. Bronson Alcott, his neighbor, spied him, "dodging about amongst the trees in his hilltop as if he feared his neighbors' eyes would catch him as he walked."[52] Walking back and forth on the path behind his house, he told Emerson that when he died, the well-worn track would be his only memorial. Again plagued by his dread of the almshouse, he husbanded his money, refusing Una drawing lessons, or spent it profligately, impelled by a self-fulfilling prophecy. He added an ill-designed third-story tower to his home for a study, importing 450 Norway spruces to build it, and then, when the assemblage was complete, rued the whole thing.

In fact, Hawthorne spent much of his adult life trying to simu-late the conditions of his more prolific early years, which he melodramatically characterized as spent in the lonely seclusion of his room. His tower, for instance, was a last, desperate effort to rise above whatever had fatally stalled his writing. Nothing happened. Hawthorne could not work. The room was too hot in summer, too cold in the winter. "He always, I believe, finds fault," observed Ellery Channing.[53] The man who wrote com-pellingly of a sense of place could find none for himself. Sitting in his study, curtains drawn, he sketched the abortive romance he was never to finish.

When he went to Boston to dine with the sages of the all-male Brahmin Saturday Club, one observed that Hawthorne "has the look all the time of a rogue who evidently finds himself in a company of detectives."[54] Furtive, out of place, afraid he was a fraud, Hawthorne anguished in the intellectual company to which he aspired. Not of their number, either financially or psychologically, he shrank from their touch. When the well-loved hostess Annie Fields (wife of Hawthorne's publisher) one day lifted her hand to brush the dust from Hawthorne's greatcoat, he flinched as though struck. He said he did not like his coat brushed, lest the material too quickly wear out.

Hawthorne's friends, already confused or disappointed by his indifference to their cause, his position on abolition, and his puta-tive sympathy for the South, could not understand why he would dedicate his collected reminiscences of England, *Our Old Home*, to Franklin Pierce. Hawthorne was unflinching. Harriet Beecher Stowe never wanted to see Hawthorne again, and Charles Eliot

Norton rationalized that the "dedication to F. Pierce—the corre-spondent of Jeff. Davis, the flatterer of traitors, & the emissary of treason,—reads like the bitterest of satires; and in that I have my satisfaction. The public will laugh."[55] The loyal Fieldses took the loyal Sophia's view: "friendship of the purest stimulates him," Annie Fields confided to her diary, "and the ruin in prospect for his book because of his resolve does not move him from his purpose."[56]

Hawthorne complained more than ever of his health. When he showed Fields a chapter from his new romance (later called "The Dolliver Romance"), Fields as ever encouraged his friend, sending Hawthorne a selection of possible titles, such as "The Deathless Man," ironically to spur the increasingly frail author onward. But, by the spring of 1864, Hawthorne could not write and scarcely was able to read; he had no appetite, slept little, and his hand shook when he wrote. Finally, when his symptoms seemed mildly better, he took a trip for his health with William Ticknor who, as misfortune would have it, died while the two were in Philadelphia. Hawthorne himself had little more than a month to live.

As if he knew as much and wanted to spare his family, Haw-thorne planned another trip, this time to New Hampshire with Franklin Pierce. "Certainly my father did not like to die, though he now wished to do so," Hawthorne's daughter Rose recalled years later.[57] The man who prided himself on his physical strength, who had once skated in freezing weather before dawn and chopped wood all afternoon, dreaded a helpless old age. When the carriage had arrived at his doorstep that spring day in May 1864, with its promise of a change of air, the furrowed, frail, white-haired man had walked out of the house with military pos-ture, upright and unaided. Sophia put her hands to her face and wept.

A home-grown expatriate, Hawthorne had long craved the comfort of home and of community, be it the Brook Farm ideal-ists or the Concord partisans, while at the same time, he compul-sively moved from house to house, as if domesticity (and its asso-ciation with women) would choke him. He resettled himself and his family in Boston, Concord, Salem, Lenox, West Newton,

Concord again, then England and Italy, before returning in 1860 to the Concord intellectuals, among whom he lived unhappily the last four years of his life. He even refused to die at home, insisting that his friend Pierce take him on a journey through New England at the very last. "Happy the man that has such a friend beside him, when he comes to die!" Hawthorne had prophetically written in *The Blithedale Romance* twelve years earlier.[58]

At the Pemigewasset House in Plymouth, New Hampshire, Nathaniel Hawthorne stopped breathing some time in the early hours of the morning of 19 May 1864, his father's birthday. Pierce said that when he had noiselessly entered Hawthorne's room, his old friend looked as though happily asleep. But just that afternoon, Pierce recalled, Hawthorne had sighed and said it would be a boon if one could pass away without a struggle. He had already informed his family they should burn old letters and provide for his remaining sister, Elizabeth.

The funeral took place on 23 May, a sunny day, at the Congregational church in Concord with James Freeman Clarke presiding. James Fields carried Hawthorne's unfinished manuscript. Pierce stayed with the family, and the pallbearers included Longfellow, Emerson, Alcott, Hillard, Holmes, and Norton. After the service, Hawthorne was buried in Sleepy Hollow Cemetery in a spot beneath tall white pines.

Though Hawthorne had for some time looked frail and ill, his death seemed to startle some of his neighbors. Emerson, for one, admitted ruefully he never really knew Hawthorne. Others clearly felt the same way. Duplicity—the sense of living double and not being what one seems or what others take one to be— were leitmotifs in Hawthorne's life. So too, were empathy, sexual passion, sorrow, and aggression, as well as the embittered loneliness of the outsider. His sensitivity to criticism, imagined and real, allowed him to identify with the objects of his hatred. And it induced a form of preemptive self-criticism, much like Dimmesdale's voluptuous self-punishment, by which he compensated for those granite traits he recognized and condemned in himself. Hawthorne was perceptive, he was beloved, he was goodhearted, but he was hostile and vengeful too—and he knew it, tempering his own severity in the balanced phrasings of his Augustan prose. His uncanny ability was to weave all these elements into the elegant writing that has touched so many.

NOTES

1. Nathaniel Hawthorne, *The Scarlet Letter*, in Hawthorne, *Collected Novels* (New York: Library of America, 1983), p. 127. All references from the novels will be taken from this volume and subsequently identified simply by the novel's title and the page number.

2. Quoted in Julian Hawthorne, *Nathaniel Hawthorne and His Wife*, vol. 1 (Boston: Houghton Mifflin, 1884), p. 95. Julian Hawthorne, it should be noted, is notoriously unreliable.

3. Henry James, *Autobiography*, ed. Frederick Dupee (New York: Criterion, 1956), p. 415.

4. Elizabeth Hawthorne to James T. Fields, 13 and 16 Dec. [1870], Boston Public Library.

5. *The Centenary Edition of the Works of Nathaniel Hawthorne* (Columbus: Ohio State University Press, 1962–97), 8:429. Subsequent references to the *Centenary* edition will give the volume and page numbers.

6. Nathaniel Hathorne to Elizabeth C. Hathorne, 7 Mar. 1820, *Centenary* 15:117.

7. Rebecca Manning, "Some Facts about Hawthorne," Phillips Library, Peabody Essex Museum, subsequently identified as Phillips.

8. *Spectator*, 21 Aug. 1820, Phillips.

9. Nathaniel Hathorne to Elizabeth Clarke Hathorne, 13 Mar. 1821, *Centenary* 15:138–39.

10. Priscilla Dike to Richard Manning, 17 Oct. 1828, Phillips.

11. *Centenary* 20:193.

12. Nathaniel Hawthorne, "Passages from a Relinquished Work," in Hawthorne, *Tales and Sketches* (New York: Library of America, 1996), p. 176. All references from the tales and prefaces will be taken from this volume and subsequently identified simply by the tale or preface's title and the page number.

13. John Neal, *American Writers: A Series of Papers Contributed to Blackwood's Magazine (1824–1825)*, ed. Frederick Lewis Pattee (Durham, N.C.: Duke University Press, 1937), p. 201.

14. "Sir William Phips," p. 12.

15. "Conversation with E.P.P.," notes taken by Julian Hawthorne, n.d., Pierpont Morgan Library.

16. Preface to *The Snow-Image*, p. 1155.

17. Nathaniel Hawthorne to Sophia Peabody, 3 July 1839, *Centenary* 15:320.

18. Louisa Hawthorne to Nathaniel Hawthorne, 11 June 1841, Henry W. and Albert Berg Collection of American Literature, New York Public Library, subsequently identified as Berg.

19. Caroline Sturgis (Tappan) to Margaret Fuller, 21 July 1842, Houghton Library, Harvard University, subsequently identified as Houghton.

20. Nathaniel Hawthorne to Sophia Peabody, 1 June 1841, *Centenary* 15:545.

21. Henry James, Senior, to Ralph Waldo Emerson, quoted in Edward Waldo Emerson, *The Early Years of the Saturday Club, 1855–1870* (Boston: Houghton Mifflin, 1918), p. 331.

22. Sophia Peabody to Margaret Fuller, 11 May 1842, Houghton.

23. *Centenary* 8:345.

24. *The Scarlet Letter*, p. 260.

25. Sophia Hawthorne to her mother, 6 Mar. 1845, Berg.

26. Sophia Hawthorne to Elizabeth Palmer Peabody, 7 Sept. 1845, Berg.

27. "The Old Manse," pp. 1124, 1147.

28. *The Scarlet Letter*, pp. 344, 261.

29. Nathaniel Hawthorne to James T. Fields, 17 June 1852, *Centenary* 16:550.

30. See Sophia Hawthorne to Mary Mann, 5 Dec. 1857, Berg: "My husband has begun to write since November."

31. Nathaniel Hawthorne to Zachariah Burchmore, 9 June 1850, *Centenary* 16:340.

32. *The House of the Seven Gables*, p. 351.

33. Nathaniel Hawthorne to E. A. Duyckinck, 27 Apr. 1851, in *Centenary* 16:421.

34. James T. Fields to Nathaniel Hawthorne, 12 Mar. 1851, Berg; Nathaniel Hawthorne to Horatio Bridge, 15 Mar. 1851, *Centenary* 16:407.

35. Nathaniel Hawthorne to James T. Fields, 25 Feb. 1864, *Centenary* 18:641.

36. Herman Melville to Nathaniel Hawthorne, 16? Apr. 1851, in *Herman Melville, Correspondence*, ed. Lynn Horth (Chicago: Northwestern University Press and Newberry Library, 1993), p. 186.

37. Herman Melville to Nathaniel Hawthorne, 1? June 1851, in *Herman Melville, Correspondence*, ed. Horth, p. 193.

38. *Centenary* 22:163.

39. Nathaniel Hawthorne to Elizabeth Peabody, 25 May 1851, *Centenary* 16:441.

40. Sophia Hawthorne to Louisa Hawthorne, 1 Dec. 1851, Berg.

41. Nathaniel Hawthorne to Zachariah Burchmore, 15 July 1851, *Centenary* 16:456.

42. Nathaniel Hawthorne to William D. Ticknor, 19 Jan. 1855, *Centenary* 17:304; Nathaniel Hawthorne to James T. Fields, 11 Dec. 1852, *Centenary* 16:624.

43. Rose Hawthorne Lathrop, *Memories of Hawthorne* (Boston: Houghton Mifflin, 1897), p. 422.

44. *Centenary* 23:416–17.

45. *Centenary* 14:513.

46. Nathaniel Hawthorne to Henry Wadsworth Longfellow, 30 Aug. 1854, *Centenary* 17:250.

47. Nathaniel Hawthorne to James T. Fields, 3 Sept. 1858, *Centenary* 18:151.

48. *The Marble Faun*, p. 1195.

49. Nathaniel Hawthorne to William D. Ticknor or James T. Fields, 27 Sept. 1860, *Centenary* 18:323.

50. Nathaniel Hawthorne to Charles Sumner, 11 Apr. 1861, *Centenary* 18:373.

51. *Centenary* 23:403.

52. Bronson Alcott, Journals, 17 Feb. 1861, Houghton.

53. William Ellery Channing to Ellen Channing, 30 Oct. 1851, Massachusetts Historical Society.

54. Henry James, Senior, to Ralph Waldo Emerson, quoted in Emerson, *The Early Years of the Saturday Club*, p. 331.

55. Charles Eliot Norton to George W. Curtis, 21 Sept. 1863, Houghton.

56. Annie Adams Fields, Diary, 26 July 1863, Massachusetts Historical Society.

57. Rose Hawthorne Lathrop, *Memories of Hawthorne*, p. 478.

58. *The Blithedale Romance*, p. 667.

HAWTHORNE
IN HIS TIME

Mysteries of Mesmerism

Hawthorne's Haunted House

Samuel Chase Coale

Nathaniel Hawthorne despised and feared mesmerism, the process in which a practitioner hypnotized his subject and put her into a trance. He found it morally and philosophically repugnant, since in his view the mesmerist could violate an individual consciousness and soul and gain power over his victim. At the same time, he recognized that the process was probably physiologically and psychologically sound. It worked. The master could manipulate his slave. Hawthorne used this mysterious force to describe the way the artist works upon a reader's consciousness. His own fictional technique emulated that process. The kind of fiction he called "romance," in his view, was essentially a mesmeric text that hovered between our recognizable daily and social world and the more phantasmagoric realm of our dreams. Despising the force, he yet recognized its true power and was simultaneously attracted to and repelled by it.

In Hawthorne's fiction, characters examine others with their powerful mesmerizing gazes. They skewer their subjects on the compulsive strength of their unnerving and deliberately concentrated observations, like vampires about to strike. In doing so, they hope to penetrate the other's social and public disguises and expose the darker self within. Whether Dr. Chillingworth focuses on the unfortunate Arthur Dimmesdale in *The Scarlet Let-*

ter, Matthew Maule entrances the vulnerable Alice Pyncheon in *The House of the Seven Gables*, the evil Westervelt paralyzes the ethereal Priscilla in *The Blithedale Romance*, or the Gothic shadow that is Miriam's model in *The Marble Faun* totally envelops her with his eyes, the pattern is repeated over and over again in Hawthorne's work.

At the same time, Hawthorne himself x-rays and probes his characters' darker psyches. He, too, penetrates their subconscious minds and grapples with the secrets and compulsions he finds there. He, too, plays master to his fictionalized slaves. And in recognizing this, he, too, saw himself as a kind of spiritual villain, a marauder of the mind, and this perspective endows all of his work in both its technique and creation with an air of brooding and ineradicable guilt.

Hawthorne constructed his romances and the best of his short stories as mesmeric texts, conjured up to ensnare the reader in a kind of dark trance as he created the dark domain of Gothic fiction and the barely discovered subconscious depths of his characters. The texts perform their mesmeric task carefully and precisely, often utilizing the hypnotic lull of a repetitive, clause-ridden style, the presence of shadows and past sins, and the fascination with strange images—birthmarks, scarlet letters, ministers' black veils, poisonous flowers, demons in gloomy midnight forests—that can never be fully explained or rationalized. No wonder he felt the chill his own characters often felt; they performed mesmeric arts together, torn between the moral horror of what they were doing and the secret delight in what they could not stop themselves from pursuing.

Where did mesmerism come from? How did it find its way to the United States in the 1830s, and why was it received so avidly by so many Americans? Why did it affect Hawthorne and so many others so completely and insistently? And, if Hawthorne were ultimately suspicious about its use, if not the scope and depth of its powers, why did he employ it so readily in his fiction?

We should begin with Franz Anton Mesmer himself and the historical context that helped produce him. Born in 1734, he wrote his dissertation for his M.D. and Ph.D., entitled "The Influence of the Planets on the Human Body," at the University of Vienna Medical School. However cosmological the title, his dissertation was strictly a scientific affair, examining the influence of gravitation on human physiology and including the suggestion of an extremely subtle "universal fluid," which permeated all things, ebbed and flowed in some kind of magnetic tidal manner, and was undetectable by the five senses. Mesmer first used the term "animal magnetism" ("animal" in the sense of "vital") in his "Letter to a Foreign Physician" on 5 January 1775. He had been experimenting with a woman who lived with him and his wife and who was suffering from convulsions, spasms, and general hysteria. In treating her, he used magnets to attract and repel the tidal waves of the universal fluid within her, within himself, and which completely surrounded them, attempting to direct this ebb and flow and thus cure her of her illness. It worked, and the young woman, Francisca Oesterlin, went on to marry Mesmer's stepson.

Mesmer probably achieved the greatest personal recognition in his lifetime when he arrived at the Place Vendôme in Paris in February 1778 and set up a successful clinic. People rushed to him for cures. He treated rich and poor alike and drove them to what he called "the crisis," as if a fever had to be broken. At the Hotel Bullion, he relied on dim lights, quiet music, and a series of four tubs called *baquets*, which contained magnetized water and iron rods around which his patients would gather. He himself—a kind of magical overseer in beautiful robes, complete with wand— wandered among them, hands outstretched. The patients would apply the rods to the sick areas of their bodies and would link themselves to one another with a rope, thus allowing the fluid to interpenetrate and communicate with each of them. Mesmer would reinforce the action of the fluid by mesmerizing the supposed poles in their bodies. There were mattress-lined crisis rooms where the critical convulsions could occur, the final event that broke the illness and relieved the patient. "Control the tidal waves entering the physiology from outside the body," Mesmer believed, "and you control the illness."[1]

Just what was this animal magnetism? Mesmer described it as

a material influence which bodies, animate or inanimate, exercise upon each other through the mediation of a universal and extremely fine fluid (the "magnetic" fluid), which underpins the phenomena of animal life in the same sort of way as air is the vehicle of sound or the ether of light. This fluid penetrates and perfuses all material bodies. . . . Glass, iron, gold, steel, silver are good conductors, and so in the animal organisms are nerves.[2]

When the circulation of this magnetic fluid is obstructed, disease results. To eradicate the disease, Mesmer often faced his patient seated, their feet touching in order to complete the magnetic circuit. With a penetrating gaze, he focused on the patient, completed the magnetic circuit, and after the crisis, the patient was cured. The iron rods, rope, and joined hands around the baquets were supposed to reproduce the same experience.

At the time, Mesmer's initial ideas were not that farfetched. Science was fascinated by invisible fluids and forces in everything from Newton's gravity to Franklin's electricity. Scientists tried to prove empirically that these universal fluids existed and tried to systematize them into one general and universal theory. Mesmer fit right into this general design of the universe in his quest "to reduce the mysteries of life to one basic principle," according to Maria Tatar, "to identify a single animating agent that at once sustains life and figures as its chief cause."[3]

The search for an ultimate theory of existence and the general atmosphere it produced can be seen in *L'Homme Machine*, Julien Offray de La Mettrie's book, published in 1747, which described "man as a mechanical entity in which psychic events are regularly produced by organic causes."[4] "The various states of the soul are always related to the body," La Mettrie asserted (*Machine* 14), and thus the mind is

> like a self-performing piano which listens to itself play, can simultaneously order the signs in a great diversity of patterns and keep present to consciousness the sensations that these evoke. . . . It can stand aside from its own sensory content and examine the arrangements it imposes on them—in a word, it can reflect. (*Machine* 27)

Such a mechanistic thesis became a *succes de scandale* in France, and La Mettrie's book was consequently forbidden to be sold there. But, by the 1760s, his ideas emerged as a broad generic concept that many people took almost for granted. His concept thoroughly undercut any divine sanctions whatsoever and reduced humanity to the inner workings of a clock, thus helping to advance science's assault on religious values. Such a stance challenged the prevailing spiritual metaphysics and belief in a divine design, since "to deny the soul's immateriality meant more or less to doubt God's existence, because the divine presence in the world was presumably discernible only to the spiritual man" (*Machine* 24).

Mesmer's magnetic fluid theoretically fused both matter and spirit, the physical and the metaphysical, and united them in a vast cosmological plan that could suggest both planetary and perhaps divine influence as well as "a universally distributed fluid, so continuous as to admit of no vacuum anywhere, rarefied beyond all comparison, and by nature able to receive, propagate and communicate all motion—this is the medium of the influence" (*Wizard* 101). Science and religion did not have to be enemies. Such a fluid became the source of light, heat, electricity, and other mysterious elements in the universe. It also suggested a possible source for the soul itself as one among these various forces, producing both visible effects and the revival of the human spirit. As Edward S. Reed suggests, "The fundamental idea animating most of these theorists was that the soul exists as some kind of force within nature" and that it probably was related to all the other natural forces in some yet-undiscovered manner.[5] Identify these forces, and somewhere the soul could be ultimately located among them. Such theorists, therefore, did not discredit religion at all and viewed themselves as positively opposed to any totally materialistic explanation of the cosmos. Though Mesmer based his theory on facts and fluids alone, his personality and reputation added to this fruitful and still mysterious union between emerging sciences and traditional religion.

"My own suspicion," Alan Gauld suggests:

is that the rationalistic physician, who had early on rejected the priesthood as a career . . . had an inner tendency to-

ward mysticism; his theory derived as much from the word-
less communings with nature . . . as from any observations
he had made himself. (*History* 16)

In such a way, both religious and scientific visions could be sup-
ported or upheld, or at least the theory could straddle both
worlds and account for the mysteries within them. As Charles
Poyen St. Sauveur, the man credited with bringing mesmerism to
the United States in 1836, described it:

This discovery . . . gives a new life to the religious principle,
and furnishes unconquerable weapons to Christianity against
materialism, which is already triumphant in some parts of the
civilized world—it opens a new and broad field to psychological speculations.[6]

In pursuit of justifying his theory and in gaining public respect
and recognition for it, however, Mesmer, "blinkered by his own
single-mindedness and the paranoid tendencies which went with
it" (*History* 17), attracted the attention of two royal commissions
assembled by Louis XVI, which produced two reports in 1784.
Paris before the French Revolution was certainly receptive to all
kinds of intellectual and metaphysical speculations—it was probably the most intellectually free city in Europe at the time—but
Mesmer's work undermined and offended official and institu-
tional medicine.

The royal reports acknowledged the fact that animal magnetism worked. The commissioners witnessed the trances, the magnetic sleep that Mesmer's patients experienced, but they could
find no evidence of the mysterious fluid that, according to
Poyen, was "so nice, active, and subtle, that we may consider it as
a spiritual substance" (*Report* xlii). The report continued, "In
these cases it was impossible not to acknowledge the power of
imagination, a power owing to which those individuals believing
themselves magnetized, felt the same effects as if they had been
so" (*Report* 92). "We may conclude with certainty, that such a
state exists, whenever it gives rise to the development of the new
faculties designated by the names of clairvoyance, intuition, pre-

vision" (*Report* 167), but the fluid itself did not. The commission's first report (11 Aug. 1784) concluded, "If this substance affects material objects, then it must be detectable; if it is too ethereal to be detected, then it cannot affect material objects" (*Spellbound* 22). In short, "The imagination without the aid of Magnetism can produce convulsions, and . . . Magnetism without the imagination can produce nothing."[7] Instead of pursuing the psychological aspects of Mesmer's powers, the commissioners pronounced his theory fatally flawed, but Mesmer, unable to relinquish his belief in the fluid, pursued his research even as he and his work were publicly rejected.

Mesmerism in France, however, continued its somewhat clandestine progress. It mingled with radical political theory, evoking Rousseau's idea of primitive nature as opposed to a decadent society, and "by 1789 this eclectic, spiritualist form of mesmerism, the form that was to be revived in the nineteenth century, had spread throughout Europe."[8] Ironically, Mesmer himself contributed to this spiritualist and metaphysical form of his theories by evoking and describing all kinds of occult practices and perceptions in his 1799 *Memoire sur la découverte du magnétisme animal*.

Discredited scientifically, Mesmer's invisible fluid slowly evaporated, but the sense he had of a single animating force that underlay all things persisted. In fact it permeated romantic theory, though one is hard-pressed to suggest which came first, Mesmer or romanticism. As Whitney R. Cross describes it, this single force contributed to the growing belief that "natural laws rather than whimsical miracles embodied God's purposes for humanity,"[9] and it may have contributed to Schelling's romantic vision, as summarized by Tatar: "The concept of nature as an organic whole, the identity between nature and the human mind . . . and the principle of polarity—came to serve as the very foundations of Romantic poetry" (*Spellbound* 71).

On 4 May 1784, the Marquis de Puysegur mesmerized a twenty-three-year-old peasant by the name of Victor Race on his estate. Race had been suffering from, among other things, inflammation of the lungs, and Puysegur's magnetism cured him. The marquis's younger brother, the comte, who had had asthma, had been cured by Mesmer in March 1780, after spending three months around the baquets, and the marquis had been intrigued. Word spread rapidly. Puysegur was able to cure people without the crisis that Mesmer's patients experienced. But the comte had guessed as early as 1783 that the success of the entire process was based upon "the importance of the will of the operator in influencing the response of the patient" (*History* 44). The marquis issued his famous imperative: "Croyez et Veuillez [Believe and Will]" (*Short* 77). Although the word *hypnotism* was not coined until 1843 (by Scottish physician James Braid in Manchester, England), Puysegur's intuition proved to be correct.

An atmosphere of fraud and charlatanism has always surrounded Mesmer, mostly because of the royal commissioners' reports but also because of his later dabbling in the occult and his insistence that the magnetic fluid actually existed. It is now known that he plagiarized most of his doctoral dissertation and, despite teaching his disciples about his theory, probably came to see that animal magnetism resided in himself, not in some invisible fluid. His persistence and his stubbornness prevented him from discovering the very real existence of hypnotism, and his various pamphlets and apologetics doomed his work to ultimate irrelevance, despite his continuing to see patients in Paris and elsewhere. He died in virtual obscurity in 1815.

Charles Poyen St. Sauveur, "a self-proclaimed Professor of Animal Magnetism," who likened himself to Galileo, Columbus, and Christ (*End* 17), arrived in Boston in March 1836 to give a series of lectures on mesmerism, thus providing the necessary link between European mesmerism and the American fascination with it. On his family-owned plantations in Martinique and Guadeloupe, he discovered that the French planters were employing magnetism and "using their slaves as subjects."[10] An evangelical abolitionist in the United States, he originally wanted to write a book about slavery, but the mayor of Lowell, Massachusetts, where he ended up teaching French and drawing lessons to the daughters of nouveau-riche mill owners, and his publisher suggested that he choose another subject. He chose mesmerism, and "the publisher agreed to print it, but only on one condition—that Dr. Poyen stir up as much excitement over animal magnetism as Dr. Spurzheim had created over phrenology."[11] Thus, in 1836, Poyen published his *Report on the Magnetical Experiments*, which was followed by his *Progress of Animal Magnetism in New England* in 1837, spurred on by his own public mesmeric exhibitions.

In 1837, Poyen began a long tour of New England, which took him to Taunton, Nantucket, and Salem. On that tour, he magnetized Phineas Parkhurst Quimby who, in magnetizing the woman soon to become Mary Baker Eddy, helped lay the groundwork for her religious discovery that, borrowing a phrase from him, she called "Christian Science." Dr. Joseph Emerson Fiske, a young dental assistant to Dr. Nathaniel Peabody, the father of Hawthorne's future wife, Sophia, heard Poyen speak, was convinced that he, too, possessed magnetic powers, and offered to help cure Sophia of her headaches. This would lead to Hawthorne's famous letter, which warned Sophia about magnetic powers and control. From Mesmer to Poyen, Poyen to Fiske, Fiske to Peabody, and Peabody to Hawthorne: the magnetic chain was complete.

Hawthorne recorded in his *American Notebooks* on 24 July 1837 his visit to the home of his friend Horatio Bridge and his discussions with a French visitor there, a Mr. Schaeffer:

> When we sit in the twilight, or after Bridge is abed, talking of Christianity and Deism, of ways of life, of marriage, of benevolence,—in short all deep matters of this world and the next . . . he generally gets close to me, in these displays of musical and histrionic talent. Once he offered to magnetize me, in the manner of Monsieur Poyen.[12]

According to the *Salem Gazette* of 12 and 15 September 1837, Poyen performed his mesmeric experiments for a Salem audience, and Hawthorne's future sister-in-law, the cause-oriented, evangelical Elizabeth Peabody, heard him. Hawthorne speculated in his 1842 diary about "questions as to unsettled points of History and Mysteries of Nature to be asked of mesmerized persons."[13]

Why was America so susceptible to mesmerism, among so many other pseudosciences of the time? According to Gilbert

Seldes, who, writing in 1928, tried to describe the general fervor of the period, Americans believed in the perfectability of man, and the drama of personal salvation was still very much part of the late-Puritan culture. Humanity was becoming more interesting to itself in a new world that was bent on self-reformation.[14] New ideas, cults, movements thrived, "uplifted by an almost euphoric optimism as to the prospects for improving man's lot in the world or assuring his comfort in the next" (*History* 179). Imminent revelation hovered in the air, and there existed no highly institutionalized authority in a culture that was still essentially rural, the population scattered and isolated in their separate communities.

Perhaps Henry Spicer in his *Sights and Sounds: The Mystery of the Day: Comprising an Entire History of the American "Spirit" Manifestations* (1853), a book on spiritualism, which turned out to be the next revelation that followed mesmerism, best expressed the state of mind that could exist in the sparse villages of snow-bound vistas on the frontier. On a coach trip to Palestine, Ohio, he described the countryside in winter as:

> wild and weird. . . . Endless woods of beech and pine, bleak hills, dismal hollows, lonely, snow-suffocated huts, and straggling, lifeless villages . . . might have contributed in some degree to engender that peculiar condition of mind . . . in the sudden, unhealthy impulse imparted to the imagination . . . said to characterize persons whose lives passed in lone and remote districts of the earth.[15]

Traveling in such places revealed "a certain track of debatable land to be struggled through, like a conquered, but not pacified, country, of which reason still reigns nominal sovereign." And in this place, one could become mesmerized, entranced, falling into a hypnotic state, which "if prolonged . . . is one of the strangest" (*Sights* 248). It is as if the setting itself had initiated the trance, an assumption not lost upon Hawthorne in describing the devil's appearance in the midnight woods of "Young Goodman Brown," the garden of poisoned plants in "Rappaccini's Daughter," or the nightmarish spectral Boston in "My Kinsman, Major Molineux."

Between 1800 and 1850, religious sects and utopian social movements erupted everywhere. Whitney R. Cross's classic study of this phenomenon, *The Burned-Over District*, reveals as much. People were ravenous for belief in gold tablets, lost Indian tribes, prophetic angels, revivalism and conversion, progress of any kind, zealous ultraism, experimental communities, or prophetic mesmerists. Some even believed, along with William Miller, that the world would come to an end on 22 October 1843. As William G. McLoughlin has explained, much of America was undergoing its "Second Great Awakening" between 1795 and 1835, and many believed that God's grace was directly available to man through revivalists and itinerant missionaries and prophets, who were eager to regenerate the faith in the individual soul and consciousness.[16] In the midst of all of this, "mesmerism offered a new faith, a faith that marked the end of the Enlightenment . . . and the dawning of the nineteenth century" (*End* 165).

The mesmerism craze caught fire. Each believer tried to attach his own term to the process. Joseph Rhodes Buchanan called it "neurology"; John Bovee Dods, a Universalist minister, who was invited to speak in the Hall of Representatives in Washington, D.C., on 12 February 1850, "electrobiology" (*Soul* 1); Dr. Fiske, "electropsychology"; J. Stanley Grimes, a medical professor, "etherology"; and LaRoy Sunderland, until 1833 a famed Methodist minister, who later became a zealous abolitionist, "pathetism."

> There appeared a new breed of mesmerists—itinerant magnetizers who made the rounds of carnivals and festivals with their trance maidens in order to cash in on the latest fad sweeping the Continent. The cruel exploitation of an innocent young girl by a shrewd mesmerist wizard was to become a pervasive theme in nineteenth-century European and American literature. (*Spellbound* 31)

Many Universalist ministers were consumed by the new revelations, believing that God would send no one to hell in any case and looking for a scientific manner in which to celebrate and expand one's individual powers. In 1855, Webster's *Dictionary* defined a Universalist as "one who affects to understand all particulars," and once more mesmerism supplied that all-animating force, part fluid, part psychological will power, part mysterious effluvium or "soul," which many suspected lay at the center of all things. As Robert Fuller suggests, mesmerism initiated

> an enduring tendency in American religious thought. The American mesmerists were the first to encourage popular audiences to abandon a scripturally-based theology in favor of psychological principles said to govern the individual's ability to inwardly align himself with a higher spiritual order. (*History* 194)

By the 1820s, a national system of book production and distribution had been established, and a huge audience for popular medical books existed. New medical systems appealed directly to a public willing to accept them or, at the very least, experiment with them. These new procedures produced their own self-appointed practitioners, who were trained outside the established medical schools, but they were also designed to be self-administered in many cases. Animal magnetism was only one of the self-declared new approaches to medicine and health, which included everything from homeopathy to hydropathy.

One of the best eyewitness accounts we have of the era appears in Robert Collyer's *Lights and Shadows of American Life* (1838), although he—at one time a British medical student—was quite determined to show how much America needed him the moment he arrived.[17] He eventually appeared at the conclusion of Hawthorne's "The Hall of Fantasy," published in February 1843, in which the narrator and his guide meet "the spirits of several persons, whom Dr. Collyer has sent thither in the magnetic sleep."[18] In 1838, Collyer found a New York City full of

> humbugs. [It is a place where] . . . much quackery abounds, where any one who has the impudence may leave his foreplane, or lapstone, or latherbrush, and become a Physician; where any unlettered biped who has sufficient cant and hypocrisy may become a Minister of the Gospel, where ignorant

and lousy pettifoggers may claim to be Lawyers, and are per-
mitted in the Courts . . . where even some of the most sacred institutions of the Government bear upon their face the
indelible blot of bribery and corruption, robbery, embezzle-
ment, and every kind of moral guilt . . . where in fact a
cloud of moral depravity has arisen so dense and high as to
eclipse from human sight the poor remains of virtue that still
exist there. (*Lights* 4)

Collyer was appalled by the "tall, red-faced man" who attended his lectures on phrenology and then went on to imitate
them, setting up his own traveling charts and skulls and lectures,
"rising out of the dense obscurity that had always enshrouded
him, and claiming to be the greatest, the most learned Phrenolo-
gist of the day" (*Lights* 17). He marveled at the fact that most of
English literature had been pirated and hawked inexpensively
with no copyright laws to impede its public progress, a practice
that appalled American writers like Herman Melville, who saw
all these works as the purest and cheapest competition for a distinctly American literature.[19] Collyer surely had his axes to grind,
but his observations of a professionally loose and open American
market for everything from ministers to prophets, novelists
to phrenologists, certainly captures the Jacksonian spirit of the
era and the manner in which apprentice cobblers could rise
to the status of publicly acclaimed prophets. "The demon of
money-making" (*Lights* 14) was everywhere apparent, and so
was the wide-open opportunity for con artist and charismatic
clairvoyant.

One apprentice cobbler who seized this opportunity was
Andrew Jackson Davis, the "Seer of Poughkeepsie." He heard
J. S. Grimes lecture in 1843, decided that he was indeed a magnetic somnambule (clairvoyant), and went on to give a series of
lectures as a professional. While a Dr. Lyon magnetized him, and
the Reverend William Fishbough wrote down what he prophe-
sied, Davis wrote a 786-page tome, *The Principles of Nature*. The
sprawling book, reviewed and praised in the *New York Tribune* by
George Bush, professor of Hebrew at New York University, became a bestseller, filled as it was with the Swedenborgian faith in

endless correspondences between this world and the next. Dictated Davis:

> The human mind should comprehend the great truth that nothing exists in the outer world except as it is produced and developed by an interior essence, and that of this essence the exterior is the perfect representation. . . . Every form invented by Man is a precise representation of the interior thought which is the cause of its creation. (*Short* 227)

Harmony reigned within all things.

On the Friday night of 31 March 1848, in the hamlet of Hydesville in upstate New York, scene of so many revelations and miracles, the American fascination with mesmerism took a sudden and unexpected turn. Spiritualism, in which somnambules became mediums in touch with the spirit world and reported back to the living what the spirits were saying, had been around as early as 1788 in Stockholm. Alphonse Cahagney, a restorer of old furniture in Paris, had mesmerized subjects, who could then describe the celestial world. But nothing like the Fox sisters had happened in the United States before.

On that March night, eleven-year-old Kate Fox heard strange rappings in the family bedroom. "Here, old Splitfoot, do as I do," she reportedly commanded. She snapped her fingers, and the spirits responded. Her mother, Margaret Fox, asked the spirits to rap twice if they were spirits. They did. Neighbors were summarily summoned and dazzled. The event took on the features of a romance by Hawthorne: the dark domain of the Fox house at night with its flickering candles; the secret deed of spiritual possession or visitation, which revealed the apparent murder of a peddler in the house years ago; the cover-up of that dastardly deed; and the power of unseen spirits over the people in the house—like Miriam's dark shadowy model in *The Marble Faun*, the Maules' mesmeric powers over the Pyncheons in *The House of the Seven Gables*, and Westervelt's power over just about everyone in *The Blithedale Romance*.

Interestingly, as mesmeric clairvoyants metamorphosed into spiritualist mediums—Andrew Jackson Davis described the Foxes' rappings as the fulfillment of his mesmeric prophecies of ultimate correspondences between all things, including the living and the dead—they were most frequently seen to be women (even though the mediums were almost equally divided between men and women at the time). The female stereotype of passivity and reception permeated the 1850s, and Hawthorne himself used it in his fiction to describe characters Alice Pyncheon, Priscilla, and Hilda, among others. It fit easily into the developing, middle-class Victorian vision of specific gender roles. Women were supposed to be passive, easily controlled by outside forces; they were far more sympathetic, "religious," and sensitive than men; self-sacrifice was their greatest role. The Reverend William H. Ferris, in his "Review of Modern Spiritualism" in February 1856, made this quite clear:

> I never knew a vigorous and strong-minded person who was a medium. I do not believe that such a one can ever become one. It requires a person of light complexion, one in a negative passive condition, of a nervous temperament with cold hands, of a mild, impressible, and gentle disposition. Hence girls and females make the best mediums.[20]

Spiritualism spread like a social disease. Isaac and Amy Post, Quaker friends of Leah Fish Fox, Margaret and Kate's older married sister, had attended the first seances and apparently taught the spirits to tap out their messages letter by letter to make them clearer. By the summer of 1850, fifty to a hundred mediums were working in upstate New York. Personal testimonies swamped newspapers and journals. The Fox sisters performed on stage to overflow audiences. Eighteen communities of 3,800 Shakers experienced spiritualist visions and trances up until 1844, usually in the presence of girls, similar in execution but not at all in substance to the uprisings in Salem in 1692. The paroxysms of religious conviction and conversion were an almost daily occurrence. And books, whose titles were almost longer than the actual text, appeared everywhere from the uplifting and relatively brief *Voices from the Spirit World* (1852) by Isaac Post to William McDonald's *Spiritualism Identical with Ancient Sorcery, New Testa-*

ment Demonology, and Modern Witchcraft: With the Testimony of God and Man against It (1866).

Hawthorne absorbed and acknowledged all of these historical facts and qualities in his *Notebooks* and fiction: the credulous country mind in its remote environment; the gender-specific role of the medium; the mesmeric trance as a genuine psychological and physiological experience with its blurring of everyday fact and dreamlike encounters. In his famous letter to Sophia Peabody on 18 October 1841, he recognized the real power of "these magnetic miracles." This power had unknown origins and uncertain consequences, and it was able to "bewilder us," and even, in writing to Sophia, if Hawthorne "possessed such a power over her, I should not dare to exercise it."[21] He seems to have believed so much in the basic psychological existence of such hypnotic powers that he came to view them as antithetical to his own as both a writer and Sophia's future husband:

> And, dearest, thou must remember, too, that thou art now a part of me, and that by surrendering thyself to the influence of this magnetic lady [Mrs. Park, who was helping Sophia overcome terrible headaches], thou surrenderest more than thine own moral and spiritual being. (*Letters* 588)

Hawthorne versus the mesmerist in a battle for Sophia's being: flip sides of the same coin? He abhorred what he saw as mesmerism's violation of an individual soul: "It seems to me that the sacredness of an individual is violated by it; there would be an intrusion into the holy of holies—and the intruder would not be thy husband!" (*Letters* 588).

The transformation of mesmerism into spiritualism provided no great obstacle for Hawthorne, for in his eyes the craze was essentially the same. In 1863, Sophia Elizabeth de Morgan declared in her book: "Every wonderful effect produced by mesmerism has since found its explanation or its counterpart in the spiritual phenomena."[22] Hawthorne would have agreed with all but the "wonderful." In effect, the spirits communicating with the medium were similar to "the work of an intelligent unseen being, acting by means of a force similar to mesmerism upon the system of the medium" (*Result* 96). Hawthorne decided as much in his *Notebook* on 1 September 1858. Spiritualist seances "seemed to be akin to those that have been produced by mesmerism, returning the inquirer's thoughts and veiled recollections to himself, as answers to his queries."[23]

In 1858 in Italy, Hawthorne summed up his attitude toward spiritualism and at the same time defined it once and for all as merely an outgrowth of the mesmeric performances he had heard and read about in the 1830s and 1840s, as described in *The Blithedale Romance*. The existence of spiritualism may have tantalized him, but it did not convince him:

> But what most astonished me is, the indifference with which I listen to these marvels. They throw old ghost stories quite into the shade; they bring the whole world of spirits down amongst us, visibly and audibly; they are absolutely proved to be sober facts by evidence that would satisfy us of any other alleged realities; and yet I cannot free my mind to interest itself in them. They are facts to my understanding (which, it might have been anticipated, would have been the last to acknowledge them), but they seem not to be facts to my intuitions and deeper perceptions. My inner soul does not in the least admit them. There is a mistake somewhere. So idle and empty do I feel these stories to be. (*Notebooks* 398–99)

At the same time, trying to plumb the depths of these strange phenomena, Hawthorne continued:

> The whole matter seems to me a sort of dreaming awake. . . . It resembles a dream, in that the whole material is, from the first, in the dreamer's mind, though concealed at various depths beneath the surface; the dead appear alive, as they always do in dreams; unexpected combinations occur, as continually in dreams; the mind speaks through the various persons of the drama, and sometimes astonishes itself with its own wit, wisdom, and eloquence, as often in dreams. . . . I should be glad to believe in the genuineness of these spirits, if I could; but the above is the conclusion to which my soberest thoughts tend. There remains, of course, a great deal for

which I cannot account, and I cannot sufficiently wonder at the pig-headedness both of metaphysicians and physiologists, in not accepting the phenomena so far as to make them the subject of investigation. (*Notebooks* 400–401)

Such a "sort of dreaming awake," like the mesmeric trance, became for Hawthorne a characteristic analogy to describe his kind of romance.

The realm where that trance can be most effective is in the kind of space into which both moonlight and firelight, imagination and actuality, intrude and intermingle, as Hawthorne explains in "The Custom-House" at the beginning of *The Scarlet Letter*. This suggests the realms of the mesmeric trance and the spiritualist seance, which become the dark and haunted domain of Hawthornian romance.

In "The Custom-House," Hawthorne describes a familiar room made unfamiliar by moonlight. The moonlight invests the room with "a quality of strangeness and remoteness," the perfect realm in which the romancer's imagination may flourish, "somewhere between the real world and fairy-land, where the Actual and the Imaginary may meet, and each imbue itself with the nature of the other." The mingling of the light of the coal fire in the room with the otherwise remote and cool moonlight helps to warm and humanize the scene, and both when reflected in the "haunted verge" of a mirror suggest the true domain of the willing romancer. Here, "if a man, sitting all alone, cannot dream strange things, and make them look like truth, he need never try to write romances."[24]

Within that domain, mesmerist-scientists with their penetrating intelligence and trance-inducing powers stalk their prey. One thinks of Ethan Brand, Rappaccini, Chillingworth, Westervelt, and Matthew Maule. Each of these males has his female victim: Brand's Edith, Rappaccini's Beatrice, Chillingworth's Hester (and, later, Dimmesdale), Westervelt's Priscilla, and Maule's Alice Pyncheon.

At the same time, the structure and texture of Hawthorne's fiction, the texts themselves, partake of such mesmeric methods as the induction into and transition toward the trance or hypnotic state. Hawthorne lures the reader into his darker realm by setting his scene and then describing it hypnotically by using repetitive clauses and eerie images. In such a shadowy domain, he then conjures up images and events from the past; Puritan Boston, the old Pyncheon house, the Veiled Lady at the beginning of *The Blithedale Romance*, the strange black veil on the face of a much-loved minister. Such a structure mimics the "hypnotic induction [which] furnishes the conditions for transition to the hypnotic state," immobilizing the reader, willing her to pay close attention to the writer's desire, to "the hypnotist's bidding." The act of reading becomes dreamlike, a "sort of dreaming awake," as the writer works on the reader's imagination. The reader's mind is almost directly controlled by the writer-mesmerist, so that the reader wills only what the writer wills in his text, perceiving the world at that moment through the writer's entrancing vision of it. As in a real trance, "the arousal of visual memories and the play of visual imagination appear to be more vivid than in the usual waking state." And, once in Hawthorne's clutches, once within his text, the reader can fall prey to "trance logic, the peculiar acceptance of what would normally be found incompatible," complete with "the loss of ties to reality," as she is drawn into a Gothic realm.[25]

Hawthorne's use of long clauses and repetition in the opening paragraph of *The House of the Seven Gables*, for example, establishes his own mesmerist-like gaze upon his material and, by creating this linguistic spell, disconnects the reader, as does the trance, from the world of everyday consciousness and experience:

> Halfway down a bystreet of one of our New England towns stands a rusty wooden house, with seven acutely peaked gables, facing towards various points of the compass, and a huge, clustered chimney in the midst. The street is Pyncheon street; the house is the old Pyncheon house; and an elm tree, of wide circumference, rooted before the door, is familiar to every town-born child by the title of the Pyncheon elm. On my occasional visits to the town aforesaid, I seldom failed to turn down Pyncheon street, for the sake of passing through the shadow of these two antiquities—the great elm tree and the weather-beaten edifice.[26]

Hawthorne situates the reader in a strange, out-of-the-way place: "halfway down a bystreet . . . for the sake of passing through the shadow" of the Pyncheon house and elm. He is almost drawn to this place against his will, the "seldom failed" suggesting the lack of personal choice that the more positive and active phrase "often succeeded" would not. He also repeats the word *Pyncheon* four times as if conjuring some spell or creating some eerie incantation. And the clauses add details to the scene that make it even stranger: "a rusty wooden house, with seven acutely peaked gables . . . a huge, clustered chimney . . . the shadow of these two antiquities."

At the beginning of the second paragraph, Hawthorne acknowledges that "the aspect of the venerable mansion has always affected me like a human countenance." We are about to enter into that domain of dark romance, the interior of a soul, the expressive shadows of the human psyche that, in Hawthorne's romance, suggest the interior of the mesmeric trance. It is almost as if that dark countenance were mesmerizing the author and transforming him into the medium of its mysteries. The process begins with the "rusty wooden house"; the repeated name of Pyncheon evokes an almost spellbinding animating principle for it; we are lured into "passing through the shadow"; and the house is transformed before our eyes into "a human countenance." The normal, everyday, sunlit world succumbs to a darker, shadowy, trancelike realm in which the author will attempt to connect us to some ancient and mysterious past, which will itself attempt to overcome and overshadow that ordinary world.

The darkness of the trance is no mystery in Hawthorne's fiction, since he associated it not only with his art but also with witchcraft, demonic possession, and the like. He purposefully set *The Scarlet Letter* during the English Civil War from 1642 to 1649, a period that he knew, from reading Sir Walter Scott, was the time of the worst persecution of witches in English history, complete with Matthew Hopkins, the "Witchfinder General." Charles Upham, in his *Lectures on Witchcraft* (1831), which Hawthorne had read, wrote in detail about the would-be witch Ann Hibbins, sister of Richard Bellingham, the deputy governor of Massachusetts, and she appears as Mistress Hibbins in Hawthorne's romance. Thus, as Richard Forrer explains, "The world portrayed in Hawthorne's fiction, rather than humanizing his characters, seems either to stunt them or to evoke and abet their demonic possibilities."[27] Such is the extent of those "demonic possibilities," incorporated into the texture and form of Hawthorne's idea and execution of the romance, that his narrators virtually "express a dualistic vision of the universe wherein the power of evil almost inevitably neutralizes, if not outmatches, the power of God" (*Conflict* 158).

There might, however, be another more practical reason for employing such mesmeric devices. Hawthorne was acutely aware that American literature was new. It could not compete with the pirated editions from England, which were sold cheaply and widely. He wanted to establish a sense of the importance of the American past for his own work, as he did in the title of his lost collection of short stories, "Seven Tales of My Native Land." At the same time, he wished to escape the simplistic moral lessons that most American literature provided as if still rooted in the didactic Puritan period of its youth. Literature in general, but American literature in particular, should reveal its own inherent powers, distinctly different from allegorical parables. It needed to proclaim its own powerful reason for being.

Hawthorne mused on the weight and the curse of his own New England past, both as part of his personal biography and as material for Gothic fiction, a literary genre that was very popular with the public. He wished to conjure up that past in his fiction with its effects and events. To do so, he may have assumed that such a power and influence were chiefly psychological, and what better way to display this power than by relying on psychological narratives, underscored by the analogous powers of the mesmeric trance? Literature could then reenact essential human dramas of which the public was already extremely aware. It could reflect the "demonic" powers of its time and thus become a truly native literature in its own right.

Several reviewers of Hawthorne's fiction, despite their impressionistic and biographical meanderings, picked up on this major strain in his prose. Typically, Richard Henry Stoddard declared in 1853 that "in the region of mystery, the wildernesses and caverns of the mind, he is at home."[28] E. P. Whipple recognized in 1852 that Hawthorne "has penetrated into mysterious regions of consciousness, a pioneer in the unexplored wildernesses of thought."[29] Other critics elaborated on these insights by exploring how Hawthorne "lures the mind from the visible and concrete to the invisible and spiritual" and into "the dim regions of twilight, where realities blend inextricably with mere phantoms."[30] Other reviewers, both American and British (and often anonymous), pursued this line of criticism. *Harper's* in 1851 described *The House of the Seven Gables* as "connecting the legends of the ancient superstition with the recent marvels of animal magnetism."[31] Commented a British critic:

> Mr. Hawthorne manages the supernatural so well, he makes it so credible by refining away the line of demarcation between the natural and the supernatural, he derives profit so ingeniously from the existing tremor of the public mind, arising from what is seen and said of mesmerism, electro-biology, spirit-rappings, and Swedenborgian psychology.[32]

Added Leslie Stephen in 1872, "Mesmerism . . . plays an important part in *The Blithedale Romance* and *The House of the Seven Gables*, though judiciously softened and kept in the background" (*Cornhill* 497).

Many attributed the powers associated with mesmerism to Hawthorne the artist. "The insight into character especially, seems at times to follow the processes of clairvoyance more than those of the waking imagination," Whipple declared in 1851.[33] In 1860, he added, "His great books appear not so much created by him as through him. They have the character of revelations. . . . His profoundest glances into individual souls are like the marvels of clairvoyance . . . a sort of meditative dream."[34] "Mr. Hawthorne's peculiar genius lies in the power he possesses to be haunted, and in his turn to haunt the reader. . . . before he has done with you you are pursued, you are possessed, you are beset with his notion: it is in your very blood," explained Richard Holt Hutton in 1860.[35] And Dorville Libby proposed in

1869 that "Hawthorne does not clear up his mysteries. The truly supernatural admits no clearing up. It is the especial privilege of the romancer to make this departure from the strictly probable, and thus avail himself of the charm of mystery."[36]

Critics related Hawthorne's mesmeric interests to the state of America as well. Wrote one typically condescending British critic in 1860: "He represents the *youthfulness* of America . . . its vague aspirations, its eager curiosity, its syncretism, its strainings after the perception of psychologic mysteries."[37] Hutton decided that Hawthorne had to investigate "the mysterious links between the flesh and the spirit, the physical and the spiritual nature, a subject on which all original New England writers have displayed a singular and almost morbid interest."[38] Railed another British wag about *The Blithedale Romance*:

> How thoroughly worn out and *blasé* must that young world be, which gets up excitements in its languid life, only by means of veiled ladies, mysterious clairvoyants, rapping spirits. [There is] nothing attractive in the pale clairvoyant Priscilla—the victim, we are led to suppose, of Mesmerism and its handsome diabolical professor.[39]

Libby suggests that Hawthorne could be casting aspersions upon all

> spiritualists [who] have seized upon this ready-made faith, swept together a multitude of occult and out-of-the-way phenomena, roughly classified the crude material, with a little addition of theory, and assumed for their so-called system the holy name of a religion. And this, too, has its devoted adherents and unquestioning believers. ("Supernatural" 454)

In many cases, critics readily agreed upon the close and sympathetic relationship between Hawthorne's art and "the law of spiritual influence, the magnetism of soul on soul," which metamorphosed "into the most elusive movement of Consciousness" (Whipple 257).

Even as Hawthorne consciously employed the mesmeric

trance and the mesmerizer as fictional structure and villain, he nevertheless voiced his concerns about the very real terrors of the process he had so readily responded to and appropriated. He did not just object to the violation of the individual soul or the probable exposure of certain secret places in the human heart and consciousness, which might otherwise remain unrevealed. The true powers of mesmerism could conjure up the "black hole" of the self and reveal to the conscious mind the pervasive and threatening absence that lurked there. He once suggested to Sophia that in hearing the voice of her dead mother in a mesmerist/spiritualist trance, she was really listening to "her own voice, returning out of the lonely chambers of her heart" (*Notebooks* 399), as Hawthorne must have recognized his own voice in the various characters he conjured up for us.

NOTES

1. Vincent Buranelli, *The Wizard from Vienna: Franz Anton Mesmer* (New York: Coward, McCann and Geoghegan, 1975, p. 114. In text as *Wizard*.

2. Alan Gauld, *A History of Hypnotism* (Cambridge: Cambridge University Press, 1992), p. 11. In text as *History*.

3. Maria Tatar, *Spellbound: Studies in Mesmerism and Literature* (Princeton, N.J.: Princeton University Press, 1978), p. 49. In text as *Spellbound*.

4. Aram Vartanian, Introduction and notes to Julien Offray de La Mettrie, *L'Homme Machine: A Study in the Origins of an Idea* (Princeton, N.J.: Princeton University Press, 1960), p. 13. In text as *Machine*.

5. Edward S. Reed. *From Soul to Mind: The Emergence of Psychology from Erasmus Darwin to William James* (New Haven, Conn.: Yale University Press, 1997), p. 82. In text as *Soul*.

6. Charles Poyen St. Sauveur, *Report on the Magnetic Experiments Made by the Commission of the Royal Academy of Medicine* (Boston: D. K. Hitchcock, 1836), pp. v–vi. In text as *Report*.

7. Frank Podmore, *From Mesmer to Christian Science: A Short History of Mental Healing* (New Hyde Park, N.Y.: University Books, 1963), p. 59. In text as *Short*.

8. Robert Darnton, *Mesmerism and the End of the Enlightenment in*

France (Cambridge, Mass.: Harvard University Press, 1968), p. 71. In text as *End*.

9. Whitney R. Cross, *The Burned-Over District* (New York: Harper and Row, 1965), p. 326.

10. Slater Brown, *The Heyday of Spiritualism* (New York: Hawthorn, 1970), p. 12.

11. Grace Adams and Edward Hutter, *The Mad Forties* (New York: Harper and Row, 1942), p. 90.

12. *Centenary* 8:58.

13. Robert C. Fuller, *Mesmerism and the American Cure of Souls* (Philadelphia: University of Pennsylvania Press, 1982), pp. 34–35.

14. Gilbert Seldes, *The Stammering Century* (New York: Harper and Row, 1928/1965), pp. 305–7, 319. In *The Popular Mood of Pre–Civil War America* (Westport, Conn.: Greenwood, 1980), Lewis O. Saum disagrees. Hawthorne and Melville, he believes:

> hardly stood in bilious isolation; they had vast company in the common men of America. . . . That abiding negation, that resignation bordering on fatalism, made Hawthorne and Melville much more attuned to their society than is frequently supposed. . . . I find an abiding moroseness. (20, 53, xxii)

15. Henry Spicer, *Sights and Sounds: The Mystery of the Day: Comprising an Entire History of the American "Spirit" Manifestations* (London: Thomas Bosworth, 1853), p. 249. In text as *Sights*.

16. William G. McLoughlin, "Revivalism," in *The Rise of Adventism: Religion and Society in Mid–Nineteenth-Century America,* ed. Edwin S. Gaustad (New York: Harper and Row, 1974), pp. 121–47.

17. Robert Collyer, *Lights and Shadows of American Life* (Boston: Redding, 1838). In text as *Lights*.

18. Taylor Stoehr, *Hawthorne's Mad Scientists: Pseudoscience and Social Science in Nineteenth-Century Life and Letters* (Hamden, Conn.: Shoe String, 1978), pp. 35–37.

19. Complained James Fenimore Cooper in *Notions of the Americans* in 1828:

> The fact that an American publisher can get an English work without money must for a few years longer . . . have a tendency to repress a national literature. No man will pay a writer for an epic, a tragedy, a sonnet, a history, or a romance, when he can get a work of equal merit for nothing.

Quoted by J. Donald Crowley, ed., *Hawthorne: The Critical Heritage* (London: Routledge & Kegan Paul, 1970), p. 2. In notes as *Heritage*.

20. Quoted in R. Laurence Moore, *In Search of White Crows* (New York: Oxford University Press, 1977), p. 120.

21. *Centenary* 15:462. In text as *Letters*.

22. Sophia Elizabeth de Morgan, *From Matter to Spirit: The Result of Ten Years' Experience in Spirit Manifestations. Intended as a Guide to Enquirers* (London: Longman, Green, Longman, Roberts, and Green, 1863), p. 49. In text as *Result*.

23. *Centenary* 14:398. In text as *Notebooks*.

24. Nathaniel Hawthorne, *The Scarlet Letter* (Columbus, Ohio: Charles E. Merrill, 1969), pp. 35, 36.

25. Ernest R. Hilgard, *Hypnotic Susceptibility* (New York: Harcourt Brace & World, 1965), pp. 49, 11, 9, 12.

26. Nathaniel Hawthorne, *The House of the Seven Gables*, ed. Seymour L. Gross (New York: W. W. Norton, 1967), p. 5.

27. Richard Forrer, *Theodices in Conflict: A Dilemma in Puritan Ethics and Nineteenth-Century American Literature* (New York: Greenwood, 1986), p. 138. In text as *Conflict*.

28. Richard Henry Stoddard, "Nathaniel Hawthorne," *National Magazine* 2 (Jan. 1853): 17–24; *Heritage* 289.

29. E. P. Whipple, "Review of New Books," *Graham's Magazine* 41 (Sept. 1852): 333–34; *Heritage* 254. In text as Whipple.

30. Eugene Benson, "Poe and Hawthorne," *Galaxy* 6 (Dec. 1868): 742–48; and Leslie Stephen, "Nathaniel Hawthorne," *Cornhill Magazine* 26 (Dec. 1872): 717–34; *Heritage* 434, 497. The latter in text as *Cornhill*.

31. Unsigned review, *Harper's New Monthly Magazine* 2 (May 1851): 855–56; *Heritage* 196.

32. Anon., "American Novels," *North British Review* 20 (Nov. 1853): 81–99; *Heritage* 300.

33. E. P. Whipple, review in *Graham's Magazine* 38 (May 1851): 467–68; *Heritage* 197.

34. E. P. Whipple, "Nathaniel Hawthorne," *Atlantic Monthly* 5 (May 1860): 614–22; *Heritage* 347, 348.

35. Richard Holt Hutton, "Nathaniel Hawthorne," *National Review* 11 (Oct. 1860): 453–81; *Heritage* 372, 373.

36. Dorville Libby, "The Supernatural in Hawthorne," *Over-*

land Monthly 2 (Feb. 1869): 138–43; *Heritage* 458. In text as "Supernatural."

37. Anon., "Nathaniel Hawthorne," *Universal Review* 3 (June 1860): 742–71; *Heritage* 365.

38. Richard Holt Hutton, "Nathaniel Hawthorne," *Spectator* 37 (July 1864): 705–6; *Heritage* 410.

39. Anon., "Modern Novelists—Great and Small," *Blackwood's Magazine* 77 (May 1855): 562–66; *Heritage* 311–12.

BIBLIOGRAPHY

Adams, Grace, and Edward Hutter. *The Mad Forties*. New York: Harper and Row, 1942.

Brown, Slater. *The Heyday of Spiritualism*. New York: Hawthorn, 1970.

Buranelli, Vincent. *The Wizard from Vienna: Franz Anton Mesmer*. New York: Coward, McCann and Geoghegan, 1975.

Collyer, Robert. *Lights and Shadows of American Life*. Boston: Redding, 1838.

Cross, Whitney R. *The Burned-Over District*. New York: Harper and Row, 1965.

Crowley, J. Donald, ed. *Hawthorne: The Critical Heritage*. London: Routledge & Kegan Paul, 1970.

Darnton, Robert. *Mesmerism and the End of the Enlightenment in France*. Cambridge, Mass.: Harvard University Press, 1968.

de Morgan, Sophia Elizabeth. *From Matter to Spirit: The Result of Ten Years' Experience in Spirit Manifestations. Intended as a Guide to Enquirers*. London: Longman, Green, Longman, Roberts, and Green, 1863.

Forrer, Richard. *Theodices in Conflict: A Dilemma in Puritan Ethics and Nineteenth-Century American Literature*. New York: Greenwood, 1986.

Fuller, Robert C. *Mesmerism and the American Cure of Souls*. Philadelphia: University of Pennsylvania Press, 1982.

Gauld, Alan. *A History of Hypnotism*. Cambridge: Cambridge University Press, 1992.

Hawthorne, Nathaniel. *The American Notebooks*, ed. Claude M. Simpson. Vol. 8 of *The Centenary Edition*. Columbus: Ohio State University Press, 1972.

————. *The French and Italian Notebooks*, ed. Thomas Woodson. Vol. 14 of *The Centenary Edition*. Columbia: Ohio State University Press, 1980.

————. *The House of the Seven Gables*, ed. Seymour L. Gross. New York: W. W. Norton, 1967.

————. *The Letters: 1813–1843*, ed. Thomas Woodson, L. Neal Smith, and Norman Holmes Pearson. Vol. 15 of *The Centenary Edition*. Columbus: Ohio State University Press, 1984.

Hilgard, Ernest R. *Hypnotic Susceptibility*. New York: Harcourt Brace & World, 1965.

Kerr, Howard. *Mediums, and Spirit-Rappers, and Roaring Radicals: Spiritualism in American Literature, 1850–1900*. Urbana: University of Illinois Press, 1972.

McLoughlin, William G. "Revivalism," in *The Rise of Adventism: Religion and Society in Mid–Nineteenth-Century America,* ed. Edwin S. Gaustad. New York: Harper and Row, 1974.

Mellow, James R. *Nathaniel Hawthorne in His Times*. Boston: Houghton Mifflin, 1980.

Miller, Edwin Haviland. *Salem Is My Dwelling Place: A Life of Nathaniel Hawthorne*. Iowa City: University of Iowa Press, 1991.

Moore, R. Laurence. *In Search of White Crows*. New York: Oxford University Press, 1977.

Podmore, Frank. *From Mesmer to Christian Science: A Short History of Mental Healing*. New Hyde Park, N.Y.: University Books, 1963.

Poyen St. Sauveur, Charles. *Report on the Magnetic Experiments Made by the Commission of the Royal Academy of Medicine*. Boston: D. K. Hitchcock, 1836.

Reed. Edward S. *From Soul to Mind: The Emergence of Psychology from Erasmus Darwin to William James*. New Haven, Conn.: Yale University Press, 1997.

Seldes, Gilbert. *The Stammering Century*. New York: Harper and Row, 1928/1965.

Spicer, Henry. *Sights and Sounds: The Mystery of the Day: Comprising an Entire History of the American "Spirit" Manifestations*. London: Thomas Bosworth, 1853.

Stoehr, Taylor. *Hawthorne's Mad Scientists: Pseudoscience and Social Science in Nineteenth-Century Life and Letters*. Hamden, Conn.: Shoe String, 1978.

Tatar, Maria. *Spellbound: Studies in Mesmerism and Literature.* Princeton, N.J.: Princeton University Press, 1978.

Vartanian, Aram. Introduction and notes to Julien Offray de La Mettrie, *L'Homme Machine: A Study in the Origins of an Idea.* Princeton, N.J.: Princeton University Press, 1960.

Hawthorne and Children in the Nineteenth Century

Daughters, Flowers, Stories

Gillian Brown

When Hawthorne rewrote the story of King Midas for his 1852 collection of children's stories, *A Wonder-Book for Girls and Boys*, he added the character of a daughter, whom he called Marygold. Midas, we are told, loved this "little maiden who played so merrily around her father's footstool. But the more Midas loved his daughter, the more he did desire and seek for wealth," thinking, "the best thing he could possibly do for this dear child would be to bequeath her the immensest pile of yellow, glistening gold, that had ever been heaped together since the world was made." Even though she is the intended beneficiary of Midas's gold, Marygold herself does not at all share her father's "insane desire for riches."[1] While Midas delights in his ability to transform flowers into gold, Marygold laments the bloom and scent lost in this transmutation: "all the beautiful roses, that smelled so sweet and had so many lovely blushes, are blighted and spoiled! They are grown quite yellow . . . and have no longer any fragrance!" (49).

Eventually, Marygold's own life is sacrificed to her father's alchemical faculty when she turns to gold from his kiss. Midas had often said, "whenever he felt particularly fond of the child, . . . that she was worth her weight in gold" (53). Once the phrase has become literally true, he realizes that the living Marygold exceeds in value all the piles of gold envisioned in his miserly fantasies. The lesson Midas learns about the follies of fetishism and miserliness is a familiar one: rather than wanting everything to be gold and wanting an endless supply of gold, he should be happy with the riches he already possesses, most especially his daughter, Marygold. And, rather than projecting his fortune into the future, he should be concerned with the life of the one upon whom his own self-perpetuation depends. At the same time that Hawthorne is reciting the well-known lessons of an ancient fable, however, he also is presenting a message familiar to his contemporary nineteenth-century readers, a reminder of the importance of children, their value to parents as beloved objects, and their cultural value as emblems and agents of goodness.

Many years before writing the *Wonder-Book*, Hawthorne had noted "the charm of childhood" upon adults. In "Little Annie's Ramble," one of the stories in his 1842 collection, *Twice-Told Tales*, he wrote, "As the pure breath of children revives the life of aged men, so is our moral nature revived by their free and simple thoughts, their native feeling, their airy mirth. . . . Their influence on us is at least reciprocal with ours upon them."[2] Child characters thus figure frequently in Hawthorne's tales, which so persistently explore moral issues.

Hawthorne began his publishing career as an author of books for children, working on Samuel G. Goodrich's Peter Parley series of educational books.[3] These books furnished easily comprehended accounts of world history and geography. What interested Hawthorne most about children, however, was not the project of educating them, but "their influence on us," the ways they can educate adults. The influence of children upon adults, though, arises not from children themselves so much as from the adult imagination of children. Put another way, Hawthorne explores the process of how adults make children into the measures of themselves. When he later writes again for children, Hawthorne portrays Midas in light of the little girl, Marygold's, moral perspective.

Before Marygold, the character of children as possessors of superior moral vision and thus as agents of moral reformation was a staple feature of early nineteenth-century temperance and abolitionist literature. Children appear as natural critics of the inhumanity of slavery, for example, because they clearly see the analogy between the commerce in persons and the commerce in animals. In a fictional dialogue between father and son published in the abolitionist paper the *Slave's Friend* (1836), the boy, Charles, asks his father if it is true that people "sell boys and girls, like Julia and me . . . by the pound, as they do pigs and fish?" The father affirms that this is the case, telling Charles that if he looks into books on slavery, he "will see [a picture of] some slaves weighing a little girl in a pair of scales." This information makes Charles consider closely the details of how slavery treats persons as commodities:

CHARLES: How much will she weigh?

PAPA: I suppose about fifty pounds.

CHARLES: How much do they get a pound for the poor slaves?

PAPA: Four dollars, and sometimes five: If that little girl weighed fifty pounds, and her master got four dollars a pound for her, she was sold for two hundred dollars.

CHARLES: Ah! that's the reason they don't want to emancipate the slaves; they get so much money by selling them. Isn't it so, father?[4]

Charles easily recognizes the economics of slavery, which rationalizes such an inhumane practice; he thus throws into relief the operation of greed in slave owners. The clarity and correctness of the child's view permeated antislavery arguments. Harriet Beecher Stowe most memorably embodied these faculties in *Uncle Tom's Cabin* (1852) with the character of Little Eva, the angelic little girl who urges her father to free his slaves.[5]

Like Little Eva, Mary Morgan, the child heroine of T. S. Arthur's popular temperance novel, *Ten Nights in a Bar-Room* (1852), has an "angel-look."[6] To her alcoholic father, Mary is "an angel," the only one who can comfort him when he suffers delirium tremens (78). Mary not only attends to her father's suffering but, in Christlike fashion, suffers for him. When she tries to get her father out of Slade's tavern, the bar where he wastes his life, she gets hit by a glass thrown at him. After this injury, she develops a fatal fever. Mary dies and, as in Eva's dying, leaves her father with the memory of her redemptive love. These daughters reveal the evils of certain forms of consumption, whether the inhumanity of the slave trade or the dangers of alcohol addiction.[7] Little girls much like Mary and Eva pervade nineteenth-century reform literature; they are also standard figures of goodness in novels, unforgettably epitomized by Louisa May Alcott's Beth and Charles Dickens's Little Nell.[8]

In turning Marygold to gold, Midas displays the depravity of his love for gold, a love that kills his most beloved possession. It is only when Midas can see the fatal consequences of substituting a golden statue for his own child that he can see his love of gold as a mistaken value, as a wrongful investment of feeling. Thus Marygold, through the transformation of her body, most explicitly teaches Midas the error of his ways. This Christlike function of the daughter, also apparent in the deaths of Eva, Mary, Beth, and Nell, enlightens her survivors, showing them the impropriety if not horror of the principles by which they have been living. Treating persons as chattel, or preferring golden objects above all others, even living ones, or living for drink alone, or maintaining old grudges—all these modes of conduct involve following a false standard by which other human beings matter less than profit, aesthetic pleasure, liquor, or pride. Placing children into this calculus, as Hawthorne and so many nineteenth-century writers do, dramatizes the moral depravity to which economic and personal desires can lead: it takes a child's death to demonstrate adults' inhumane preoccupations and to steer them toward reformation.

By inventing Marygold and making the Midas story revolve around her, Hawthorne successfully modernizes the old story from Ovid's *Metamorphoses* into a familiar nineteenth-century moral tale about avarice.[9] Perhaps, the tale is even a reminder of how evil endures, the subject that Hawthorne had just explored in *The House of the Seven Gables* (1851), his novel about the repercussions of individual crimes of greed upon subsequent generations. Moreover, in making the child the point of departure and the occasion for Midas's reformation, Hawthorne both engages in and expounds on the nineteenth-century cultural formation of the salvific child. His own literary practice of employing children in the labor of adult reformation comes under his scrutiny as Hawthorne considers what it means to invest children with so momentous a purpose. The significance of Marygold, for Hawthorne's work and for nineteenth-century American culture, consists in the questions she raises about adult assignments of the child's role in moral reformation. Marygold, as Hawthorne fashions her, functions not as an exemplar to child readers but as a standard by which to appraise Midas. Writing about children, Hawthorne both exemplifies and criticizes the nineteenth-century American imaginative practice of making children witnesses and saviors of humans who err. To see how Hawthorne's own fiction develops a case against (even as it relies on) the enormity of expectations placed upon children, it is useful to consider some works prior to "The Golden Touch" as well as the historical context in which his portrayals of children appeared.

Saintly Children

Stories of exemplary children, particularly stories of saintly children who die and leave their shining models of virtue to their survivors, regularly appear in religious literature and sermons beginning in at least the seventeenth century. The Protestant Reformation, advocating unmediated individual readings of God's words in the Bible, encouraged widespread literacy. At the same time, Protestantism spread through the new literacy made possible by the invention of the printing press, which made literature available to unprecedented numbers of persons. Thus Protestant doctrine as well as Protestant conversion aims relied on and promoted education to furnish and direct reading skills.[10] Stressing the individuality of human relations to the deity, Protestant sects and churches also tried to ensure that individuals, from generation to generation, would choose the same religious affiliations. Thus, the early education and influence of children became a crucial project, resulting in the emergence of a religious children's literature. Best exemplified by James Janeway's popular *A Token for Children* (1671), this literature followed the earlier format of lives of the saints and martyrs but focused on child protagonists.[11] Puritan emigrants to America read this book to their children while their ministers quoted from it in their sermons, describing the holy lives and joyful deaths of children, such as eleven-year-old John Harvy, who died counseling his siblings on "the danger of pride." Cotton Mather thought it important for children in the colonies to have exemplars more local than Janeway's English youth and accordingly published his *A Token for the Children of New England* (1700). He included within his catalog of child piety the case of his own brother Nathanael, who died in his teens, leaving the example of his piety as "a Mirrour, wherein you may see what *may* be done by a young person."[12]

Because most American Protestant groups originally upheld the Calvinist emphasis on original sin, the child's religious state at death, especially in the case of early death, greatly mattered. The familiar phenomenon of infant mortality made Puritan parents want to be assured of their children's acceptance *of* God and possible merciful acceptance *by* God. Narratives of children's piety and happy deaths clearly offered parents a form of consolation for their loss and their fears for their children's fates after death. One effect of this narrative tradition of saintly children was to question the Calvinist notion of persons as born sinful, in other words, to think of the possibility that children might indeed be born as good as the paragons in the stories. In fact, the doctrine of child depravity continually troubled and divided Protestant churches. By the end of the eighteenth century, most descendants of the early American Puritans no longer held to the doctrine of children as innately evil. From changes within Puritan practices (such as more lax requirements for church membership and acceptance of individual members into church membership on the basis of family connections) as well as the colonial experience of generations forging new customs in response to a new environment, a much more benign and hopeful account of humans as not only redeemable but innately good emerged.[13] Even in the more familiar ethos of England, the changing views of child competence generated by and in tandem with new inter-

ests in literacy and education led to a sense of children's originality, the romantic sense of childhood so vividly recorded by
Blake and Wordsworth. Blake's images of children in *Songs of Innocence* (1789) and Wordsworth's description of children in *Intimations of Immortality* (1807) as "trailing clouds of glory" stand as
poetic landmarks for the romantic view of childhood as innately
good, if not superior to the adult condition.[14]

   While Little Eva and Mary Morgan clearly descend from the
reformation religious literary tradition, which continued to pro-
liferate in the early nineteenth century through Sunday School
tracts and juvenile magazines,[15] they also recall the more secular
eighteenth-century child heroes and heroines, such as Goody
Two-Shoes and Giles Gingerbread, whose industry and virtue
bring them wealth and happiness as adults. These prototypes
for the later nineteenth-century Horatio Alger suggest the remarkable worldly faculties and accomplishments of individual
children.[16] The child's role in reform literature, an established
feature of nineteenth-century culture, thus stems from representational patterns of childhood used in secular as well as religious
publications of the preceding centuries. It is not just the paradigm of saintly children but the sense of children's efficacious-
ness that makes them such suitable moral agents for reform
discourses.

   One of Hawthorne's earliest tales, "The Gentle Boy," revolves
around an innocent and beautiful child, a boy named Ilbrahim,
whose sweetness and patience resemble the qualities of the children in the Puritan piety narratives. Yet Hawthorne makes this
boy the victim of Puritan intolerance, the object of their bigotry
even though he exemplifies the very characteristics of Christianity that they profess to value and honor. Based on historical
accounts of Quaker persecutions in seventeenth-century New
England, Hawthorne's portrait of Ilbrahim is one of his most
devastating indictments against early American Puritans.[17] To
make his case, Hawthorne employs the literary conventions invented and relied upon by the Puritans against the historical
record of their practices. He offers a narrative of a saintly boy
not to console or celebrate a religious community, but to shame
it: Ilbrahim, Hawthorne writes, "was a sweet infant of the skies,

that had strayed away from his home, and all the inhabitants of this miserable world closed up their impure hearts against him" (14).

The orphaned son of persecuted Quakers—orphaned because the Puritans have executed his father and banished his mother—Ilbrahim arouses the compassion and love of a childless Puritan couple, who protect and adopt him. In the household of Tobias and Dorothy Pearson, Ilbrahim finds shelter and love. But the Puritan community in which they live treats the child with "scorn and bitterness" (23). At the forefront of this tale is the terrible suffering to which the boy is subjected: besides the loss of his parents, he is continually ostracized by the community and treated cruelly by other children. When the loving little Ilbrahim, "with a look of sweet confidence on his fair and spiritual face," tries to join neighboring children at play, he is savagely stoned and beaten (25). The persecution of the child extends to his foster parents, who are shunned and reviled. Displaying the malignity of Puritan orthodoxy, "The Gentle Boy" powerfully denounces religious intolerance.

Hawthorne's objection to religious prejudice is not limited to Puritanism, however, for the story explicitly also criticizes what he repeatedly calls the "fanaticism" of Quakers (19, 20, 32, 36). Ilbrahim's mother, Catharine, who abandons him so she may wander as a prophet for her faith, epitomizes an irrationality and inhumanity as misguided and tragic as the Puritan abusive treatment of Ilbrahim. In contrast to Dorothy, who with her "rational piety" manages to adhere to both her Puritan faith and her sense of maternal duty to Ilbrahim, even in the face of intolerance, the "enthusiast" Catharine "violated the duties of the present life, and the future, by fixing her attention wholly on the latter" (20). This critique of Catharine makes clear that the problem with extreme religious visions lies in forsaking present responsibility while attempting to shape the future. If the Puritans' commitment to furthering their faith and history leads them to inhumane behavior, the Quaker sense of mission similarly misleads Catharine. Both misguided religious practices result in the abuse of the child Ilbrahim. Setting up his attack on religious bigotry thus as an advocacy of proper parenting, Hawthorne exposes the inhumanity of subjecting children to parental religious commitments.

In Ilbrahim's case, the very life of the child is sacrificed to parental beliefs, beliefs Hawthorne describes as fanatic even as he generates sympathy for the Quakers. Initially, the tale seems to be suggesting that the gentle boy works as an agent of conversion, causing his foster father, Tobias, to doubt his Puritan faith and to sympathize with the Quakers, even to consider joining that sect. Tobias, though he comes to shelter and respect Quakers, at much danger to himself, cannot find comfort in the Quaker relation to God. To underscore the story's refusal to prefer one religion over another, and to reiterate its brief for humane childrearing, Hawthorne includes the example of an old Quaker man, who recounts having left his dying daughter to pursue his religious mission and his subsequent torment at the thought that he had erred in so doing. Highlighting this monitory message to both Tobias and the reader, Catharine returns to find her son dying and confesses to her own terrible mistake in having left her child. Ilbrahim dies in his mother's arms, comforted only by that embrace and not by any prayers, Puritan or Quaker. Then, in the tradition of pious dying children, he comforts her:

In a moment, his mother was kneeling by the bed-side; she drew Ilbrahim to her bosom, and he nestled there, with no violence of joy, but contentedly as if he were hushing himself to sleep. He looked into her face, and reading its agony, said, with feeble earnestness, "Mourn not, dearest mother. I am happy now." And with these words, the gentle boy was dead. (36)

Both recalling the Puritan child piety narrative and setting the paradigm for death scenes of children like Little Eva in nineteenth-century fiction, this vignette of the child's death stresses the influence of the child on the parent. "As if Ilbrahim's sweetness yet lingered round his ashes; as if his gentle spirit came down from heaven to teach his parent a true religion, her fierce and vindictive nature was softened by the same griefs which had once irritated it" (36). Catharine (as Hester Prynne does in *The Scarlet Letter*) later settles in the community that persecuted her and her child and is eventually treated with "pity" and "little kindnesses" (36). The narrator of the tale concludes by noting the improvement in the Puritan community as well as the improvement in Catharine, "a triumph of our better nature," which gives him "a kindlier feeling for the fathers of my native land" (37).

The critique of Puritan intolerance and parenting developed in "The Gentle Boy" bespeaks Hawthorne's lifelong literary and personal concern with how adults treat and affect children, especially in their attribution of special or salvific powers to children. Precisely because children do influence adults, Hawthorne thinks that adults must respect the lives of children, neither neglecting them for, nor overburdening them with, their own needs or expectations. While Hawthorne readily admits and richly describes the influence of children upon adults, following and contributing to the imagery of salvific children in American culture, his worries about improper parenting extend beyond his Puritan forebears (the "fathers" of his native land) to contemporary nineteenth-century customs. Violated children and insensitive, if not abusive, parents continue to appear in his fiction throughout his career.

Endangered Daughters

A long-standing example of the folly of avarice and miserliness, Midas in Hawthorne's treatment also typifies bad parenting. Though he loves his daughter, he wrongfully casts her as the reason and recipient of his desire for more gold. Wanting to bequeath her the greatest possible fortune in gold, Midas uses his relation to Marygold to justify his own obsession. In this way, he resembles Catharine and the Puritan parents whose interests in future salvation lead them to subordinate their children to their personal visions. Even after the waning of Puritan doctrine and pedagogy, Hawthorne continues, in the middle of the nineteenth century, to register an anxiety about the effect of parental desires and ambitions upon children. For the custom of parental investment in children both pre-dates and perseveres after Puritanism, persisting most prominently in nineteenth-century America in the proclivity for reform, which regularly makes children both the objects and agents of designs for improving the world. Describing Eva as "your only true democrat" in *Uncle Tom's Cabin*, Harriet Beecher Stowe reiterates the contemporary sense of children's superior social and spiritual virtues, which pervaded abolitionist and temperance literature.[18]

Though never a participant in the movements that made antebellum America known as the Age of Reform—except for his brief membership in the communitarian living experiment at Brook Farm—Hawthorne lived in a circle of friends and relations who actively pursued political, religious, economic, and educational reforms. His relatives by marriage included some of the foremost revisionary commentators on childrearing: sister-in-law Mary Peabody Mann wrote a treatise on parental responsibilities to children called *The Moral Culture of Infancy* (1864). Her husband, Horace Mann, initiated the public school movement in the United States. Another sister-in-law, Elizabeth Peabody, introduced the kindergarten system and with Bronson Alcott designed and founded the alternative Temple School in Boston. Hawthorne also was familiar with the new dietary and disciplinary philosophies of childrearing practiced by Alcott in his family when they lived as neighbors in Concord. Louisa May Alcott would later recall the ways she and her mother and sisters suffered under Alcott's enthusiasms, which often left them hungry and poor.[19] Hawthorne and his wife, Sophia, held their own distinct ideas about the upbringing of children, which included home-schooling and intensive parental attention to every aspect of their children's lives.[20] All these concerns with childhood, however differently defined and directed, stemmed from the conviction of the basic goodness of children. As Mary Mann declared, a bad child seems "an anomaly of nature"; such a being could only emerge from bad parenting.[21] The problem that she noted of "parents not having the right views of their parental duties" recurs in Hawthorne's tales as the subjection of children to parental preoccupations, whether religious, economic, scientific, political, intellectual, or aesthetic.

As nineteenth-century reformers emphasized the excellence of children and expounded different views of proper childrearing, Hawthorne continued to consider how even the best intentions of parents—such as the Puritan hope for children's salvation or Midas's desire to leave a fortune for his daughter—could harm their children. In nineteenth-century America's abiding though reconceived interest in children, Hawthorne still finds evidence of the adult tendency to impose visions and values upon children. Inventing Marygold and adding her to the Midas story, Hawthorne draws attention to the persistence of wrongful parental investments, a phenomenon that he recognizes not only in Puritan history and contemporary cases but also in the seemingly enlightened cultural practice of idealizing or sanctifying children, particularly girls.

By the time Hawthorne wrote the stories for *A Wonder-Book*, there was a catalog of well-known child heroines in nineteenth-century children's literature; besides the angelic Little Eva and Mary Morgan, saintly girls pervaded popular novels and stories by early nineteenth-century American writers such as Catharine Maria Sedgwick, Eliza Leslie, A. J. Graves, Maria McIntosh, and Susan Warner. The title character of Emma Catherine Embury's *Constance Latimer; or, The Blind Girl* (1837) epitomizes the moral excellence of the young heroines, who in the face of all difficulties, including physical disabilities, behave with grace and charity. These heroines emerge with and reflect the feminization of virtue, the alignment of moral values with women and the domestic sphere.[22] As domestic women come to embody goodness for nineteenth-century America, presexual little girls even better approximate the ideal of the angel in the house, the agent of spiritual reformation for the family and society. With the gendering of virtue as feminine, the figure of the saintly little boy generally gives way to more mundane boy characters, who struggle to improve themselves, like J. C. Abbott's Rollo in the series of that title, or, as the century proceeds, to frankly mischievous heroes like Tom Sawyer.[23]

Following this trend, Hawthorne never fashions another Ilbrahim, even though he continues to explore the problem of the effects of parenting upon children. For Hawthorne, the femininity of the nineteenth-century child paragon aptly dramatizes the vulnerability of children to parental influence. The selfishness of parental investments in their offspring, typified by Midas's desire to transmit his wealth to Marygold, particularly plagues girls in Hawthorne's fiction. In the father-daughter relationship, Hawthorne finds an effective paradigm of parental misuse of children. Fathers, in depending upon their children for self-perpetuation and glory, whether worldly or spiritual, display an appalling unseemliness, which appears in Hawthorne's stories as both self-centered and sexual. This is not to say that Hawthorne is implying that fathers sexually abuse their children, but to point out that Hawthorne is studying an excessive self-love, which perverts all aspects of paternal love. This parental condition is fatal to children. The golden touch which so gratifies Midas's greed contaminates even the loving gestures through which a father expresses devotion to a child. It is by kissing Marygold that Midas turns his daughter into a golden statue. The father's economic excess—his greed and miserliness—infects and alters his familial relations, making Marygold just like the gold he desires. Literally objectified into Midas's most valued love object, Marygold epitomizes the futile logic of Midas's affiliation of love, gold, and futurity. Sacrificing his daughter's life to his mania, Midas deprives himself of both the purpose and the means of preserving and transmitting his fortune.

Hawthorne's young heroines regularly suffer for the sins and manias of their fathers (or husbands, who similarly control women) as Marygold is petrified by Midas or Alice Pyncheon is subjected by her father to another man's mesmeric control or Beatrice Rappaccini is experimented upon by her father. Georgiana in "The Birthmark" dies under her husband's cosmetic surgery; a young girl morally deteriorates under Ethan Brand's psychological scrutiny.[24] Marygold manages to survive her subjection to her father's desire after he repents his avarice, having realized "how infinitely a warm and tender heart, that loved him, exceeded in value all wealth that could be piled up betwixt the earth and sky" (53). Having learned his lesson, Midas wishes to be rid of the golden touch. His wish is granted (by the same stranger who gave him the golden touch), and everything is restored to its prior condition. Along with the roses, Marygold revives, and the only residue of the golden touch that remains is a permanent "golden tinge" in her hair, which also appears in the "rich shade of gold" of the "glossy ringlets" that her children inherit from her (57). As is the case in so many Hawthorne tales, the younger generation bears the physical marks of the character and actions of an ancestor. Even if the Calvinistic doctrine of original sin seems to no longer apply to children in the nineteenth century, Hawthorne retains a notion of inherited evil. Children themselves are morally innocent but marked by the sins of their parents. The bad parenting Mary Mann saw as productive of anomalies of the inherent good nature of children appears in Hawthorne's work as a genetic inheritance.

In Hawthorne's imagination, individual attributes and acts have lasting consequences, particularly for those who are the biological effects of an individual. Children contract something of their parents from their parents. So, from a child's point of view—which is, by definition, every person's point of view—parental character and behavior are crucial concerns. The weight of the past so often appears pressing or painful in Hawthorne's stories because it physically bears on each new generation. In owing their existence to their parents, that is, in issuing from the desires and acts of their parents, children represent the agency of their forebears. Children's representation of their progenitors includes the unchosen condition of embodying and signifying some aspect of their ancestors. Inheritance of this kind subjects each generation to the past, to the sins of the fathers, which do not so much repeat as quite literally *reappear* in their children. The condition of children is inheritance; they embody the principle of their existence, benefiting or suffering from it.

It is this parental persistence—the heritability of the effects of agency—that haunts and informs Hawthorne's negative vision of inheritance and kinship. Daughters in Hawthorne's stories do not always survive their fathers' legacies to transmit any signs of ancestral agency to future generations. As the primary agents of transmission, women are in an especially precarious situation. Because they serve as the mediums through which their fathers' histories are displayed and perpetuated, they seem—and are used as—canvases for their fathers' experiments in self-portraiture. To be a daughter, in Hawthorne's fictional world, is to be the heiress to the effects of paternal desire and behavior—just as Alice Pyncheon becomes a medium in subjection to the mesmeric commands of Matthew Maule as a result of her father's greed, which motivated him to give Maule access to his daughter. The habitual practices that represent paternal will and intention thus come to be represented in the daughter's condition but not in a direct mimesis, for what the daughter inherits is not her father's agency but the consequences—usually negative—of that agency. Long before implementing any forms of childrearing, parents thus can endanger their offspring in the very fact of generation. Sons as well as daughters accordingly suffer in Hawthorne's stories: Clifford Pyncheon, much like little Ilbrahim, also bears the negative effects of his lineage. I would suggest, though, that Hawthorne usually figures subjection as a female experience; his works feature women victimized by men. When Hawthorne describes male victims, such as Clifford and Ilbrahim, he represents their experience in the customarily feminine conditions of passivity and weakness. If, for nineteenth-century America, little girls best represent ideal human qualities, for Hawthorne, little girls best reveal the harms that humans inflict and deed to their children.[25]

Manufactured Children: Daughters and Flowers

The endangerment of daughters, without the mitigating restorations achieved in the fairytale narratives of "The Golden Touch" and *The House of the Seven Gables*, is the subject and tragedy of "Rappaccini's Daughter." In this story, the biological transmission of paternal character into filial physiology implicit in Marygold's name takes an even more literal form as Beatrice is transformed into one of her father's botanical creations. If Marygold's flower name suggests the naturalization and moral transformation of Midas's love of gold, Beatrice's metamorphosis into a flower literalizes the daughter/heiress's condition as the organic representation of paternal obsessions and habits. The subject of

Dr. Rappaccini's horticultural experiments, Beatrice embodies his scientific practices and ambitions: "Her father . . . was not restrained by natural affection from offering up his child . . . as the victim of his insane zeal for science."[26]

Rappaccini's aim was to make his "earthly child" identical with "the offspring of his science, of his intellect," a beautiful poisonous flowering shrub (123). To this end, Beatrice "grew up, and blossomed with the plant, and was nourished by its breath" (123). By her father's scientific experimentation, which substitutes for maternal nurture, Beatrice became the plant's "human sister" (97), a hybrid of human and plant, who lives and thrives on the poisonous fragrance of the plant, which she also comes to emit. Rappaccini's transformation of Beatrice magnifies as it epitomizes the transmission of the daughter's paternal inheritance. Completely her father's daughter, Beatrice becomes, like the plant, his creation. With no mother at all, neither an attentive Dorothy nor neglectful Catharine, Beatrice represents only her father. It is not enough that Rappaccini's daughter signify something of her father; in his vision of inheritance, she must *be* the result of his science. The process of generation must be supplemented by invention to ensure the father's perpetuity. And this invention improves upon generation, producing in the "daughter of [Rappaccini's] pride and triumph" a woman "redundant with life, health, and energy," a woman "apart from ordinary women," "who is able to quell the mightiest with a breath" (127, 97, 127).

Because generation is the channel of future self-representation, Rappaccini must also fashion a husband for his daughter. Hence, the young man, Giovanni, becomes "the subject of one of Rappaccini's experiments" (107), as he is exposed to Beatrice's "fatal breath" (124). In the course of pursuing his own desire for Beatrice, Giovanni becomes heir to her paternal legacy, transformed like her into a "poisonous thing," what he calls "a world's wonder of hideous monstrosity" (124). To underscore Beatrice's transmission of her condition to Giovanni, the bringing of the young man into the family, the tale supplies a Lamarckian scene of Giovanni's inscription with the Rappaccini touch. According to Lamarck, whose zoological theory was popular throughout the nineteenth-century, organisms acquire their traits through their activities. The long necks of giraffes, for example, derive from the habit of stretching their necks to get food from tall trees; their physical condition thus bears witness to their experience. After meeting with Beatrice, Giovanni discovers on "his right hand—the very hand which Beatrice had grasped in her own . . . a purple print, like that of four small fingers, and the likeness of a slender thumb upon his wrist" (115). His habitual encounters with her reproduce her in his body. In this lateral transmission of Rappaccini's creation, the possibility of vertical descent is achieved. That this mode of self-reproduction requires making a new race, or at least significant transformations in the race, suggests the extent to which generations owe not only their existence but the aspects of their state to prior self-representational projects. From the perspective of Hawthorne's tale, persons stem from other people's machinations. Rappaccini's horticultural development of Beatrice shows that both biology and culture compose persons, to quite frightening degrees.

Though drawn into Rappaccini's garden by his own desire and curiosity, Giovanni bitterly blames Beatrice for enticing him "into her region of unspeakable horror" (124). His role in completing Rappaccini's system of transmission demonstrates how the heiress's husband also functions in service to the paternal legacy. He may blame female sexuality for his entrapment in the paternal design, but the story also makes clear that the rightful object of Giovanni's outrage is Rappaccini's will, realized in his science.

From the start, Giovanni is given reason—or at least rumor—to keep away from Rappaccini. His father's old friend, Professor Baglioni, warns that Rappaccini "will hesitate at nothing" for "the interest of science" (119). What Baglioni does not tell the young man is "that there was a professional warfare of long continuance between him and Dr. Rappaccini, in which the latter was generally thought to have gained the advantage" (100). When Baglioni intervenes to save Giovanni, giving him an antidote to the poison Beatrice breathes, he acts not just to protect the son of his old friend but to "thwart Rappaccini," whose practice as "a vile empiric" he thinks should not "be tolerated by those who respect the good old rules of the medical profession"

(119–20). To stop Rappaccini, he destroys his perpetuity, his daughter. His gossipy characterization of Beatrice as so learned in her father's science that "she is already qualified to fill a professor's chair" (101) bespeaks his recognition of Beatrice's importance to her father's reputation. When he jokes that "perchance her father destines her for mine" (101), he further reveals the threat Rappaccini's daughter poses for his own future. Consistent with the logic of transmission to which Rappaccini is so horrifically devoted, Baglioni conducts the professional rivalry on the grounds of the future, over control of the younger generation. It is to Baglioni's science that Beatrice is ultimately sacrificed when she drinks the antidote with which he has provided Giovanni. Giovanni as well as Beatrice unwittingly enters into not just one scheme of individual ambition but into competing plots, both intent on making a mark across generations.

So, children may be subjected both to their fathers' legacies and to those of their fathers' rivals. In this way, children appear doomed to figure in prearranged scenarios. Yet the exigencies of inheritance do not obviate agency and intentionality in the younger generation. After all, the fathers are also the generation of other (prior) fathers. Though "the poor victim of man's ingenuity and of thwarted nature, and of the fatality that attends all such efforts of perverted wisdom" (128), Beatrice insists on herself as different from and independent of whatever her father has "striven to mingle with [her] being" (127). As for Giovanni, she takes him not for her fellow victim but at his word—for the character conveyed through his "blighting words" to her. Responding to his "words of hatred," her final words to him are appropriately reproachful: "Oh, was there not, from the first, more poison in thy nature than in mine?" (127). Maintaining a metaphysical truth—a truth not bound to the physical attributes of her body—Beatrice illuminates the dimensions of character operating apart from, and sometimes against, inheritance. One is not simply and only the embodiment of one's progenitor.

The horticulture through which Beatrice becomes "redundant with life" may technologically mirror botanical generation and exhibit her father's expertise, but it does not eliminate her "spirit" (97, 125). If "Rappaccini's Daughter" works as a horror tale about heredity (or at least about patrilinear heredity), about one's parents and what they have done (which is always potentially what they have done to oneself), it also repudiates the purely deterministic account of individuals. In doing so, the story reveals and explicates the necessity of the metaphysical, of incorporeal qualities, to the process of human transmission (which Rappaccini would literalize as a purely physical operation). For progeny always introduces new individuals, and in order for these individuals to represent their ancestors, they must be understood metonymically—as bodies symbolizing their progenitors. That is, individuals signify their ancestry by some inherited attribute. Yet the acquisition of a heritable attribute depends upon the existence of a distinct person, the difference embodied by each and every generation. With inherited traits, each generation also possesses its own characteristics, thus representing both past and present intentions, and indeed, the principle of intention through which physiology is continually reshaped. It is the malleability of the inherited body that Rappaccini's daughter ultimately signifies: the prominence of agency in even what appears the most paternally determined of life forms.

It might be said that Hawthorne's story dramatizes and preserves the importance of intentionality in inheritance in order to undo the limits implied by the process of representing intentionality, which inheritance entails. If the daughter is the fruit of the father's desires, she also can terminate or transcend those desires. To transcend Rappaccini's desire, Beatrice terminates her own life, recognizing that only in metaphysical form can she undo her patrimony, her father's representational project. That daughters can reshape themselves, rewriting their inheritances, is their power, though a power that often imperils their lives. Having examined the sinister aspects of paternal investments in daughters, Hawthorne suggests a way out of inheritance. As parents idealize (and objectify) children, children can take that idealization and redirect it. In bearing the weight of signifying parental goals, good and bad, children in the nineteenth-century imagination also have the capacity to signify differently. Thus within the cultural investment in children, within the manufacturing of children into saviors or new species of life, still lies the possibility of children improving upon the world of their fathers, of shaping alternative histories. Beatrice may be her father's ideal, but by her death she reforms his notion of perfection.

Children and Stories

Marygold does not need to rewrite her inheritance because her father has already done so. Unlike Beatrice, Marygold does not have to leave life forever in order to make her father see his insanity (Hawthorne uses this same word for both men's obsessions). Her time as a statue is more like a fairytale heroine's sleep than a death: everyone lives happily ever after, once she revives. As in Shakespeare's dramatic use of pretended deaths and statues in *The Winter's Tale*, reformation effects a restoration of all that was good before certain foolish and tragic acts. Then, the movement forward to the perpetuity of "happily ever after" can occur; life can go on, and new generations can be born. Midas gets his grandchildren, to whom he tells the story of his experience with the golden touch. Hence his lesson, rather than his greed, passes into the future, to his descendants.

Marygold still bears the mark of the golden touch in "the golden tinge" of her hair. But for Marygold, "this change of hue was really an improvement," reflecting the moral improvement in her father's character as well as the color of his miserly desire. Marygold's hair now appears "richer than in her babyhood" (57), a pleasing refinement upon nature like those Midas, "in his earlier days, before he was so possessed of [the] insane desire for riches," had produced in his garden: "the biggest and beautifullest roses that any mortal ever saw or smelt" (41) and that Marygold so loved. Midas's gardening displays a proper application of nurture from which his avidity for gold temporarily estranges him. While children like Rappaccini's daughter, who is not accorded the benefits of a father's redemption, may perish from parental transmissions, Hawthorne's version of the Midas tale shows that they also may benefit from their inheritance, if that inheritance is the parent's reformation. "The Golden Touch" depicts the transmission of a benign patrimony, the story of

Midas's transformation, which succeeds and annuls Marygold's transformation. What Midas finally imparts to Marygold is a slight physical alteration that serves to remind him of his past folly, an insignia of his experience and reformation. Her highlights signify her father's change in values: "ever since that morning" on which he turned everything he touched to gold, Midas reports, "I have hated the sight of all other gold, save this"—the golden hair of Marygold and her children (57).

Ending "The Golden Touch" with Midas as the teller of his own story to his grandchildren, Hawthorne returns to the narrative frame of *A Wonder-Book*. The book arranges his revisions of Greek and Roman myths as a series of stories told to a group of New England children by a young man named Eustace Bright. A student at Williams College, Eustace "had won great fame among the children as a narrator of wonderful stories" (7). Eustace describes the stories he tells as "the nursery tales that were made for the amusement of our great old grandmother, the Earth, when she was a child in frock and pinafore" (9). These ancient tales can be found in "musty volumes of Greek," but Eustace thinks they belong in "picture books for little girls and boys" (9). He thus presents the opinion that Hawthorne announces in the opening sentence of the preface to *A Wonder-Book*: "The classical myths [are] capable of being rendered into very capital reading for children" (3). Through Eustace and then Midas, Hawthorne draws attention to the retelling of already known stories. Such retellings, as Hawthorne's, Eustace's, and Midas's relation of tales in *A Wonder-Book* demonstrate, include the inventions and alterations of the storyteller. The telling of stories thus offers a paradigm of change even as it bears witness to the past.

Like "The Golden Touch," "Rappaccini's Daughter" is set in a narrative frame, which emphasizes the status of the story as a retold tale. The preface with which the story begins purports to be an editor's introduction to a translation of the tale *Beatrice; ou la Belle Empoisonneuse* by the French author M. de l'Aubépine. The title of Hawthorne's story in its original edition, in fact, was "From the Writings of Aubépine," and all later editions of "Rappaccini's Daughter" retain this designation as a subtitle.[27]

Aubépine is French for the hawthorne plant, and the narrative of Aubépine's literary productions details Nathaniel Hawthorne's actual literary works. His *Twice-Told Tales* appear as Aubépine's *Contes deux fois racontées* while the well-known story "The Artist of the Beautiful" becomes *L'Artiste du Beau; ou le Papillon Mécanique*. With the name "Aubépine," Hawthorne translates and puns his own authorial identity, drawing attention to his role as a storyteller.

The identities that language can establish with names, aligning persons with words, display a variety of references from which to choose one's identity. As *Aubépine* may signify a plant or a person, any name can serve as a person's—or plant's—identity. In *A Wonder-Book*, Hawthorne indulges in what he calls his "love" of "odd names" by giving the invented daughter of Midas the flower name Marygold (which of course also refers to the saint and to Midas's beloved substance). He also employs the allegorical and allusive aspect of words in his naming of Eustace's child friends. The children who listen to Eustace's stories are called Primrose, Periwinkle, Sweet Fern, Dandelion, Blue Eye, Clover, Huckleberry, Cowslip, Squash-blossom, Milk-weed, Plaintain, and Buttercup. The variety of references and metamorphic faculties that Hawthorne finds in language can furnish refuge from the fixity of identity produced by family names. Hawthorne is the name Hawthorne chose for himself when he altered the spelling of his inherited name from "Hathorne" to "Hawthorne." He thereby set himself apart from his family, particularly from their historical part in the Puritan intolerance that Hawthorne noted and excoriated in his writing. One ancestor, William Hathorne, participated in the persecution of Quakers as described in "The Gentle Boy," ordering the whipping of a Quaker woman named Ann Coleman.[28] By distinguishing his name from the Hathorne family, Hawthorne also sought to make himself, like children in the nineteenth-century ideal, independent of ancestral inheritance. Giving explicitly allegorical names both to his own daughters—Una and Rose—and to his fictional children, he accented the range of association that individuals can realize through their names. Obviously, the parent or author who names children is expressing his own range of definition; the children who bear the chosen names have to define themselves against or in accordance with their given names.[29] Because names can refer to various objects, and because names can change, they are a mutable and not necessarily binding inheritance.

In the sketch of Aubépine, Hawthorne presents an account of the origins of "Rappaccini's Daughter" that ironically describes the story as a translation, clearly a translation of Hawthorne himself by himself. He sets up the notion of the origins of the tale as a trick, a maneuvering of names and details. By this artifice, Hawthorne stresses both his own inventiveness and his, or any writer's, indebtedness to prior stories. Hawthorne significantly does not use his prefatory device to promote any parental model of authorship, patrilinear or matrilinear. Instead, the framing of the tale of "Rappaccini's Daughter" (itself a fable of patrilinear production) in a fictional narrative of authorial identity serves to identify authors with children, the inheritors and reformers of culture. If, by his own inventiveness, an author can reproduce and transform himself as Hawthorne translates himself into Aubépine, writing fiction can be an effective way of taking control over one's inheritance. Like Beatrice, who chooses a different fate from the one that her father has designed for her, the writer Aubépine suggests how stories can be recast, even if only by altering the name of the author. From the example of Beatrice, Hawthorne derives a model of writing based upon the child's condition. Agents of both repetition and difference, daughters like Beatrice and Marygold are emblematic of the literary techniques of recitation and revision, which make all storytelling, even of the most ancient stories, retelling.

After writing of the repercussions of Puritan history in the novels *The Scarlet Letter* and *The House of the Seven Gables* and of the dire situation of children in "The Gentle Boy" and "Rappaccini's Daughter," Hawthorne confidently described a new pattern of parental legacies in which parents themselves, and thus their children, improve. The burden of signification and salvation has moved from the child to the parent, leaving children free to be themselves. In "The Golden Touch," this takes the form of the child auditors, who criticize the storyteller. As the adult figures, Midas and Eustace, tell stories, the children who listen become literary critics. The epilogue following the Midas tale, called "Shadow Brook: After the Story," describes the reception of Eustace's story by the children. Primrose complains that "some people have what we may call 'The Leaden Touch,' and make everything dull and heavy that they lay their fingers upon" (58). Periwinkle offers an improvement upon the plot: she suggests that the golden touch would be a desirable faculty if the right forefinger had "the power of turning everything to gold" while the left forefinger had "the power of changing it back again, if the first change did not please" (59). The boy Sweet Fern wants more realistic details: "how big was Marygold, and how much did she weigh after she was turned to gold?" (59). The children thus express their own viewpoints and point to further transformations an author might make in the tale.

Hawthorne's renderings of children, which this chapter has traced through three tales and through the literary history of child characters, established the importance of the child's independence, the touchstone of subsequent American children's literature. Questioning the representation of childhood in Puritan tradition and in nineteenth-century customs that retain features of that tradition, Hawthorne's stories inaugurated a new tradition.

NOTES

1. Nathaniel Hawthorne, *A Wonder-Book for Girls and Boys* (1852), rpt. *The Centenary Edition of the Works of Nathaniel Hawthorne* (Columbus: Ohio State University Press, 1972), 7:40–41. All references to "The Golden Touch" are to this edition and will appear parenthetically within the chapter.

2. Nathaniel Hawthorne, "Little Annie's Ramble," *Twice-Told Tales* (Boston: James Munroe, 1842), p. 167. This narrative was one of Hawthorne's 1835 magazine pieces; it did not appear in the first edition of *Twice-Told Tales* (1837).

3. Nathaniel Hawthorne, *Peter Parley's Universal History, on the Basis of Geography*, vols. 1 and 2 (London: John W. Parker, 1837). An American edition appeared three months later. Hawthorne's sister

Elizabeth also worked on these books. The Boston edition of *Peter Parley's Universal History*, which differs slightly from the London edition, appears with her name as the author. As he was simultaneously working on these books, Hawthorne was writing short stories; after separate publication in journals, they became his first collection, *Twice-Told Tales* (1837). In 1828, he had completed a novel, *Fanshawe*, which he published at his own expense and quickly repudiated. Before he wrote his well-known novels, he published three children's books in the early 1840s: *Grandfather's Chair, Famous Old People*, and *Liberty Tree*. So, at the beginning of his career, Hawthorne was most successful in his ventures at children's literature. See Nina Baym, *The Shape of Hawthorne's Career* (Ithaca, N.Y.: Cornell University Press, 1976).

4. "Selling Slaves by the Pound," in the *Slave's Friend* (New York: Antislavery Office, 1836), excerpted in *Pictures and Stories for Forgotten Children's Books*, ed. Arnold Arnold (New York: Dover, 1969), p. 52. For an informative account of antislavery articles for children, see Carolyn L. Karcher, "Lydia Maria Child and *The Juvenile Miscellany*," in *Research about Nineteenth-Century Children's Books*, ed. Selma K. Richardson (Urbana: University of Illinois Press, 1980).

5. Ann Douglas describes the nineteenth-century cult of Little Eva in *The Feminization of American Culture* (New York: Knopf, 1977), pp. 1–13, 24–72.

6. T. S. Arthur, *Ten Nights in a Barroom* (1852; rpt. Cambridge, Mass.: Harvard University Press, 1964), p. 87. Subsequent references to this text will appear parenthetically within the chapter.

7. Judith Pascoe presents an insightful reading of T. S. Arthur's temperance tract as part of an ongoing critique of his fiction aimed at nineteenth-century consumerism in "T. S. Arthur and the American Girl," in *The Girl's Own: Cultural Histories of the Anglo-American Girl, 1830–1915*, ed. Claudia Nelson and Lynne Vallone (Athens: University of Georgia Press, 1994), pp. 34–51.

8. A detailed discussion of the ideal child of early nineteenth-century American children's fiction can be found in Anne Scott MacLeod, *A Moral Tale: Children's Fiction and American Culture, 1820–1860* (1975; rpt. Hamden, Conn.: Archon, 1990). This discussion is extended forward into modern children's fiction in her next book, *American Childhood: Essays on Children's Literature of the Nineteenth and Twentieth Centuries* (Athens: University of Georgia Press, 1994).

In a recent study of youthful heroines, Lynne Vallone sees nineteenth-century literature continuing to follow and engage with the paradigm of "virtue rewarded" set forth in Richardson's *Pamela*. See her *Disciplines of Virtue: Girls' Culture in the Eighteenth and Nineteenth Centuries* (New Haven, Conn.: Yale University Press, 1995).

9. In addition to nineteenth-century editions of Ovid's *Metamorphoses*, Hawthorne consulted the 1844 *Classical Dictionary* edited by William Smith. Roger Lancelyn Green describes Hawthorne's departures from these texts in his postscript to *The Complete Greek Stories of Nathaniel Hawthorne* (New York: Franklin Watts, 1963), pp. 349–52.

10. The rise of Protestantism, pedagogy, and publishing proceed integrally. The significance of print upon culture has been well-treated by Lucien Febvre and Henri-Jean Martin, *The Coming of the Book: The Impact of Printing, 1450–1800* (London: New Left Books, 1976), and Elizabeth L. Eisenstein, *The Printing Press as an Agent of Change*, 2 vols. (Cambridge: Cambridge University Press, 1979). On Protestantism and the education of children, see C. John Somerville, *The Discovery of Childhood in Puritan England* (Athens: University of Georgia Press, 1992); Sanford Fleming, *Children and Puritanism: The Place of Children in the Life and Thought of the New England Churches, 1620–1847* (New Haven, Conn.: Yale University Press, 1933); Philip Greven, *The Protestant Temperament: Patterns of Childrearing, Religious Experience, and the Self in Early America* (New York: Alfred A. Knopf, 1977); Peter Gregg Slater, *Children in the New England Mind in Death and Life* (Hamden, Conn.: Archon, 1977); and Edmund S. Morgan, *The Puritan Family: Religion and Domestic Relations in Seventeenth-Century New England*, rev. ed. (Westport, Conn.: Greenwood, 1966).

11. James Janeway, *A Token for Children: Being an Exact Account of the Conversion, Holy and Exemplary Lives, and Joyful Deaths of Several Young Children* (London, 1671). On Janeway and Puritan children's literature, see Gillian Avery, "The Puritans and Their Heirs," in *Children and Their Books*, ed. Gillian Avery and Julia Briggs (Oxford: Clarendon, 1989), pp. 79–93.

12. Cotton Mather, *A Token for the Children of New England* (Boston: Timothy Green, 1700), p. 3. The memoir of Mather's brother also appeared as a separate publication called *Early Piety Exemplified in the Life and Death of Nathanael Mather* (London, 1689).

13. The best account of the Puritan experience in America, espe-

cially of the declension and secularization of Puritan doctrine, remains Perry Miller, *The New England Mind: From Colony to Province* (Cambridge, Mass.: Belknap Press of Harvard University Press, 1953). On childhood in eighteenth-century America, also see John F. Walzer, "A Period of Ambivalence: Eighteenth-Century American Childhood," in *The History of Childhood*, ed. Lloyd deMause (New York: Psychohistory Press, 1974), pp. 351–82 and Bernard Wishy, *The Child and the Republic: The Dawn of Modern American Child Nurture* (Philadelphia: University of Pennsylvania Press, 1968). Important general studies of changes in conceptions of childhood during the eighteenth century are Phillippe Aries, *Centuries of Childhood*, trans. Robert Baldrick (New York: Vintage, 1962), and Lawrence Stone, *The Family, Sex, and Marriage in England, 1500–1800* (New York: Harper Colophon, 1975).

14. Wordsworth provides his own complex portraits of adult investments in children, especially in such poems as "We Are Seven." Here, I am referring not so much to Wordsworth's own sense of childhood as to the romantic conception of childhood commonly attributed to his poetry.

15. Gillian Avery furnishes an informative account of the ongoing religious influence upon nineteenth-century American children's literature in *Behold the Child: American Children and Their Books, 1621–1922* (Baltimore: Johns Hopkins University Press, 1994), pp. 65–120.

16. *The History of Goody Two-Shoes; Otherwise Called Mrs. Margery Two-Shoes* (1765) and *The Renowned History of Giles Gingerbread* (1764) were two of the most often reprinted stories of the popular children's books first published by John Newbery in London. (Newbery's name is best known today for the award annually given to the best children's book.) Horatio Alger's popular Ragged Dick Series, stories of poor boys who made good, were published first in the juvenile magazine the *Student and Schoolmate*, then in book form in 1868, and thereafter reprinted many times. See Edwin P. Hoyt, *Horatio's Boys: The Life and Work of Horatio Alger* (New York: Stein and Day, 1974).

The emergence and development of children's literature in England and America is well documented in F. J. Harvey Darton, *Children's Books in England* (Cambridge: Cambridge University Press, 1958); Monica Kiefer, *American Children through Their Books: 1700–1835*

(Philadelphia: University of Pennsylvania Press, 1948); and Samuel F. Pickering, Jr., *Moral Instruction and Fiction for Children, 1749–1820* (Athens: University of Georgia Press, 1993).

17. Originally intended as part of a projected collection to be called "Provincial Tales," "The Gentle Boy" first appeared in print in Samuel Goodrich's annual literary magazine, *The Token* (Boston, 1832). Hawthorne then included the (somewhat revised) story in his 1837 collection *Twice-Told Tales* as well as reprinting it separately in 1839 with illustrations by Sophia Peabody, whom Hawthorne married in 1842. All references to "The Gentle Boy" will be to the original 1832 text, reprinted in *Young Goodman Brown and Other Tales*, ed. Brian Harding (New York: Oxford University Press, 1987), pp. 3–37. On Hawthorne's sources for this tale, see G. Harrison Orians, "The Sources and Themes of Hawthorne's 'The Gentle Boy,'" *New England Quarterly* 14 (1941): 664–78.

18. Harriet Beecher Stowe, *Uncle Tom's Cabin; or, Life among the Lowly* (1852; rpt. New York: Viking Penguin, 1981), p. 273.

19. On the Alcotts, see Madeleine Stern, *Louisa May Alcott* (Norman: University of Oklahoma Press, 1950). An informative account of nineteenth-century reform movements with which Hawthorne was familiar is furnished in Anne Rose, *Transcendentalism as a Social Movement, 1830–1850* (New Haven, Conn.: Yale Universtiy Press, 1981). Also see Ronald G. Waters, *American Reformers, 1815–1860* (New York: Hill and Wang, 1978).

20. Clearly fascinated by children and much engaged in the process of childrearing, Hawthorne recorded many details about his own children, Una, Julian, and Rose, in his *Notebooks*, letters, and private writings. He and his wife, Sophia, wrote their observations of their children in a joint journal from 1842 to 1854; Sophia also made the children the chief subjects of her regular correspondence to friends and relations. While I am not pursuing a biographical account of Hawthorne's interest in children, that record certainly exists and furnishes another important measure of Hawthorne's response to nineteenth-century ideas of childrearing, as well as to the particular difficulties encountered with his own children. His daughter Una suffered from psychic disorders, which continually concerned her parents. On the childrearing practices of the Hawthornes, see T. Walter Herbert, *Dearest Beloved: The Hawthornes and the Making of the Middle-Class Family* (Berkeley: University of California Press, 1993).

21. Mary Peabody Mann and Elizabeth Palmer Peabody, *The Moral Culture of Infancy, and Kindergarten Guide* (Boston: Burnham, 1864), pp. 156–57.

22. Ellen Montgomery, the ten-year-old heroine of Susan Warner's *The Wide, Wide World* (1850) stands as another exemplary girl, though Warner is careful to describe the effort involved in Ellen's goodness. Nina Baym discusses the works of Warner and contemporary women writers in *Woman's Fiction: A Guide to Novels by and about Women in America, 1820–1870* (Ithaca, N.Y.: Cornell University Press, 1978), pp. 51–174. While most popular fiction was authored by women in this period, it is worth noting that male writers, especially in religious and reform literature such as T. S. Arthur's *Ten Nights in a Bar-Room*, likewise idealized girl characters.

On the emergence of the cult of domesticity and its feminization of virtue, see Nancy C. Cott, *The Bonds of Womanhood: Woman's Sphere in New England, 1780–1835* (New Haven, Conn.: Yale University Press, 1977); Barbara Welter, "The Cult of True Womanhood," in her *Dimity Convictions: The American Woman in the Nineteenth-Century* (Athens: Ohio University Press, 1976), pp. 21–41; and Nancy Armstrong, "The Rise of the Domestic Woman," in her *Desire and Domestic Fiction* (New York: Oxford University Press, 1987), pp. 59–95.

23. Though well intentioned, Rollo repeatedly and often comically fails at the lessons he attempts. For example, in *Rollo at Work; or, The Way for a Boy to Learn to Be Industrious* (1839), Rollo neglects his father's advice and tries out what he thinks are better ways of moving a pile of wood; he ends up making a huge mess. He then acknowledges that he should have obeyed his father. Tom Sawyer and his avatars determinedly embark on ventures they know to be forbidden. See Gillian Avery, "Frank and Manly: Ideals of Boyhood," in her *Behold the Child*, pp. 184–210; Anne Scott MacLeod, "Bad Boys: Tom Bailey and Tom Sawyer," in her *American Childhood*, pp. 69–76; and Alice M. Jordan, *From Rollo to Tom Sawyer* (Boston: Horn Book, 1948).

24. "The Birthmark" appeared in the journal the *Pioneer* (1843), then in the collection *Mosses from an Old Manse* (1846). "Ethan Brand" was first published in the *Boston Weekly Museum* (1850), reprinted in the *Dollar Magazine* (1851), and again reprinted as part of the collection *The Snow-Image* (1852).

25. In *The Scarlet Letter*, Hawthorne produced the most interest-

ing of his fictional little girls: the wild child Pearl, daughter of an adulterous union. Though Pearl very much fits the pattern of a child overdetermined by the past—and victimized for the circumstances of her birth and the sins of her mother—she is also a difficult child, not at all saintly. With Pearl, Hawthorne presents a much more complex child character, who breaks out of the nineteenth-century mold of evangelical girls. The case of Pearl merits an essay of its own.

26. "Rappaccini's Daughter" was first published in the *Democratic Review* (1844), then republished in the collection *Mosses from an Old Manse* (1846). References to this story will be to the 1846 edition, reprinted in *The Centenary Edition of the Works of Nathaniel Hawthorne* (Columbus: Ohio State University Press, 1974), 10:119.

A slightly different version of this reading of "Rappaccini's Daughter" appears in my article "Hawthorne's Endangered Daughters," *Western Humanities Review* (Winter–Spring 1997): 327–31.

27. In another play on fact and fiction, Hawthorne's narrator reports that *Beatrice* first appeared in *La Revue Anti-Aristocratique*—Hawthorne's Frenchification of the *Democratic Review*. On the publishing history of this story, see Arlin Turner, *Nathaniel Hawthorne: A Biography* (New York: Oxford University Press, 1980).

28. Other Hathornes were active in the Salem persecution of witches. See Paul Boyer and Stephen Nissenbaum, *Salem Possessed: The Social Origins of Witchcraft* (Cambridge, Mass.: Harvard University Press, 1974).

29. As T. Walter Herbert has shown, Hawthorne's naming and nurturing of his own daughters quite tragically limited their sense of self-definition. Both suffered from psychic illnesses. See *Dearest Beloved*, pp. 151, 218, 224, 238, 265, 275, 280–83. The point I am stressing in this chapter is that, as a writer, Hawthorne was very interested in the ways names can limit, expand, or alter the range of self-definition.

Hawthorne and the Visual Arts

Rita K. Gollin

"The Art-Conditions and Prospects of America"

Nathaniel Hawthorne was born into a confident and rapidly expanding America where the visual arts were of little importance.
There were no major collections of art, no government patronage of the arts nor generous private patrons, no academies
where aspiring artists could develop their skills. Benjamin West
and John Singleton Copley had done fine work in America, but
then both moved to London and remained there for the rest of
their lives. English-born portraitists like John Smibert had pros-
pered in colonial times, and Gilbert Stuart's reputation soared
when he returned from England to the new republic. During the
early decades of the nineteenth century, talented painters like
John Vanderlyn and Washington Allston spent long stretches of
time in France and Italy. When they returned home, they were
imbued with European standards of High Art, which preferred
sacred, mythological, and historical subject matter to representations of present-day realities. Not until Hawthorne began
publishing in the 1830s did an original artist attain maturity in
this country without recourse to Europe: Thomas Cole, the so-
called father of American landscape, whose canvases capture
much of America's distinctive natural grandeur. And not until

then did anyone attempt a serious assessment of America's art and artists.

William Dunlap's pioneering *History of the Rise and Development of the Arts of Design in the United States* (1834), spoke for the burgeoning nation. He argued that American art had steadily improved since colonial times and would continue to do so, helping the young republic reach a glorious maturity. His aesthetic was consistent with the country's Jacksonian optimism and the Emersonian moral conviction of his time. Since, as Emerson put it, "nature is the opposite of the soul, answering to it part for part for part," Dunlap believed that good artists penetrate beyond surfaces to convey underlying spiritual truths. The best artist is by definition a moral agent, a man of "the highest mental powers, united to the keenest physical perceptions of the good and beautiful," while "the good artist who is not a good man, is a traitor to the arts, and an enemy to society" (1:176, 169).

This was notably true of portrait painters, as Dunlap's long section on Gilbert Stuart makes clear. Portrait painting "recommends itself to the household affections of all mankind" though it commands mainly "the time and purses of the rich," Dunlap pragmatically observed. He acknowledged that Stuart "favored the renowned, the rich, and the fashionable" but nevertheless admired him as a highly perceptive man and an extraordinary artist. Stuart could elicit "revealing traits of character" from his sitters and then "animate his canvas . . . with that peculiar, distinctive life which separates the humblest individual from his kind. He seemed to dive into the thoughts of men—for they were made to rise, and to speak on the surface" (221–22). The best painters, Dunlap assured his readers, look through outward and visible signs toward inward and spiritual realities.

But, in mid–nineteenth-century America, feelings of cultural inferiority far outweighed pride in American art and artists. Most ambitious artists believed they could perfect their craft only in Europe. And most people of refinement believed they could most fully cultivate their taste and moral sensibilities only in the presence of the great works of art that could be seen only abroad.

These seemed self-evident truths. As their most cosmopolitan spokesman, James Jackson Jarves, affirmed in the most influential of his many books, *The Art-Idea* (1864), art is essential to the refinement of mankind, and the best art imparts wisdom. "In art as well as in literature, the most enduring things and endearing are those which best intimate an existence above the level of the worldly and vulgar," he declared. Artists who depict the world we inhabit but substitute "the beautiful, good, and permanent" for "the coarse, sensual and superficial" can help elevate sympathetic viewers to "the full stature of manhood" (181–82).[1]

But America and Americans had a long way to go, Jarves believed. The country was "but half rescued from the wild embrace of the wilderness" and still "choked by the stern cares and homely necessities of an incipient civilization." There was none of the "antecedent art" that enriched the lives of Europeans, no adequate collections of European art "to guide a growing taste," no adequate art schools, no dependable patronage, and few discerning critics (148–51). Yet America's wild beauty was "inspiriting," and the country's very lack of antecedent art could promote independence and originality. As "a vital principle of life," art remained crucial to the nation's "moral welfare and complete education" (165).

Jarves's specific "Inquiry into the Art-Conditions and Prospects of America" included perspicacious analyses of its earliest painters, from Benjamin West to Washington Allston, and of the "new school," which included Cephas Thompson, George Loring Brown, and many others by then known to Hawthorne. A spokesman for period standards, who also helped to shape them, Jarves reserved his highest praise for art that portrays two kinds of truth:

> Realism . . . best satisfies those who confide in what they consider as the substantial and tangible in nature, holding to epidermal representation as the end and aim of art; while idealism alone will content those who believe that its legitimate purpose is the expression of inner life or the soul of things. The art which most happily combines the two is the most successful with mankind at large. Whether they comprehend its principles or not, their instincts recognize them.

Even more congruent with Hawthorne's beliefs is Jarves's conclusion that the best art is participatory:

> The effect of high art is to sink the artist and spectator alike into the scene. It becomes the real, and, in that sense, true realistic art, because it realizes to the mind the essential truths of what it pictorially discloses to the eye. The spectator is no longer a looker-on . . . , but an inhabitant of the landscape. (203–6)

By the time Jarves said so in 1864, many American landscapists, including Thomas Cole and Thomas Doughty, were honored and exhibited, if not widely exhibited, as were genre painters, including William Sidney Mount and George Caleb Bingham. Portrait painting, nevertheless, predominated. Anyone who could paint a recognizable likeness, whether a self-trained local limner or a renowned English artist, could find employment even in colonial times. Portrait painting "recommends itself to the personal vanity and the household affections of all mankind," as Dunlap had remarked, and the new nation was also eager for icons of its heroes: George Washington and other founding fathers. By the mid–nineteenth century, the country was also eager for portraits of its most eminent writers. But an *Atlantic Monthly* reviewer made a crucial distinction—while praising recent portraits of Emerson, Whittier, and Bryant—between the mere "likeness-maker," who produces only a "representation of something seen" and the true portraitist, who also produces "something felt." As Dunlap had said about Gilbert Stuart, a true portrait penetrates to the inner life of the sitter and thus attains "full insight and representation of character."[2] As a writer of fiction, Hawthorne set himself the same goal.

Portraiture

Portraits were part of Hawthorne's environment from his childhood on. Miniatures of his father and his father's father were among his family's prized possessions, and ancestral portraits were on prominent display in many of the houses he visited. Pencil portraits or silhouettes of family members might also be on display, and many books included engravings of historical and mythological figures. Meantime, commissioned portraits of George Washington and other national heroes were exhibited in the city's government buildings and public spaces, embodiments of the country's heroic past and its hopes for the future, as were the dozens of old portraits at the Essex Historical Society.

As his life branched out, so did Hawthorne's access to the visual arts. Bowdoin College owned a modest collection of European paintings and engravings, and the growing permanent collection at the Boston Athenaeum included a similar mix of copies and originals. The Athenaeum's annual exhibitions might include a Copley portrait and a Cole landscape alongside copies or imitations of Old Masters. Engravings of famous paintings were sold in bookstores and auction houses and printed in *The Token* and other publications alongside Hawthorne's early tales and sketches. During his six-month editorship of the *American Magazine of Useful and Entertaining Knowledge* in 1836, Hawthorne's burdensome task was to produce text to accompany engravings of uneven merit.

That same year, Hawthorne read Dunlap's *History*,[3] and allusions to art began to enter into his writings. Dunlap told about Gilbert Stuart capturing a general's incipient madness in a portrait, and this became the germ of "The Prophetic Pictures" (1837), Hawthorne's story about a portrait painter's similar disturbing insight into a sitter's sanity. A sketch of Benjamin West's childhood was the first of Hawthorne's *Biographical Stories for Children* (1842), and John Singleton Copley plays a sympathetic role in his "Drowne's Wooden Image" (1844). In *The House of the Seven Gables*, Hawthorne invented an Edward G. Malbone miniature of his character Clifford Pyncheon consistent with Dunlap's comment that Malbone's miniatures are imbued with "the grace, purity and delicacy" of his own character and Dunlap's regret that the miniatures are preserved for private viewing and so "comparatively, little seen" (2:145). Such issues would resurface in many of Hawthorne's fictions and journal entries, most notably in *The Marble Faun* and the *French and Italian Notebooks*.

What primarily engaged Hawthorne's attention during a visit to the Essex Historical Society in the fall of 1837 was the literal and representational character of art:

> Governor Leverett, a dark mustachioed face, the figure two-thirds length, clothed in a sort of frock-coat, buttoned, and a broad sword-belt girded round the waist. . . . Sir William Peperell in English regimentals, coat, waistcoat, and breeches all of red broadcloth, richly gold-embroidered; he holds a general's truncheon in his right hand. . . . Endicott, Pyncheon, and others in scull-caps [*sic*], etc. Half a dozen, or more, family portraits of the Olivers, some in plain dresses, brown, crimson, or claret, others with gorgeous gold embroidered waistcoats. . . . Ladies, with lace ruffles, the painting of which, in one of the pictures, cost five guineas. . . . Miniatures in oil, with the paint peeling off, of stern, old, yellow faces.

His only comment about artistry per se was that the clothing of the Oliver family was "generally better done than the faces." In none of them did he discern any intimation of the sitter's character. As a group, however, they provoked a generalization that anticipates a major theme of *The House of the Seven Gables*:

> Nothing gives a stronger idea of old worm-eaten aristocracy, of a family's being crazy with age, and its being time that it was extinct, than these black, dusty, faded, antique-dressed portraits. (23:176–79).

Soon after making that entry, Hawthorne met his fellow Salemite Sophia Amelia Peabody. A romantic idealist who idolized Emerson, Sophia had learned to paint by copying the work of three of her successful contemporaries: Thomas Doughty, Chester Harding, and Washington Allston. By the time she met Hawthorne in the winter of 1837, those copies and her copies of European masters had won widespread praise, as did her Flaxmanlike outline drawings and her pencil portraits. Evidence of their growing intimacy includes his evident pleasure in the pencil sketch she made of him in December 1838:

S. A. P.—taking my likeness, I said that such changes would come over my face, that she would not know me when we met again in Heaven. "See if I don't!" said she, smiling. (23:214)

A month later, another picture inaugurated a new kind of partnership. When Sophia showed Hawthorne her line drawing of Ilbrahim, the title character in "The Gentle Boy," he assured her that he would never see Ilbrahim otherwise. He then had the story republished with an engraving of her drawing, assuring readers that "whatever of beauty and pathos he had conceived, but could not shadow forth in language, have been caught and embodied in the few and simple lines of this sketch" (9:568).

A year later, engaged to marry her and living in Boston, awaiting two oil paintings she was producing "expressly for him," he assured her:

> I never owned a picture in my life; yet pictures have always been among the earthly possessions (and they are spiritual possessions too) which I most coveted. . . . I have often felt as if I could be a painter, only I am sure that I could never handle a brush;—now my Dove will show me the images of my inward eye, beautified and etherealized by her own spirit. (15:397–98)

When the paintings arrived, he pronounced them "perfect." He praised not her imitative romantic landscapes but the figures painted in the foreground. They were images of his "inward eye": a white-clad solitary figure in one of them was Sophia's "veritable self," he exulted, and the couple in the other represented their unchangeable selves: "Years cannot alter us, nor our relation to each other" (15:414, 402).

In 1840, Salem's leading portraitist, Charles Osgood, produced the first of what would be four oil paintings of Hawthorne, the image of a handsome and sensitive young man, which delighted his family. We can only guess what Hawthorne thought of it, or of any of his earlier portraits, or of any of the painters for whom he had sat. In 1850, while sitting for Cephas Thompson, he mused that his earlier portraits had dissatisfied "those most familiar with my phiz" (presumably Sophia and himself), then reached a pessimistic conclusion: "there is no such thing as a true portrait; they are all delusions." (8:491).

Nonetheless, Hawthorne respected Thompson as "a man of thought" with "truth in himself," who seemed "to reverence his art, and to aim at truth in it," and who shared his belief that closely observed details can intimate underlying truths. Toward the end of one sitting, Thompson began "painting with more and more eagerness, casting quick, keen glances at me, and then making hasty touches on the picture, as if to secure with his brush what he had caught with his eye," and this Hawthorne recognized as "akin to what I have experienced myself in the glow of composition" (8:498–99). His publishers would later buy Thompson's portrait and present it to the author, the only oil painting of himself that Hawthorne would ever own.

His publishers commissioned an engraved copy of that Thompson portrait for an expanded collection of *Twice-Told Tales*, and it delighted his children as a "likeness." Though Sophia thought it lacked "cheerfulness," Hawthorne remarked that the look of "bedevilled melancholy" befitted the author of *The Scarlet Letter*. He asked his publishers to include it in presentation copies of his new novel, *The House of the Seven Gables*, which centers on truths that portraits can convey, and commented that he was struck by an expression in it that he did not recall seeing in the original. It bore "a singular resemblance . . . to a miniature of my father" (16:400).

The Truths of Portraits

Even before he met Sophia, Hawthorne's interest in the truths that portraits can convey had surfaced in a few tales. The first and most heavily Gothic is "The Prophetic Pictures" (1837). The story's unnamed eighteenth-century artist reputedly

> captures not merely a man's features, but his mind and heart. He catches the secret sentiments and passions, and throws them upon the canvass, like sunshine—or perhaps, in the portraits of dark-souled men, like a gleam of infernal fire. (9:167)

As the young couple, Walter and Elinor, prepare to sit for their portraits, those on display in the artist's studio confirm his reputation for producing portraits that seem preternaturally endowed with life: "the whole mind and character were brought out on the countenance, and concentrated into a single look, so that, to speak paradoxically, the originals hardly resembled themselves so strikingly as the portraits did" (9:170).

The story then focuses on the expressions that the couple's portraits finally assume: Elinor's is sad and anxious and Walter's unwontedly "lively." As the painter tells Elinor:

> "I have painted what I saw. The artist—the true artist—must look beneath the exterior. It is his gift . . . to see the inmost soul, and, by a power indefinable even to himself, to make it glow or darken upon the canvas." (9:175)

According to connoisseurs, the two portraits are "among the most admirable specimens of modern portraiture." But more problematically, "people of natural sensibility" are arrested by the "look of earnest import" on Walter's face, "though no two explained it alike" (9:176–77).

"It is the idea of duration—of earthly immortality—that gives such a mysterious interest to our own portraits," the narrator muses, though that is not what the story is about. A central concern is with the painter, who is "insulated from the mass of human kind" except as they are "connected with his art." At the climax of the story, the painter sees the couple assume the precise expressions that he had captured on canvas; but when the now-maddened Walter aims a knife at his wife, the painter steps between them "like a magician, controlling the phantoms which he had evoked" (9:184). The story raises questions about a painter's responsibilities to his subject and about portraits as vehicles for truth, issues that would concern Hawthorne for the rest of his life.

Other tales similarly turn on the inner realities rendered through the surface appearances of portraits. In the much slighter and more sentimental tale "Sylph Etherege" (1838), a young girl's fiancé presents her with a delicate miniature portrait ostensibly of himself but actually embodying her own ethereal loveliness. When the ugly fiancé finally presents himself as the reality and crushes the miniature, Sylph too is destroyed. As he "sneeringly" claims, "I did but look into this delicate creature's heart; and with the pure fantasies that I found there, I made what seemed a man,—and the delusive shadow has wiled her away" (11:118). His antithesis is the woodcarver in "Drowne's Wooden Image" (1844), whose love of a beautiful woman briefly opens a "well-spring of inward wisdom," which empowers him to create a beautiful statue, which seems indistinguishable from the woman herself. In "Edward Randolph's Portrait" (1838), a time-darkened portrait rumored to be of the devil is literally of a seventeenth-century official, who had earned "the curse of a People" by obtaining an annulment of the Massachusetts charter. In the story's eighteenth-century present, the young girl who cleans it briefly releases Randolph's tormented visage from the "void darkness." Her uncle, Thomas Hutchinson, also betrays the colonists and dies with the same tormented expression on his face. In all these tales, Hawthorne uses art and artists primarily for Gothic effect, to tell ghost stories that ominously connect this world to another.[4]

Portraits that capture and preserve hidden truths about their sitters are central to *The House of the Seven Gables*, especially an oil painting of Colonel Pyncheon, the wicked seventeenth-century builder of the house, but also a daguerreotype of his wicked descendant, Judge Pyncheon, and, incidentally, a miniature of his gentle cousin, Clifford. The ancestral portrait that hangs on the wall in *The House of the Seven Gables* is invested with meaning from the moment it appears in the seventeenth-century prologue to the nineteenth-century narrative. From then on, its "stern, immitigable features [which] seemed to symbolize an evil influence" reinforce the moral Hawthorne tentatively proposes in his preface: "the wrong-doing of one generation lives into the successive ones" (2:21, 2).

Colonel Pyncheon's portrait depicts "the stern features of a Puritanic-looking personage, in a scull-cap, with a laced band and a grizzly beard," a Bible in one hand and "a more successfully painted sword in the other" (2:33), an evocation of many of the stern-faced portraits that Hawthorne had confronted at the Essex Institute. Its time-darkened surface paradoxically displays the sitter's cold-hearted greed: "the painter's deep conception of his subject's inward traits has wrought itself into the essence of the picture, and is seen, when the superficial coloring has been wrought off by time" (2:59). It has become a true portrait of an ostensibly upright person, who has in fact conspired in another man's death to obtain a piece of property.

Consistent with Gothic literary convention, the portrait seems to have a life of its own. The aging spinster, Hepzibah Pyncheon, trembles under its eye, reluctant to judge the ancestor she had once revered as harshly as her new "perception of the truth compelled her to do." Yet that dark truth is central to the novel: if her cousin Jaffrey Pyncheon were to don a costume like his ancestor's, "nobody would doubt that it was the old Pyncheon come again!" (2:59).

That identification of the present with a past evil is dramatically confirmed through her young cousin Phoebe's response to a daguerreotype. When the daguerreotypist, Holgrave (Hepzibah's roomer), shows it to the country-bred Phoebe, she assumes it is a copy of the ancestral portrait whose "stern eye has been following me about, all day" but with its attire somehow changed. She is literally wrong but essentially right. The essential character of Judge Pyncheon has been fixed by sunshine on a chemically treated plate, a process that the Frenchman Louis Daguerre had introduced in 1839. Required to hold his pose for about thirty seconds, the judge dropped his benign mask to reveal "a truth that no painter would ever venture upon, even could he detect it." As Holgrave says, "Here we have the man, sly, subtle, hard, imperious, and withal, cold as ice." Presumably, Hawthorne's own dismay at a recent stern-faced daguerreotype of himself underlies Holgrave's question to Phoebe: "Look at that eye! Would you like to be at its mercy?" (2:91–92).[5] The eye in question is of course literally Judge Pyncheon's, as Phoebe realizes when the judge drops his initially benign expression and looks just like the old Colonel Pyncheon in his portrait (2:119).

Hawthorne gives a comically Gothic spin to that portrait in Holgrave's inserted narrative about an eighteenth-century Pyncheon, whose eagerness for a valuable tract of land makes him willing to give up the house. At that point, the portrait "magically built into its walls" frowns, clenches its fist, and is "averred to have lost all patience, and to have shown itself on the point of descending bodily from its frame" (2:197-98). Subsequently, when Judge Pyncheon dies while seated beneath the portrait (as his ancestor had done), Hawthorne introduces a more surreally comic fantasy in which the old colonel returns to gaze at his portrait and shakes its frame. Fact and Gothic fantasy most fully coincide when the malevolent portrait falls on its face.

Utterly different is the delicate miniature on ivory of the young Clifford Pyncheon garbed in a silk dressing gown. By attributing it to the period's preeminent miniaturist, Edward Malbone, Hawthorne displays his own aesthetic sophistication and credits his readers with sharing it. We see Hepzibah tenderly remove it for consolation and contemplation shortly before Clifford returns after thirty years of unjust imprisonment for presumably murdering the Pyncheon who then owned the house. As we eventually learn, Judge Pyncheon himself had inadvertently caused that Pyncheon's death from the same hereditary disease that had killed the colonel and had then allowed the blame to fall on Clifford. When Hepzibah cautiously shows the miniature to Phoebe, the girl immediately perceives what Malbone had captured and what Hepzibah loves: a sweet-faced man with "something of a child's expression," who should be protected from suffering (2:75). It does not take her long to realize that the wasted man who soon returns to the house is "the original of the beautiful miniature." However fleetingly, he displays "the same expression, so refined, so softly imaginative, which Malbone—venturing a happy touch, with suspended breath— had imparted to the miniature!" (2:91). Malbone's art has preserved Clifford's essential character.

Another kind of portrait appears in Holgrave's story-within-the-story to characterize the doomed aristocrat Alice Pyncheon at the threshold of her sacrifice to her father's greed:

A portrait of the young girl, painted by a Venetian artist and left by her father in England, is said to have fallen into the

hands of the present Duke of Devonshire, and to be now preserved at Chatsworth; not on account of any associations with
the original, but for its value as a picture, and the high character of beauty in the countenance. (2:200–201)

As Hawthorne assumed his gentle readers knew, no eighteenth-
century American artist could possibly have painted such a portrait, and his allusion to the major collection of portraits at
Chatsworth lays claim to connoisseurship. The man who created
the novel's colonial portrait, the Malbone miniature, and the
"unamiable" daguerreotype, all revealing truths of character hidden to the casual eye, was more than ready for the deeper immersion in art that awaited him in England and Italy.

Hawthorne as Connoisseur

Hawthorne's European sojourn began when he arrived in England in 1853 to begin a four-year term as American consul to Liverpool and ended when he returned to America in 1860. During
this time, he dramatically expanded and refined his acquaintance
with the visual arts. In England, his efforts were most intense
during a six-week stay in Manchester in the summer of 1857, yet
even that was essentially a prelude to his immersion in art during
his year and a half in Italy.

A casual 1854 notebook reference to a display of "modern
artists, comprising some of Turner, Wilkie, Landseer, and others
of the best English painters" suggests his certainty about which
artists were the "best" and suggests how much sophistication he
had achieved in less than a year abroad. A reference to Turner's
"airiness" conveys his determination to see with his own eyes and
form his own judgments, undeterred by John Ruskin's influential
conception of Turner as a major moral prophet (21:133). That determination to see for himself resurfaced whenever he visited
London's major repositories of art, where he tried repeatedly to
"get up a taste." But it culminated during the summer of 1857,
when he moved to Manchester to devote six weeks to the Manchester Exhibition of Art, then celebrated as "the largest and

most valuable collection of works of art, Ancient and Modern, ever collected."[6] Hawthorne was one of more than a million visitors to that vast display of the finest art held in British collections, selected by Prince Albert, Ruskin, and the most distinguished of still-living English artists. In Manchester, his self-education in art really began.

Soon he began to like "good things, and to be sure that they were good," and he began to acquire a rudimentary ability "to distinguish the broader differences of style; as . . . between Rubens and Rembrandt," even to see "a sort of illumination" in some pictures "that makes me see them more distinctly." But he repeatedly complained about his limited "receptive faculty," and a nagging question recurred that challenged a dominant assumption of his age: whether becoming a "man of taste" really made anyone "truer, wiser, or better" (22:356–57).

The English historical portraits he saw in Manchester, including "cold and stiff" early ones and graceful Vandykes, provoked another haunting doubt, one that had assailed him while sitting for Cephas Thompson years before: he wondered whether any portrait really "gives you a genuine idea of the person purporting to be represented." Painters distorted the truth by flattering their sitters, following ephemeral standards of taste or projecting themselves into their canvases. More problematically, "no face is the same to any two spectators." Yet the next day, after inspecting canvases by Murillo, Velasquez, and Titian, Hawthorne could concede that "a portrait may preserve some valuable characteristics of the person represented" (22:349–50, 354). The simple assumption of the earlier tales and *The House of the Seven Gables*—that a portrait displays some core truth—was beginning to fracture.

Only one group of paintings gave him immediate and unmitigated pleasure in Manchester: the seventeenth-century Dutch masters. "The closer you look, the more minutely true the picture is found to be," he marveled. "These Dutchmen get at the soul of common things, and so make them the types and interpreters of the spiritual world" (22:356). That was certainly not true of the contemporary English painter William Etty, who depicted nudes with such "enormously developed bosoms and bottoms . . . that one feels inclined to kick them" (22:357). Nor was it true of the pre-Raphaelites, whose meticulous but unselected details lacked "life and reality" and pressed "baldly and harshly upon the spectator's eyeballs" (22:347).

A few months after steeping himself in art in Manchester, Hawthorne took his family to Italy, where they lived for the next year and a half. In Italy, Hawthorne internalized the still-prevailing neoclassical theories of Sir Joshua Reynolds, which placed grand representations of sacred and heroic subjects at the top of the aesthetic hierarchy and realistic depictions of ordinary life at the bottom. His ongoing pleasure in the Dutch now seemed a sign of low taste. Yet he wished for the impossible: that Dutch minuteness might be combined with the grandeur of a painting like Raphael's *Transfiguration*.

The connection with his goals as a writer is obvious. Time would only strengthen his basic conviction that the best works of art present truths of this world but also intimate truths beyond it. Time would also increase his already intense concern with the interrelationship of artists, works of art, and spectators. That conviction and that concern animate his last completed novel, *The Marble Faun*.

Like his countrymen, who came to Italy in increasing numbers at midcentury, Hawthorne arrived with high expectations. He was fulfilling one of Sophia's lifelong dreams, which was also his, one typical of the period: by contemplating the Western world's most celebrated works of art, they expected to refine their tastes and improve their moral sensibilities. In that anticipation, Hawthorne saturated himself in art as never before by visiting museums, churches, and palaces, befriending American artists—including Cephas Thompson—and discussing art with them, measuring his own responses to acknowledged masterpieces against those in Murray's guidebooks and his friend George Hillard's *Six Months in Italy* (1853) (and also against Sophia's), and trying to achieve that "generous surrender of myself which . . . is essential to the proper estimate of anything excellent" (14:110–11).

Raphael's *Transfiguration*, for example, Murray's guidebook to Rome informed him, was "justly considered the first oil painting in the world, its simultaneous portrayal of earth and heaven perfect in intent, because suffering humanity should look to heaven for relief and consolation" (Murray 238). Hillard concurred, though he thought the two kneeling figures in the upper half (supposedly of Cosimo de Medici's father and uncle) "are a blot in this magnificent work" (Hillard 251–52). "Approaching it," Hawthorne wrote in his *Notebook*, "I felt that the picture was worthy of its fame, and far better than I could at once appreciate." The more closely he examined it, the more fully he admired its "great lifelikeness and reality, as well as higher qualities." But, unlike Murray and Hillard, he was "not convinced of the propriety of its being in two so distinctly separate parts" (14:186–88). For Hawthorne, spiritual truth was not distinctly separable from earthly reality.

By the time he wrote *The Marble Faun*, his novel about artists residing in Rome, he believed that meaning in art is collaborative, perceived in a two-way exchange between the artist's achievement and the spectator's participating imagination. "It is the spectator's mood that transfigures the Transfiguration itself," the sculptor Kenyon says at the outset. "I defy any painter to move and elevate me without my own consent and assistance." The passionate Miriam thinks this proves Kenyon "deficient of a sense," but Hawthorne had learned this from experience (4:17).

What he called his "receptive faculty" could be sated by overexposure or desensitized by an inappropriate mood, and he was often disappointed by what he saw. When he tried to interpret a painting then considered a masterpiece and attributed to Michelangelo—*Three Fates*—he reluctantly concluded, "If it means one thing, it seems to mean a thousand, and often opposite things" (14:335). Yet he also believed we should give a work of art credit for what "it makes us feel in our best moments" and never judge it in "the coldness and insensibility of our less genial moods" (14:308–9).

Hawthorne came to believe that meaning is ultimately indeterminate: no spectator can be certain of perceiving the underlying truths that an artist intended or perhaps involuntarily projected, and a painting or statue might seem alive one day and dead the next. Yet he continued to believe also that an artist's humble submission to the phenomenal universe can produce "miraculous" insight into life's mysteries, which a sympathetic spectator can come to share. Like Jarves, he was convinced that the best works of art combine truth to nature (including human nature) with intimations of deeper truths. Such truths were there in a great work but not always accessible.

That was as true of a statue as a painting, though he thought the permanence of marble demanded a higher and more care-fully deliberated conception. The three-dimensionality of a statue provoked additional concerns commonly discussed during the period, which ranged from whether a frozen moment of high action, such as the *Laocoön*, was appropriate for a static medium to whether modern figures should be clothed in mod-ern dress or classical robes. As in the case of Michelangelo's *Lorenzo de Medici*, any statue that brought Hawthorne "highest enjoyment" also brought "grief and impatience, because I feel that I do not come at all which it involves, and that by-and-by I must go away and leave it forever." The *Lorenzo*'s "naturalness" seemed impossible to describe, "as if it came out of the marble of its own accord, with all its grandeur hanging heavily about it, and sat down there beneath its weight." Hiram Powers—the popular American sculptor who was Hawthorne's friend and neighbor in Florence—attributed its grandeur and mystery solely to a trick: the helmet threw the upper face into shadow. But Hawthorne reached his own conclusion: Michelangelo "wrought the whole statue in harmony with that little part which he leaves to the spectator's imagination," reaching "a point of excellence above the capability of marble" (14:327–28, 336).

Two otherwise very different statues more directly sparked Hawthorne's creative imagination. Even when his friend Wil-liam Wetmore Story's *Cleopatra* was "only fourteen days ad-vanced in the clay," Hawthorne was impressed by the "grand subject," which suggested "something deeper in his art than merely to make beautiful nudities" (14:73). He would later ap-propriate Story's defeated yet still fiercely magnificent queen for his fictional sculptor Kenyon. And the copy of Praxiteles' mar-ble *Faun* at the Capitoline Museum—"a natural and delightful link betwixt human and brute life, and with something of a divine character intermingled"—made Hawthorne's imagination soar:

> The whole person conveys the idea of an amiable and sensual nature, easy, mirthful, apt for jollity, yet not incapable of being touched by pathos. The faun has no principle, nor could comprehend it, yet is true and honest by virtue of his simplicity; very capable, too, of affection.

"The idea keeps recurring to me," he said, "of writing a little romance about it" (14:174, 191–92).

As usual, Hawthorne was most moved by art that confirmed his own deep-seated if provisional faith that this world is a place of grief and guilt but also of love and beauty, beyond which lies a perfect eternity. That explains his passionate response to *Christ Bound to the Pillar* by Sodoma, the "most illustrious" Sienese painter. The lonely figure so "utterly worn out with suffering, that his mouth has fallen apart from mere exhaustion" and who "is only kept from sinking down upon the ground by the cords that bind him" was "redeemed by a divine majesty and beauty," Hawthorne marveled. "Sodoma almost seems to have reconciled the impossibilities of combining an Omnipotent Divinity with a suffering and outraged humanity." But, as he also acknowledged, "the spectator's imagination completes what the artist merely hints at" (14:451–52, 491–92).

Hawthorne certainly had his limits. The preference for "a lifelike illusion," which he shared with most of his contemporaries, precluded sympathetic engagement with Fra Angelico, Cimabue, and Giotto, for example, painters whose work followed other conventions. And the period's notions of decency and propriety precluded sympathetic surrender to Titian's *Magdalen* or any other nude that seemed "indecorous." As a connoisseur, he said, *Magdalen* was a "splendid" painting, singling out its lifelike hands and glorious golden hair. But the woman whom Titian had made visible to his eye was dismayingly "coarse and sensual," an impudent and impenitent woman who "so carefully let those two voluptuous breasts be seen." He then added an afterthought: Titian must have been "a very good-for-nothing old man" (14:333–34).

Even more typically Victorian was Hawthorne's fascination with one of the period's most celebrated paintings: the sentimental portrait then believed to be of Beatrice Cenci, a young girl supposedly raped by her father and then implicated in his murder, attributed to the then-illustrious painter Guido Reni.[7] "Its spell is indefinable," Hawthorne affirmed, as did Sophia and virtually everyone else they knew. "She is like a fallen angel, fallen, without sin. . . . It is the most profoundly wrought picture in the world. . . . Guido may have held the brush, but he painted better than he knew." Hawthorne nonetheless wished "it were possible for some spectator, of deep sensibility, to see the picture without knowing anything of its subject or history, for no doubt we bring all our knowledge of the Cenci tragedy to the interpretation of the picture" (14:92–93). His skepticism raised one of the primary problems of any aesthetics of representation: how much of the art being seen is created by the perceiver?

Such concerns permeate his last completed novel, *The Marble Faun*, and Hawthorne's feeling that the portrait of Beatrice Cenci had "a life and consciousness of its own" helped him construct his two heroines. Miriam is a painter of limited technical ability whose impassioned work has attained "good acceptance among the patrons of modern art" in Rome (4:20). As we soon learn, all her work is a form of self-portraiture. When the novel's four main characters contemplate Praxiteles' *Faun* in the opening scene, she imagines "how happy, how genial, how satisfactory would be his life, enjoying the sensuous, earthy side of Nature . . . as mankind did in its innocent childhood, before sin, sorrow, or morality had ever been thought of!" (4:13). But all of her own art implies sin, sorrow, and morality.

She often includes in it the ominous features of a bearded character called "the Model," who haunts her footsteps and whose unspecified guilt is somehow also hers; she often portrays such biblical heroines as Jael in the act of avenging themselves against men; and her many "sketches of common life, and the affections that spiritualize it" include images of herself only as a sad onlooker. More explicitly self-defining is Miriam's "portrait of a beautiful woman, . . . so beautiful, that she seemed to get into your consciousness and memory, and could never afterwards be shut out, but haunted your dreams." This is the only self-portrait in Hawthorne's fiction. "It is yourself!" Miriam's enraptured young admirer, Donatello, exclaims, resorting to the word "witchcraft" to account for its remarkable lifelikeness. To his great dismay, however, the picture soon "gazes sadly forth at me, as if some evil had befallen it in the little time since I looked last" (4:43–49). Donatello's recognition of that sadness is the beginning of his moral education and of his implication in Miriam's guilt.

By contrast with the "original" painter, Miriam, whose sad "heart-knowledge" informs all of her work, Hilda is a self-abnegating copyist. An idealized version of Sophia-as-copyist, Hilda feels "through and through" a great picture as if through its creator's eyes, then selects "some high, noble, and delicate portion" to copy and render "with her whole soul" and thus make it available to mankind (4:56–59). Yet her own spiritual purity limits what she perceives and produces.

The only work by Hilda that the novel presents is an amazingly accurate copy of the haunting *Beatrice Cenci*. While contemplating it in Hilda's studio, Miriam feels such "painful sympathy" with the doomed Beatrice that her expression becomes "almost exactly that of the portrait," and she begs Hilda to cover it (4:64–67). Like the disturbing portraits in "The Prophetic Pictures," "Edward Randolph's Portrait," and *The House of the Seven Gables*, as well as Miriam's self-portrait, it seems preternaturally alive. When Miriam asks if she can account for its mysterious force, Hilda confides that, while making her copy, she had felt that the real Beatrice was trying to escape her gaze. But when she glimpses her own face and Beatrice's in a mirror after witnessing the Model's murder, she fancies in horror that "Beatrice's expression . . . had been depicted in her own face" (4:205). As that final variation on the Gothic trope asserts, Hilda has joined the ranks of guilt-stained innocents. But Hawthorne displays his own connoisseurship by using one of the period's most celebrated yet most perplexing portraits to say so.[8]

The now-despondent Hilda "sometimes doubted whether the pictorial art be not altogether a delusion" (as Hawthorne often did). She "saw beauty less vividly, but felt truth, or the lack of it, more profoundly," and therefore she abandons her role as copyist (4:338–40). But she seeks spiritual consolation in a picture "peculiarly adapted to her character": Reni's *Archangel Michael Subduing the Demon*, which depicts "the immortal youth and loveliness of Virtue, and its irresistible might against ugly Evil" (4:352).

To say that Hawthorne's beliefs about art were those of his time does not mean they were simple, consistent, or unambiguous. Like most of his contemporaries, he read pictures primarily for referential meaning rather than aesthetic value, increasingly attending to his own role as spectator. He constructed his two heroines as differentiated spectators. Initially, both women agree that *Archangel Michael* is a fine picture (though Hawthorne-as-connoisseur remarks that it is not as fine as Hilda believes). Yet their different responses to it after the Model's death reflect their different experiences, emotional needs, and moral beliefs. When Miriam again confronts it, she faults its "moral and intellectual aspect" more than she had done before, insisting that the archangel should be stained and wounded after battling his powerful antagonist (as she has been stained and wounded by battling hers) (4:183–84). But when Hilda later seeks consolation from a mosaic copy of the same familiar picture, she is so overwhelmed by the archangel's unruffled "heavenly severity" that she involuntarily drops to her knees and prays.

Hilda is on the verge of becoming more fully human, and as Hawthorne's ultimately ideal spectator, she is enabled by sympathy to see "the Perfect, through a mist of imperfection," to realize that in art as in literature, the "highest merit is suggestiveness." Thus she can discern in her suitor, Kenyon's, unfinished marble bust of the now guilt-stricken Donatello what is also occurring in her: an advance "towards a higher state of development" (4:379–80).

But with Miriam's self-portrait, Hawthorne raises more provocative issues. It is a true portrait, a convincing likeness that also conveys a skillful painter's piercing insights into a sitter's inner life. More than that, as a fictive spectator and reader surrogate, Hawthorne-as-narrator says its beauty haunts "your" dreams, then lingers over the dark eyes "you" could look into "as deeply as your glance would go, and still be conscious of a depth you had not sounded." A glance at the "dark glory" of the young woman's possibly "Jewish hair" then triggers a densely allusive rhapsody:

> Gazing at this portrait, you saw what Rachael might have been, when Jacob deemed her worth the wooing seven years, and seven more; or perchance she might ripen to be what Judith was, when she vanquished Holofernes with her beauty, and slew him for too much adoring it. (4:48)

As a connoisseur familiar with "self-painters," the fictive narrator assumes that Miriam's portrait contains "intimate results of her heart-knowledge," and he wonders with Miriam whether the innocent Donatello can perceive it (4:48–49). If the sadness he soon sees is not exactly what the fictive narrator saw, it is equally true. With that intimation, Hawthorne went beyond the essentialism of his earlier fictions in which a portrait reveals a single core truth. Truth is never simple and always intimates itself ambiguously. What a spectator sees—whether in a person, the natural world, or a work of art—depends on that spectator's own character and prior experience.[9]

A recurrent complaint about *The Marble Faun* from the time it first appeared is that its concern with art weighs it down, a complaint that Hawthorne anticipated in his preface when he disingenuously claimed that he "was somewhat surprised to see the extent to which he had introduced descriptions of various Italian objects, antique, pictorial, and statuesque" (3). The novel is replete with references to famous works other American tourists sought out and pondered—not only *Beatrice Cenci*, *Archangel Michael*, and *Transfiguration*, but the paintings and statues of Michelangelo and classical statues, including the *Apollo Belvedere* among scores of others Hawthorne had struggled to assimilate into his own sensibility. His explanation was equally disingenuous: "these things fill the mind, everywhere in Italy, and especially in Rome" (4:3). More consequentially, they serve to define his protagonists and advance a "thoughtful moral," which includes much of what he had been led to believe and everything he had subsequently discovered about the moral value of art itself.

Through and beyond the layered artifice of his last completed novel, in concert with such seminal critics as Jarves and Ruskin, Hawthorne professed a faith in art as a locus of moral perception and self-perception that contested his ongoing doubts about the value of any work of art and, indeed, about the value of any work of literature, including his own. He claimed in his preface that references to art simply flowed out on the pages of his "fanciful story." In fact, he had shrewdly used art as his age used it, as a mode of edification, spiritual awareness, and moral refinement and therefore (in Jarves's words) as "a vital principle of life" (165).

NOTES

1. Whether or not Hawthorne read *The Art-Idea* when it first appeared in 1864, the same ideas had appeared in Jarves's earlier works, including *Art-Hints, Architecture, Sculpture and Painting* (1855), and it is even possible that they met in Italy, where they moved in the same circles of expatriate artists and writers.

2. *Atlantic Monthly* 3 (May 1859): 653–54. Although the "notice" was specifically of "Rowse's Portrait of Emerson. Published in Photograph," "Durand's Portrait of Bryant. Engraved by Schoff & Jones," and "Barry's Portrait of Whittier. Published in Photograph," the reviewer also stated that the copies offered "full insight and representation of character."

3. Hawthorne checked out Dunlap from the Salem Athenaeum on 9 Mar. 1836 and again on 21 May. Gollin and Idol, *Prophetic Pictures* 17, 38, 45.

4. "The Artist of the Beautiful" (1844) offers a heavily platonized variant. Owen Warland creates "Nature's ideal butterfly," which his pragmatic society cannot appreciate. Though he has put his "whole being" into the preternatural butterfly, he does not mind seeing it destroyed because "his spirit possessed itself in the enjoyment of the reality." The story's one reference to a conventional work of art is to the ambitious painting that Washington Allston had not lived to complete, sad proof that earthly accomplishments are at best "exercises and manifestations of the spirit" (*Centenary* 10:467).

5. For a provocative discussion of truth in "the mirror image" of daguerreotypes, see Trachtenberg, "Seeing and Believing," pp. 460–81.

6. *The Art-Treasures Examiner: A Pictorial, Critical, and Historical Record of the Art-Treasures Exhibition, at Manchester, in 1857* (Manchester, England: A. Ireland, 1857). See also Gollin and Idol, *Prophetic Pictures*, pp. 69–82, 124–26.

7. The painting is no longer attributed to Reni, and one of the current hypotheses is that it is not a portrait of Beatrice Cenci but "probably represents a Sybil." See *Centenary* 14:746–47.

8. He did so again by having a young artist capture Hilda's deep expression of sorrow in a portrait that connoisseurs assume was based on Guido's *Beatrice*.

9. This point is well amplified by Wendy Steiner in her chapter on *The Marble Faun* in *Pictures of Romance*, pp. 91–120.

BIBLIOGRAPHY

Baker, Paul R. *The Fortunate Pilgrims: Americans in Italy, 1800–1860.* Cambridge, Mass.: Harvard University Press, 1964.

Dunlap, William. *A History of the Rise and Progress of the Arts of Design in the United States,* 2 vols. New York: George P. Scott, 1834. Rpt. (3 vols.), ed. Rita Weiss. New York: Dover, 1969.

Gollin, Rita K., and John L. Idol, Jr., eds. *Prophetic Pictures: Nathaniel Hawthorne's Knowledge and Uses of the Visual Arts.* New York: Greenwood, 1991.

Harris, Neil. *The Artist in American Society: The Formative Years, 1790–1860.* New York: George Braziller, 1966.

Hawthorne, Nathaniel. *The Centenary Edition of the Works of Nathaniel Hawthorne,* ed. William Charvat et al., 23 vols. Columbus: Ohio State University Press, 1962–97.

Hawthorne, Sophia Peabody. *Notes in England and Italy.* New York: Putnam, 1869.

Hillard, George Stillman. *Six Months in Italy,* 2 vols. Boston: Ticknor, Reed and Fields, 1853.

Jarves, James Jackson. *The Art-Idea.* New York: Hurd and Houghton, 1864. Rpt., ed. Benjamin Rowland, Jr. Cambridge, Mass.: Harvard University Press, 1960.

Larkin, Oliver W. *Art and Life in America.* New York: Holt, Rinehart, and Winston, 1960.

Lubin, David M. *Picturing a Nation: Art and Social Change in Nine-*

teenth-Century America*. New Haven, Conn.: Yale University Press, 1994.

Murray, John. *A Handbook for Travellers in Central Italy*, 2 vols., 7th ed. London: John Murray, 1867.

———. *A Handbook of Rome and Its Environs*, 8th ed. London: John Murray, 1867.

Norton, Charles Eliot. *Notes of Travel and Study in Italy*. Boston: Ticknor and Fields, 1860.

Novak, Barbara. *Nature and Culture: American Landscape and Painting 1825–1875*. New York: Oxford University Press, 1980.

Stein, Roger B. *John Ruskin and Aesthetic Thought in America, 1840–1900*. Cambridge, Mass.: Harvard University Press, 1967.

Steiner, Wendy. *Pictures of Romance: Form against Context in Painting and Literature*. Chicago: University of Chicago Press, 1988.

Trachtenberg, Alan. "Seeing and Believing: Hawthorne's Reflections on the Daguerreotype in *The House of the Seven Gables*," *American Literary History* 9 (Fall 1997): 460–81.

Wolf, Bryan Jay, *Romantic Re-Vision: Culture and Consciousness in Nineteenth-Century American Painting and Literature*. Chicago: University of Chicago Press, 1982.

Hawthorne and the
Slavery Question

Jean Fagan Yellin

Beguiled, perhaps, by his brilliant self-portrayal of the artist as politically disengaged, critics generally have neglected examining Hawthorne's failure to participate in the historic effort of his generation to end chattel slavery. They apparently have assumed that, unlike his Concord neighbors Emerson, Thoreau, and Fuller, he was largely unaware of the great moral struggle going on all around him. Yet there is considerable evidence to the contrary. In the years before he wrote the great romances, Hawthorne became intimately acquainted with the essential facts of chattel slavery, as well as with the debate raging around it. This chapter will explore why this knowledge fails to show itself in the great romances, where it might naturally be expected to illustrate their major theme of psychological bondage.[1]

Hawthorne's *Notebooks* yield a consistent, if partial, record of his awareness of the issue of black slavery. In his earliest journal (1836–37), he notes the sale of a young woman in seventeenth-century England: "In an old London newspaper, 1678, there is an advertisement, among other goods at auction of a Black girl of about 15 years old, to be sold."[2] Writing at Litchfield in 1836, he recorded his consciousness of the history of slavery and racial segregation in his own New England:

In a remote part of the grave-yard—remote from the main body of dead people—I noticed a humble, mossy stone, on which I traced out—"To the memory of Julia Africa, servant of Rev." somebody. There were the half-obliterated traces of other graves, without any monuments, in the vicinity of this one. Doubtless the slaves here mingled their dark clay with the earth.[3]

Like many New England seaports, Hawthorne's Salem had fed on slavery. Local historian Joseph Felt reported ships directly engaged in the "Guinea" slave trade in 1773, 1785, 1787, and 1792. After 1795, when Jay's treaty curtailed East Indian shipping, many more Salem ships became active in the larger "triangular trade," selling New England rum for African slaves and, in turn, exchanging the slaves for West Indian sugar. In the smaller triangular trade, they marketed New England rum for West Indian slaves and molasses, then sold the slaves in Charleston and other southern ports and carried the molasses back home. Whatever booty Hawthorne's acclaimed privateer forebear, the "bold" Daniel Hathorne, plundered on the high seas remains a mystery, but records show that Hawthorne's father, Captain Nathaniel Hathorne, was briefly involved in the West Indian trade before Hawthorne's birth. Although there is no evidence to suggest that he carried slaves, everyone in the West Indian trade, like everyone in Hawthorne's Salem, understood that the slave trade was a fact of international commerce. Felt writes that at least some of Hawthorne's fellow citizens were as ashamed of Salem's historic involvement in the Guinea trade as they were of Salem's historic involvement in the persecution of "witches."[4] Like most New England towns, Hawthorne's Salem was home to blacks as well as whites. It is not clear precisely when the community was established that local historian William Bentley characterized in Hawthorne's youth as "our black town," but records show that the first Africans were imported as slaves in 1638, two centuries before Hawthorne began making his *Notebook* entries.[5]

In "Old News" (1835), an early sketch, Hawthorne describes these black residents of Salem as contributing "their dark shade to the picture of society." This inclusion of their presence perhaps indicated to his readers that he was setting his scene in America, in much the same way that contemporary artists were including representatives of three races—red, black, and white—within a single painting to signal their work as American.[6]

"Old News" presents peculiarly contradictory views of blacks. Hawthorne portrays them as content, writing, "The slaves, we suspect, were the merriest part of the population, since it was their gift to be merry in the worst of circumstances; and they endured comparatively few hardships." This sounds much like John Pendleton Kennedy's plantation novel *Swallow Barn*, published three years earlier, which pictured the blacks as gay and their bondage as light.[7] Unlike Kennedy, a proslavery apologist, Hawthorne includes some of the more brutal aspects of slavery. After quoting from numerous advertisements for slaves, he makes the neutral comment that "there must have been a great trade in these human commodities." Discussing the separation of mothers from their infants, he adopts a manner that, for the modern reader, fails both as satire and as whimsy: "When the slaves of a family were inconveniently prolific,—it being not quite orthodox to drown the superfluous offspring, like a litter of kittens,— notice was promulgated of 'a negro child to be given away.'" (He repeated this shocking image some years later in *Grandfather's Chair* [1841]: "As for the little negro babies, they were offered to be given away like young kittens.") Observing that blacks rebelled by escaping and that their masters tried to catch them, he notes that a repeated runaway "carried with him an iron collar rivetted around his neck, with a chain attached."[8]

While not ignoring the violence of slavery routinely omitted from plantation fiction, Hawthorne does not exhort his readers to act to end human bondage, as William Lloyd Garrison had been doing in his newspaper the *Liberator* every Friday since 1831, publishing accounts of the atrocities of slavery and urging its immediate abolition.

Later in 1831, Nat Turner had led the bloodiest slave revolt in American history, jolting the nation into an awareness that insurrection could occur in this country.[9] But Hawthorne's "Old News" ignores the danger of armed conflict over slavery. Instead,

Hawthorne proposes a peaceful accommodation to it, writing that fugitives would do better not to attempt escape but to submit to their condition, "performing their moderate share of the labors of life, without being harrassed [*sic*] by its cares." Asserting that the whites included their slaves within the family circle, Hawthorne's final comment echoes contemporary proslavery accounts like *Swallow Barn* (1832) in claiming that the masters' kindness "modified and softened the institution, making it a patriarchal, and almost a beautiful, peculiarity of the times."

By Hawthorne's day, all of the black residents of Salem were free, although some of the older people had been held as chattel before the Massachusetts Constitutional Convention of 1780 ended all slavery in the commonwealth.[10] The presence of this free black population was not as dramatic as the slave trade or domestic slavery had been, but Salem felt it. At the beginning of the nineteenth century, when Hawthorne was born, little more than 300 of the town's approximately 10,000 residents were nonwhite; by 1840, the white population had grown half again as large while the black population had stayed approximately the same. Although small, this black community was stable. During Hawthorne's childhood, Black Salem organized and formed an African Society. By the time he returned home from college, Salem, like Boston, was enmeshed in a series of racial controversies. Its black population, which included the abolitionist Remond family, was asserting its political rights and protesting against segregation in schools, churches, and burial grounds.[11]

Then in 1830, local race relations became strained by the sensational murder of Captain Joseph White. Because the captain had made his fortune in the slave trade, at first it was thought that he had been killed by a vengeful black. (Ultimately, it was the Crowninshields, Hawthorne's distant cousins, who were convicted of the crime.) Racial tensions surfaced that year when white Salemites opposed the efforts of their black neighbors to enroll their daughters in the new girls' high school. There were more protests in 1834 when blacks again tried to attend the schools. The blacks persisted, however; finally, in 1843, Salem schools were desegregated.[12]

Like other Anglo Americans of his place and time, Hawthorne interacted with blacks all of his life. Although his casual childhood encounters with the residents of Little Guinea or New Africa at the Salem end of the turnpike have not been documented, we do know that William Symmes, his friend during his carefree boyhood summers in Maine, was black. Further, we know that during Hawthorne's college years, among his fellow students at Bowdoin was John Russwurm, who would later found the first African-American newspaper, *Freedom's Journal*. Another student later recalled walking with Hawthorne to Russwurm's room outside the village, remarking that their black classmate did not return their visits because of "his sensitiveness on account of his color." Later, during Hawthorne's brief stay at the transcendentalists' utopian commune Brook Farm—which, unlike Shaker settlements, had no black members—he documented his own "sensitiveness on account of . . . color" by writing that a child had an "almost mulatto complexion." This same Notebook entry also attests to his awareness of the racial stereotyping current in American popular culture—and to the associationists' participation in it. Referring to minstrel Thomas D. Rice's popular blackface character, he wrote of a Brook Farm masquerader, who had disguised himself as "a negro of the Jim Crow order."[13]

Although essentially conservative, Hawthorne's Salem had its share of controversy over abolition, and both antislavery and antiabolitionist sentiments were represented in the town. Black Salem women were first in the nation to create a female antislavery society. Later reorganized to include both blacks and whites, this group sent delegations to all three conventions of American Women against Slavery. In 1835, antiabolitionist whites protested against the appearance of a prominent antislavery lecturer by mobbing a meeting at Howard Street Church. But two years later, local abolitionist women scheduled four full days of activities featuring Sarah and Angelina Grimké, southern aristocrats who embraced William Lloyd Garrison's doctrine of immediate emancipation from slavery. The Grimké sisters' speaking tour made them notorious for defying the taboos against women addressing "promiscuous" audiences of both sexes. At Salem, they spoke at the Friends' Meeting House, met with "colored members of the Seaman's and Moral Reform Society," addressed an audience of more than a thousand at the Howard Street Meeting House, and talked with children and adults at the "colored Sabbath School." Still, Clarissa C. Lawrence, a black Salem delegate to the 1839 convention of American Women against Slavery, testified that she and other blacks "meet the monster prejudice *every where.*"[14]

Sophia Peabody, the townswoman Hawthorne would later marry, did not involve herself in the female antislavery movement at Salem or anywhere else. Endorsing the domestic ideology assigning women to the "private sphere," she later expressed her disapproval of abolitionist women and their efforts to intervene in the public debate over slavery when, married and pregnant, she wrote to her mother from nearby Concord about her arrangements for an inexpensive layette:

> The ladies of the antislavery society take sewing in Concord and do it very cheaply. So shall I employ them, for I have no manner of scruple about making them take as little as possible; while I could not think of not giving full and ample price to a poor person, or a seamstress by profession.[15]

Later, at the Old Manse, she commented to her mother that she was thinking of hiring a domestic, a mature black woman whom Mrs. Peabody had mentioned to her. Referring to her former maid, a fresh-faced young Irish woman, who she believed dishonest, Sophia Peabody Hawthorne wrote:

> My husband says he does not want me to undertake to keep anybody who is apparently innocent, after my late sore experience. He says the old black lady is probably as bad already as she ever will be. If you find the blackey not disinclined to come to such poor folks, I will take her in September.

Whether this woman joined the Hawthornes at Concord, I do not know, but records show that when they moved to Lenox after publication of *The Scarlet Letter*, they hired the black Mrs. Peters as a domestic.[16]

Hawthorne acknowledges Mrs. Peters's presence in his 1851 journal, when he records his brief experience caring for his five-year-old son while his wife was away. These entries indicate that, in addition to cooking, cleaning, and serving unexpected guests, Mrs. Peters had considerable responsibility for little Julian. Nonetheless, Hawthorne generally ignores the black woman's presence and names not her, but the child's pet, in the title of his journal entry: "Twenty Days with Julian and Little Bunny by Papa."

Hawthorne usually showed little interest in servants, and he was not particularly interested in Mrs. Peters. His fullest comment, which describes her exchanges with Julian, sketches a distanced relationship that follows established patterns of racial etiquette. Although he defies convention by not using her first name, in this passage Hawthorne suggests that Mrs. Peters was careful to adhere to accepted patterns of race and class even in her dealings with her employers' child:

> Mrs. Peters is quite attentive to him, in her grim way. Today, for instance, we found two ribbons on his old straw hat, which must have been of her sewing on. She encourages no familiarity on his part, nor is he in the least drawn towards her, nor, on the other hand, does he exactly seem to stand in awe; but he recognizes that there is to be no communication beyond the inevitable—and, with that understanding, she awards him all substantial kindness.[17]

Mrs. Peters had evidently taken the job with the Hawthornes as a favor, and the following winter, she wanted to quit. Only when Sophia, who was again pregnant, promised to teach her to read did she agree to stay on until after the birth of their third child. Many years later, the Hawthornes' daughter Rose recalled Mrs. Peters as "an invaluable tyrant, an unloaded weapon, a creature who seemed to say, 'Forget my qualities if you dare—there is one of them which is fatal!'" The force of this extraordinary comment suggests that Mrs. Peters may have embodied the re-

pressed fury that has fueled much of African-American literature. Even after achieving literacy, however, she apparently left
no record of her responses to America's writer of moral romances. This, like Hawthorne's failure to explore and to render
the distancing and "grim" intensity that he sensed in the black
woman, is a loss to our national letters.[18]

Hawthorne's routine exchanges with free black New Englanders like Mrs. Peters and Prince Farmer, a Salem Democrat and
restaurateur whose oysters he relished, did not, of course, provide him with information about the slave trade or chattel slavery.[19] But through other sources, he became extremely knowl-
edgeable about slave life in Cuba, about international policing of
the outlawed African trade, and about efforts to colonize freed
slaves in Liberia.

On his first visits to the Peabody house in 1837, Hawthorne
was shown the "Cuba Journals." These were letters written
home to Salem a few years earlier by the invalid Sophia Peabody,
who had gone to Cuba for her health, and by her sister Mary,
who had accompanied her. During their year-and-a-half residence on a sugar plantation, the Peabody sisters recorded their
impressions of Cuban slavery. They commented on the overwhelming black presence, on the picturesqueness of the Africans
at play, and on the oppressiveness of slave labor. They cited evidence of the brutality of the system: a coffle of chained Africans
on a road, "fiercely trained dogs," and "one poor negro . . . actually bitten to death." They wrote about the sexual exploitation
of slave women, noting a slaveholder's double families, one le-
gitimate, free, and white and the other illegitimate, slave, and
black; and they discussed the slaves' desperate resort to infanti-
cide, noting that the deaths of twenty or thirty infants on the
plantation where they were staying had resulted in a brutal punishment for the slave mothers whose babies had died. In the
Cuba journals, Hawthorne was confronted with information
as shocking as the exposés appearing each week in Garrison's
Liberator.[20]

A decade after reading these firsthand descriptions of Cuban
slavery, Hawthorne edited an eyewitness narrative describing international efforts to suppress the African slave trade and detail-

ing conditions in Liberia (recently established as a "homeland" for African former slaves expatriated by the American Colonization Society). This was the *Journal of an African Cruiser*, written at Hawthorne's suggestion by his lifelong friend Horatio Bridge.[21]

Hawthorne was trying hard to win a federal appointment in the early 1840s. Pointing to the *Journal's* implicit endorsement of the efforts of the ACS, which proposed sending blacks "back to Africa" despite opposition by the free black community, critics have speculated that Hawthorne used the book to advance himself with pro-ACS Democrats.[22] This seems entirely likely.

After winning the Salem Custom House job, he of course became even better informed about the slave trade. As surveyor, in 1846 and again in 1847, he complained to his superiors about the inaccuracy of the hydrometer used to test the proof of export liquor. His friend, the poet Ellery Channing, who visited the custom house during this period, recalled Hawthorne measuring the strength of a consignment of rum and boasting, "'I am determined the niggers shall have as good liquor as anyone gets from New England.'"[23] This comment establishes Hawthorne's awareness that the rum was destined for Africa and expresses his sense of moral responsibility to guarantee its purchaser a fair measure. But it also shows him avoiding the larger moral question about the commodities the rum would be traded for. Ivory? Slaves, called "black ivory"?

It was not necessary to work in the custom house or to read a friend's firsthand account of Liberia or Cuba, however, to be informed about African slavery during the years of Hawthorne's literary apprenticeship. The controversy over abolition brought the issue home to New England. Along with everyone else, Hawthorne was aware, for example, of the mobbing of the Boston Female Anti-Slavery Society in 1835. The Boston women, like the Salem reformers subjected to violence that year, had announced that the British abolitionist George Thompson would address their public meeting. In response, local merchants, spurred by anti-British feeling and eager to demonstrate their allegiance to their southern business partners, promoted a riot. Despite this open threat of antiabolitionist violence, the mayor refused police protection, and the mobbed women evacuated their besieged building, walking out through the crowds in racially integrated pairs. Rioters seized Garrison and had a rope around his neck before he was rescued and taken into protective custody.[24]

Like most Boston publications, the *American Monthly Magazine* denounced not the mob but the abolitionists. Under the headline "Reported Riot in Boston," it reported that the reformers had organized the meeting "as if to court danger and persecution." Although claiming to deplore public violence, *American Monthly* declared that the abolitionists' "incendiary and revolutionary doctrine" should not be tolerated and warned that if the abolitionists "are so mad and so regardless as to continue . . . they at least cannot complain of any harsh treatment."[25] When Hawthorne edited the *American Monthly* the following year, he reprinted "Mobs," which can be read as another comment on the riot. This piece—which claims that mobs are not a natural outgrowth of America's democratic institutions although "the public opinion in America is law"—blandly expresses confidence that enlightened public opinion will end public disorders.[26]

The violence was viewed differently by abolitionists. Though never one of them, Sophia Peabody was, before marrying Hawthorne, part of a circle that included members of the Boston Female Anti-Slavery Society, like the Sturgis sisters and Maria White, who converted her fiancé, poet James Russell Lowell, to abolitionism. To these women—and to Sophia's circle at Concord, which included Female Anti-Slavery Society women like the Alcotts and Lidian Emerson, whose abolitionist ideas influenced her famous husband—the mobbed women were "martyrs." British writer Harriet Martineau, who had met the reformers in Boston, used this term to describe them in the *London and Westminster Review*. Shortly after the riot, she cut short her American trip in the wake of newspaper attacks against her endorsement of their antislavery principles. Three years later, when the antislavery women were again mobbed at Philadelphia, all of reform New England gossiped about the collapse of the prominent Boston abolitionist Maria Weston Chapman after her failed attempt to speak at Pennsylvania Hall, her red shawl flaming against the Quaker gray worn by the besieged abolitionists trapped inside, and her voice drowned out by the mob.[27]

Other well-publicized incidents involved failed abolitionist efforts to rescue fugitive slaves. In 1845, Jonathan Walker, a white Massachusetts sea captain, was arrested in Florida and convicted of aiding fugitives. Walker's punishment was to be enchained, displayed on the pillory, and branded "SS" (slave stealer). Captain Walker's "branded hand" was daguerreotyped by Southworth and Hawes, and his ordeal inspired John Greenleaf Whitter to write a poem in which the signification of Walker's brand is reversed from negative to positive, from "slave stealer" to "salvation to the slave" and likened to "armoreal hatchments." In 1848, New England sensibilities were again aroused by the seizure of two young black women and the arrest of officers of the schooner *Pearl*, caught transporting them to freedom. To raise money for the Edmondson sisters' manumission, the Reverend Henry Ward Beecher staged a mock slave auction at his Brooklyn church—permitting the congregation to experience the joys of beneficence by helping to emancipate slaves while simultaneously experiencing the delights of sin by bidding for females exposed on the block. After a highly publicized trial, Captain Edward Sayer and Mate Daniel Drayton were convicted for aiding the fugitives. Sentenced to heavy fines, which they could not pay, the men spent four years in jail before being pardoned.[28]

Two of these sensational events personally involved members of Sophia Peabody Hawthorne's family. Hawthorne's future sister-in-law, Sophia's eldest sister, Elizabeth Palmer Peabody, had been a guest in the house where Martineau was staying and had burned the Boston newspapers to spare the Englishwoman the embarrassment of reading their attacks on her antislavery ideas. (Martineau later wrote that Peabody had begged her to modify her antislavery statements in order to retrieve at least a degree of respectability. When she refused, her American tour collapsed.) In the case of the *Pearl*, it was Hawthorne's brother-in-law, Horace Mann, the antislavery congressman married to Sophia's sister Mary, who defended Sayer and Drayton in court. As a literate New Englander, Hawthorne was doubtless aware of these highly publicized incidents; as Sophia Peabody's husband, he had direct knowledge of them.[29]

During the years before his marriage, Hawthorne testified to his familiarity with abolitionist discourse by adopting its language to discuss his own situation. Complaining to Sophia about his job at the Boston Custom House, he wrote that her "husband" felt "the iron of his chain"; after quitting, he exulted, "I have broken my chain and escaped." Later, planning to leave Brook Farm, he wrote that he was looking forward to being "free from this bondage. . . . Even my Custom House experience was not such a thraldom and weariness; my mind and heart were freer!"[30] The *Notebooks* written between 1842 and 1845 reveal that Hawthorne considered using the problem of slavery as a literary subject. The references to this theme testify to his fascination with the attempt to manipulate and enslave another morally and psychologically:

> To point out the moral slavery of one who deems himself a free man.

> A moral philosopher to buy a slave, or otherwise get possession of a human being, and use him for the sake of experiment, by trying the operation of a certain vice on him.

> Sketch of a person who, by strength of character, or assistant circumstances, has reduced another to absolute slavery and dependence on him. Then show, that the person who appears to be the master, must inevitably be at least as much a slave, if not more, than the other. All slavery is reciprocal, on the supposition most favorable to the rulers.[31]

Although the origins of Hawthorne's major works are present in these jottings, any recognition of a link between this metaphorical slavery and the literal enslavement of blacks is conspicuously absent here—and throughout Hawthorne's writings.

Long before, in Cuba, Sophia had recorded her conscious decision not to think about African slavery:

> I do not allow myself to dwell upon slavery for two reasons. One is, it would certainly counteract the beneficent influences, which I have left home and country to court, and another is, that my faith in God makes me sure that he makes up to every being the measure of happiness which he loses thro' the instrumentality of others. I try to realize how much shorter time is, than eternity and then endeavour to lose myself in other subjects of thought.[32]

And, like Sophia Peabody in Cuba, it appears that Hawthorne deliberately avoided thinking about black slavery in antebellum America.

In his major writings, he characteristically defines as sinful the effort of one human being to usurp the will of another; he dramatizes this not by focusing on an individual madman (as Poe did) but by locating his characters within a social context that is inevitably oppressive. Yet, again and again, he distances this drama in time and/or space instead of connecting it to the context with which every New Englander of his generation would unavoidably have associated it: American chattel slavery.

One reason for this conspicuous omission may be that, although he was well acquainted with the reformers, Hawthorne did not like them much. A journal entry written years before his brief involvement with the Brook Farm idealists testifies to his lack of sympathy for reformers and for their reforms, and, in equating advocacy of cold-water bathing with opposition to slavery, he demonstrates his failure to distinguish among their causes:

> A sketch to be given of a modern reformer—a type of the extreme doctrines on the subject of slaves, cold-water, and other such topics. He goes about the streets haranguing most eloquently, and is on the point of making many converts, when his labors are suddenly interrupted by the appearance of the keeper of a mad-house, where he has escaped. Much may be made of this idea.[33]

Hawthorne included critical presentations of reformers in more than a half dozen of the short pieces published after he left Brook Farm. His fullest condemnation is in "Earth's Holocaust," which presents a vision of ultimate destruction not uncommon in a period of social change like Hawthorne's—and our own.[34] In this sketch, the final conflagration is fueled neither by an accident nor by oppressors desperate to maintain power but by reformers, who begin by attacking social corruption and end by attacking society's most valuable institutions and achievements.

Hawthorne would return to this theme in works as diverse as "The Birthmark" and *The Blithedale Romance*. He, in fact, never moved beyond it, never changed his view that reforms are ineffective and reformers are dangerous.[35] His recurrent criticism was that they suffer from a false vision of the world. In an early sketch, his narrator asserts that reformers must "cease to look through pictured windows," must stop mistaking their distorted illumination for "the whitest sunshine."[36] More than a dozen years later, he used this same figure of speech in writing to his antislavery sister-in-law Elizabeth Palmer Peabody:

> I do assure you that like every other Abolitionist, you look at matters with an awful squint, which distorts everything within your line of vision; and it is queer, though natural, that you think everybody squints except yourselves. Perhaps they do; but certainly *you* do.[37]

Earlier, in the Berkshires, Hawthorne had contemptuously dismissed the abolitionist press, commenting that since he had not seen "a single newspaper (except an anti-slavery paper) . . . I know no more of what is going on than if I had migrated to the moon."[38]

It has been assumed that during his years abroad (1853–60), Hawthorne was unaware of the heightening struggle over abolition. But correspondence testifies that Elizabeth Palmer Peabody made persistent efforts to enlighten Hawthorne and her younger sister Sophia about the slavery controversy. This correspondence documents Hawthorne's hostility toward abolitionism (and toward Elizabeth), as well as his proprietary attitude toward his wife. Reading it, we learn that when the Hawthornes were in England, Elizabeth sent Sophia an antislavery pamphlet she had written, and Hawthorne returned the manuscript to her, commenting, "I do not choose to bother Sophia with it, and yet should think it a pity to burn so much of your thought and feeling. . . . to tell you the truth, I have read only the first line or two." When Elizabeth mailed the manuscript back to her sister, Hawthorne again responded, writing that he has now read her pamphlet: "Upon my word, it is not very good; not worthy of being sent three times across the ocean; not so good as I supposed you would always write, on a subject on which your mind and heart were interested." He then concedes, "However, since you make a point of it, I will give it to Sophia, and will tell her all about its rejection and return."[39]

Just as Hawthorne had censored his wife's mail, in 1860 Sophia Peabody Hawthorne announced that she would not permit their daughter to read her sister's pamphlet. Claiming that, although she can tolerate its antislavery arguments, she will not allow them to be inflicted on Una, she asserts that both she and Hawthorne are conversant with the reformers' attacks on American slavery and with reports of slave sales:

> As you wrote once that I probably never heard anything that was going on in America, even from newspapers, I told [Una] when she wrote you to tell you that we saw the most liberal newspapers all the time. But we do not allow the children to read newspapers. . . . And you would display before . . . [my daughter's] great, innocent eyes a naked slave girl on a block at auction (which I am sure is an exaggeration for I have read of those auctions often and even the worst facts are never so bad as absolute nudity.)[40]

If a distaste for the reformers and their tactics perhaps made it difficult for Hawthorne to make the connection between the slavery question and his concern with psychological bondage, his racial attitudes perhaps made it impossible. When editing the *American Monthly Magazine*, he had included three pieces treating skin color as a subject of inquiry. "Effect of Colour on Heat" reports the speculation in a recent issue of a London journal about the effect of climate on skin color, discusses Africans' adaptation to heat by means of "insensible persperation [*sic*]," and asserts that this "insensible persperation" causes "the peculiar odour of the coloured race." A follow-up, "Effect of Colour on Odours," suggests that "negroes . . . suffer more in proportion to their numbers, than whites, by all sorts of pestilence and unwholesome smells." "Pie-Bald Negroes" is a filler that describes black people with white spots on their skin.[41]

Better clues to Hawthorne's racial attitudes appear in his *Notebooks*, which were not written for publication. Discussing a violent racist incident that occurred during a trip to western Massachusetts in 1838, he writes that "some of the blacks were knocked down and otherwise maltreated" and then describes three of the men. One is "a genuine specimen of the slave-negro, a queer thing of mere feeling, with some glimmerings of sense." A second, who had spoken of "the rights of his race" when confronted by "a half drunken [white] fellow," suddenly assumed the role of a clown. The third was drunk. After describing the complex reactions of a member of a group of "well dressed and decent negro wenches," who encountered this "disgrace to her color," Hawthorne records his own response. Although the woman's face had expressed "scorn, and shame, and sorrow, and painful sympathy" for the drunken man, Hawthorne neither shares her reactions to the man's presence nor does he feel any "painful sympathy" for her. On the contrary. "I was," he writes, "amused." He then adds, "On the whole, I find myself rather more of an abolitionist in feeling than in principle."[42] What can we make of this self-analysis? Is he saying that, unlike abolitionist "principle," abolitionist "feeling" may find black degradation amusing? This entry suggests that, despite a lifetime of casual contacts with blacks, he feels no common humanity either with the drunken black man or with the "decent" black woman.

A subsequent notation at first appears more sympathetic. Watching a man who, except for his color, is unexceptional among the travelers at a tavern, Hawthorne hears a white man comment, "I wish I had a thousand such fellows in Alabama" and again records his response. This incident, he writes, "made a queer impression on me—the negro was really so human—and to talk of owning a thousand like him." On examination, however, his words demonstrate that even here Hawthorne distances himself. He fails to explore the moral implications of his response, does not even try to examine what it means to write, "the negro was really so human." Does this signify that the black man was indeed human? Does it signify that, although inhuman, he was very like a man?[43]

More than a dozen years later, while editing the manuscript of Bridge's *Journal of an African Cruiser*, Hawthorne responded to his friend's report of his participation in a punitive expedition. Apparently, when Bridge's commander was meeting with a group of African chiefs to discuss the plundering of an American ship and the murder of its captain and crew, a shot was fired. During the fight that broke out, the chief of Little Berebree and two other Africans were killed. In retaliation for the attacks on the meeting and for the earlier attacks on the ship, Bridge's commander ordered that the town of Little Berebree be burned and its population dispersed; later, he ordered four additional towns burned. Writing to his friend, Hawthorne expresses concern for Bridge's safety and expresses pleasure because this incident, he thinks, will enliven the *Journal*. Then, recording some reservations about the validity of the American attack, Hawthorne voices uncertainty about the humanity of Africans:

> A civilized and educated man must feel somewhat like a fool, methinks, when he has staked his own life against that of a black savage, and lost the game. In the sight of God, one life may be as valuable as another; but in our view, the stakes are very unequal. Besides, I really do consider the shooting of these niggers a matter of very questionable propriety; and am glad, upon the whole, that you bagged no game on either of those days. It is a far better deed to beget a white fellow-creature, than to shoot even a black one.[44]

In a piece written years later, during the Civil War, Hawthorne's language demonstrates that he was still uncertain of the full humanity of blacks. Describing a group of contrabands in Virginia, he writes:

They were unlike the specimens of their race whom we are accustomed to see at the North, and, in my judgment, were far more agreeable. So rudely were they attired—as if their garb had grown upon them spontaneously—so picturesquely natural in manners, and wearing such a crust of primeval simplicity, (which is quite polished away from the northern black man,) that they seemed a kind of creature by themselves, not altogether human, but perhaps quite as good, and akin to the fauns and rustic deities of olden times. I wonder whether I shall excite anybody's wrath by saying this? It is no great matter.[45]

The consistency of Hawthorne's racial responses and of his failure to subject them to analysis is worth noting because he is capable of intense self-scrutiny in relation to other issues. It is also notable because it persists throughout a period when other white New Englanders were painfully examining their responses to slavery and race, making moral judgments on these issues, and acting on their judgments. In 1837, Ralph Waldo Emerson—never a Garrisonian abolitionist—had speculated about the effect of the agitation against the slave trade. Were the horrors of the Middle Passage itemized to sensationalize, he wondered, or to force an awareness of the moral obligation to acknowledge what slavery was, and to make this awareness a central moral concern?

How can such a question as the Slave Trade be agitated for forty years by the most enlightened nations of the world without throwing great light on ethics into the general mind? . . . The loathsome details of the kidnapping; of the middle passage; six hundred living bodies sit for thirty days betwixt death & life in a posture of stone & when brought on deck for air cast themselves into the sea—were those details merely produced to harrow the nerves of the susceptible & humane or for the purpose of engraving the question on the memory that it should not be dodged or obliterated & securing to it the concentration of the whole conscience of Christendom?[46]

If Emerson's efforts to confront his moral responsibility anticipate the efforts of a later generation adequately to respond to the Holocaust, Hawthorne presents a stark contrast. In 1842, he expressed astonishment at the appearance of Longfellow's *Poems on Slavery*: "I was never more surprised than at your writing poems about Slavery. . . . You have never poeticized a practical subject, hitherto."[47] Nine years later, after the Compromise of 1850 had destroyed the Missouri Compromise and promulgated a new Fugitive Slave Law—and, as all around him, northern intellectuals were taking a stand on the slavery question—he wrote that he remained unsure of its moral significance:

> There are a hundred modes of philanthropy in which I could blaze with intenser zeal. This Fugitive Law is the only thing that could have blown me into any respectable degree of warmth on this great subject of the day—if it really be the great subject—a point which another age can determine better than ours.[48]

In Emersonian terms, he apparently never could stop dodging and obliterating.[49]

Yet, while he never endorses the reformers' ideas, their themes and images are ubiquitous in his strongest book. Although the symbol of oppression in *The Scarlet Letter* is a piece of needlework and not an iron chain, from its beginning, recurrent references to the embroidered symbol as a "brand" force its connections to the instruments of chattel slavery. Later, the narrator's language irrevocably links Hester to the slavery issue: "The chain that bound her . . . was of iron links and galling to her inmost soul." Hawthorne's New England readers may have responded to the redness of Hester's embroidery by recalling the red shawl of the besieged abolitionist Maria Weston Chapman at Pennsylvania Hall or linked Hester's "branding" to Jonathan Walker's barbarous punishment. Hawthorne's *The Scarlet Letter*, no less than Stowe's *Uncle Tom's Cabin*, which was published two years later, portrays an American society where publicly, officially, and institutionally, one of God's reasonable creatures is transformed into a thing, and where, privately, one individual tyrannizes over another in this world and threatens the salvation of his victim in the next.[50]

At the beginning of *The Scarlet Letter*, the drama in Hawthorne's Market Place is heightened because the community condemning Hester appears monolithic. While Native Americans are present, their society is not presented as an alternative to Boston (although Hester will later suggest this to Arthur). But, as Hawthorne knew, in addition to the Native Americans and transplanted Europeans his narrator shows in the Market Place, the population of seventeenth-century New England had included another group: the Africans. By obliterating this historic black presence, Hawthorne's narrator helps guarantee Hester's absolute isolation.

He does, of course, suggest a black community of a kind. In *The Scarlet Letter*, Hawthorne, in fact, presents a classic displacement: Here, color is the sign not of race but of grace—and of its absence. Black skin is seen as blackened soul. Instead of an African-American alternative to Euro-American Boston, we are shown a diabolical black reversal. This satanic conspiracy, like establishment Boston, is patriarchal; it is ruled by a male—the Black Man—whose purpose seems to be to enslave others, particularly women. That he wants their bodies as well as their souls is suggested by Hester's statement to Pearl that he is the child's father. It is tempting to play with connections between dark unpredictable Pearl and the untamed exotic dark females of our nineteenth-century letters. Central here are commonly shared notions about women and the sinfulness of female sexuality on the one hand, and about blacks and the sinfulness of black sexuality on the other, notions that suggest added significance to the nineteenth-century phrase coupling "women and negroes."

Members of this subversive group live in the town, but their activities in the forest suggest the international slave trade, with the colors of its participants reversed. Here, the names of whites are signed in a book belonging to the Black Man, and whites are branded with the Black Man's mark. They suggest, too, travelers' reports of black Africans, of wild dancing in the woods.[51] Although this diabolical society is never taken seriously, when "black" is read as a racial, and not a moral, descriptive, the text of *The Scarlet Letter* reveals an obsessive concern with blacks and blackness, with the presence of a dangerous dark group within society's midst—a concern that is characteristic of much American writing in the last decades before emancipation.

In *The Scarlet Letter*, the portrayal of Hester's official transformation from woman to thing dramatizes a negation identical to the negation central to the institution of chattel slavery: the denial of the humanity of one of God's creatures, the denial that Hawthorne's abolitionist neighbors saw as sin. Hawthorne's narrator, however, although recognizing the corruption in the world he pictures, can in his conclusion only point vaguely toward something better:

> At some brighter period, when the world should have grown
> ripe for it, in Heaven's own time, a new truth will be revealed.
> (201)

Hawthorne would echo both the meter and the matter of these phrases two years later in his campaign biography of Franklin Pierce. Paralleling his rejection of the possibility of social reform in the world of *The Scarlet Letter* with a rejection of abolitionist reform in his own day, he would write that a wise man:

> looks upon slavery as one of those evils which divine Provi-
> dence does not leave to be remedied by human contrivances,
> but which, in its own good time, by some means impossible to
> be anticipated, but of the simplest and easiest operation,
> when all its uses shall have been fulfilled, it causes to vanish
> like a dream.[52]

In 1863, Emerson and others condemned Hawthorne for dedicating *Our Old Home* to President Pierce, whose recently published correspondence, it was charged, had encouraged Jefferson Davis to commit treason.[53] Following Hawthorne's death, however, most seem to have decided to forgive—or to ignore—his refusal to confront slavery, the great moral issue of his day. But, in an essay that Hawthorne's publisher reportedly refused to print, George W. Curtis addressed the problem. Noting that eight years after the appearance of *Uncle Tom's Cabin*, Hawthorne could still write that it was difficult trying to conceive romances "'about a country where there is no shadow, no antiquity, no mystery, no picturesque and gloomy wrong, nor anything but a common-place prosperity, in broad and simple daylight, as is happily the case with my dear native land,'" Curtis asked:

> Is crime never romantic, then, until distance ennobles it? Or were the tragedies of Puritan life so terrible that the imagination could not help kindling, while the pangs of the plantation are superficial and commonplace?

Pressing his condemnation of Hawthorne's avoidance, Curtis continued:

> That the Devil, in the form of an elderly man clad in grave and decent attire, should lead astray the saints of Salem village, two centuries ago, and confuse right and wrong in the mind of Goodman Brown, was something that excited his imagination, and produced one of his weirdest stories. But that the same Devil, clad in a sombre sophism, was confusing the sentiment of right and wrong in the mind of his own countrymen he did not even guess.[54]

Despite Hawthorne's antipathy for the reformers, however, and despite even his racism, he finally had guessed—not the significance of slavery and race in his own day but their significance in the American past. In the same Civil War essay where he speculated whether blacks are perhaps "not altogether human," he included this passage:

> There is a circumstance, known to few, that connects the children of the Puritans with these Africans of Virginia, in a very singular way. They are our brethren, as being lineal descendants from the May Flower, the fated womb of which, in her first voyage, sent forth a brood of Pilgrims on Plymouth Rock, and, in a subsequent one, spawned Slaves upon the southern soil,—a monstrous birth, but with which we have an instinctive sense of kindred, and so are stirred by an irresistible impulse to attempt their rescue, even at the cost of

blood and ruin. The character of our sacred ship, I fear, may suffer a little by this revelation; but we must let her white progeny offset her dark one—and two such portents never sprang from an identical source before![55]

Although this pregnant metaphor locates in the past the vital connections between black and white Americans, although it fails to specify the monstrous element in the second birth (was it blackness? was it slavery?), and although it envisions passive black slaves and active white rescuers who must "offset" them, nevertheless it testifies that Hawthorne finally did respond imaginatively to the centrality of race and slavery in America.

But of course, he wrote this long after he had produced his great romances, where any direct recognition of these issues is conspicuously lacking. The studied ambiguity of these works, generally understood as the result of deliberate artistic decisions, must also be considered as a strategy of avoidance and denial. Hawthorne, it appears, could not acknowledge the necessary engagement of politics and art, of life and letters—the engagement that Emerson demanded of his generation and of all generations. Instead, Hawthorne devised an elaborate refusal to connect the great moral problem, which is his literary subject, with what the Garrisonians called "the American national sin."[56]

NOTES

I am grateful to the National Endowment for the Humanities for a summer research fellowship, which enabled me to work on Hawthorne; to Neal Smith, executive director of the Hawthorne Project at Ohio State University; and to my colleagues H. Daniel Peck, Roger B. Stein, Gloria Oden, Rita Gollin, and the late Frederick C. Stern for commenting on early versions of this chapter.

1. Critics who have not neglected this issue include Jonathan Arac, "The Politics of *The Scarlet Letter*," in *Ideology and Classic American Literature*, ed. Sacvan Bercovitch and Myra Jehlen (Cambridge: Harvard University Press, 1986), pp. 247–66; Deborah L. Madsen, "'A' for Abolition: Hawthorne's Bond-Servant and the Shadow of Slavery," *Journal of American Studies* 25 (1991): 255–59; Jennifer Fleis-

chner, "Hawthorne and the Politics of Slavery," *Studies in the Novel* 23 (1991): 96–106; Jay Grossman, "'A' Is for Abolition? Race, Authorship, *The Scarlet Letter*," *Textual Practice* 7 (1993): 13–30; Nancy Bentley, *The Ethnography of Manners: Hawthorne, James, Wharton* (Cambridge: Cambridge Universtiy Press, 1995), pp. 246–67; and John F. Birk, "Hawthorne's Mister Hooper: The Veil of Ham?" *Prospects* 21 (1996): 1–11. Among critics who have examined parallel issues, in addition to those cited, are Milton R. Stern, "Conservative after Heaven's Own Fashion," in *Essays in Honor of Russel B. Nye*, ed. Joseph Waldmeier (East Lansing: Michigan State University Press, 1978), pp. 195–225; and Sacvan Bercovitch, *The American Jeremiad* (Madison: University of Wisconsin Press, 1978). Central to my project is Toni Morrison, *Playing in the Dark: Whiteness and the Literary Imagination* (Cambridge: Harvard University Press, 1992). Earlier versions of sections of my chapter appeared in my *Women and Sisters* (New Haven: Yale University Press, 1989), pp. 125–50; and *The Green American Tradition*, ed. H. Daniel Peck (Baton Rouge: Louisiana State University Press, 1989), pp. 75–97.

2. *Centenary* 8:21. This text is identical in *Hawthorne's Lost Notebook, 1835–41*, transcribed by Barbara S. Mouffe (University Park: Pennsylvania State University Press, 1978), p. 28.

For biographical information, I have relied on standard works, including Robert Cantwell, *Nathaniel Hawthorne: The American Years* (New York: Rinehart, 1948); James R. Mellow, *Nathaniel Hawthorne in His Times* (Boston: Houghton Mifflin, 1980); and Louise Hall Tharp, *The Peabody Sisters of Salem* (Boston: McIntosh and Otis, 1950), and on Joseph B. Felt, *Annals of Salem* (Salem: W. & S. B. Ives, 1827), p. 416.

3. *American Notebooks*, 9 Sept.–24 Sept. 1838, *Centenary* 8:150. Approximately fifteen years later, when Hawthorne went through the old Gosport church records, among the items he copied without comment were the baptismal records of two black infants: *Centenary* 8:550.

4. Vernon Loggins, *The Hawthornes: The Story of Seven Generations of an American Family* (New York: Columbia University Press, 1951), pp. 197–98. Although Captain Nathaniel was homeward bound from the East Indies when his son was born, the following year he sailed the *Neptune* from Trinidad with a cargo that included slave-produced molasses and sugar; in 1807, he sailed to French Guiana,

where he traded for molasses, cocoa, and cotton; see Loggins, *The Hawthornes*, pp. 203–5. For trade in the years before 1816, see James D. Phillips, *Salem and the Indies* (Boston: Houghton Mifflin, 1977); and Felt, *Annals of Salem*, pp. 265, 288–89, 291, 296.

5. William Bentley, *Diary*, 4 vols. (Gloucester, Mass.: P. Smith, 1962), quoted in "A Brief History of the Negro in Salem, Prepared for the Salem Committee on Racial Understanding, 1969," typescript (Salem, 1969), p. 1. I am grateful to the Essex Institute for this source.

6. "Old News" first appeared in the *New-England Magazine* 1–3 (Feb.–May 1835); in 1852, it was collected into *The Snow-Image* (*Centenary* 11:132–60; quotation on 134). See, for example, artist John Lewis Krimmel's *View of Centre Square, on the 4th of July, c. 1810–12*.

7. See Jean Fagan Yellin, *Intricate Knot* (New York: New York University Press, 1972), chap. 4.

8. "Pomps and Vanities," in *Grandfather's Chair* (1841); Hawthorne again registered awareness of black slavery in the colonial period in his letter to Sophia of 16 Sept. 1841; see *Centenary* 15:573.

9. For the Nat Turner insurrection, see Herbert Aptheker, *Nat Turner's Slave Rebellion* (New York: Humanities Press, 1966), and Henry Irving Tragle, ed., *The Southampton Slave Revolt of 1831: A Compilation of Source Materials* (Amherst: University of Massachusetts Press, 1971).

10. For the end of slavery in Massachusetts, see John Daniels, *In Freedom's Birthplace* (rpt. New York: Negro Universities Press, 1969), p. 8.

11. The statistics come from Dorothy B. Porter, "The Remonds of Salem, Massachusetts," *American Antiquarian Society Proceedings* 95, pt. 2 (Oct. 1985): 259–95.

12. For black Salem, see Felt, *Annals of Salem*; Bentley, *Ethnography*; Lorenzo J. Greene, *The Negro in Colonial New England* (New York: Columbia University Press, 1942); Porter, "The Remonds of Salem" and "Sarah Parker Remond, Abolitionist and Physician," *Journal of Negro History* 20 (July 1935): 287–93; Ruth Bogin, "Sarah Parker Remond: Black Abolitionist from Salem," *Essex Institute Historical Collections* 110 (Apr. 1974): 120–50; and Gloria C. Oden, "*The Journal of Charlotte L. Forten*: The Salem-Philadelphia Years (1851–1862) Reexamined," *Essex Institute Historical Collections* 114 (Apr. 1983): 119–36. For a black female minister's experiences in Salem in 1829–30, see Zilpha Elaw, *Memoirs* . . . (1846; rpt. as *Sisters of the*

Spirit, ed. William L. Andrews, Bloomington: Indiana University Press, 1986). For responses to the White murder, see Loggins, *The Hawthornes*, p. 244.

13. For Symmes, see Mellow, *Nathaniel Hawthorne*, n.20, pp. 104–5; for Russwurm, see Horatio Bridge, *Personal Recollections of Nathaniel Hawthorne* (New York: Harper, 1893), p. 30; for black Shakers, see *Gifts of Power: The Writings of Rebecca Jackson*, ed. Jean McMahon Hunez (Amherst: University of Massachusetts Press, 1981). Hawthorne's comment is in *Centenary* 8:202, 203; for another reference to skin color in relation to race, see the entry of 8 May [1850], 8:503.

14. Although well documented in the holdings of the Essex Institute, the history of the Salem, Massachusetts, Female Anti-Slavery Society has not been written. See the *Liberator* (Boston), 7 Jan. 1832 and 17 Nov. 1832; Angelina Grimké to Jane Smith, 16 July 1837, Grimké-Weld papers, Clements Memorial Library, University of Michigan; and *Proceedings of the Anti-Slavery Convention of American Women* (1837, 1838, 1839). Lawrence's comment is in *Proceedings* (Philadelphia: Merrihew and Thompson, 1839), pp. 8–9.

15. Sophia Peabody Hawthorne to her mother, 15 Nov. 1843, p. 3. Unless otherwise stated, quoted passages from Sophia Peabody Hawthorne's correspondence are from collections at Ohio State University, the Henry W. and Albert A. Berg Collection, New York Public Library, and Astor, Lenox and Tilden foundations. For Sophia Peabody Hawthorne and the ideal of domesticity, see T. Walter Herbert, *Dearest Beloved: The Hawthornes and the Making of the Middle-Class Family* (Berkeley: University of California Press, 1993).

16. Sophia Peabody Hawthorne to Mrs. Peabody, 20 Aug. [1844], in Rose Hawthorne Lathrop, *Memories of Hawthorne* (1897; rpt. New York: AMS Press, 1969), p. 74; also see *Centenary* 16:64.

17. *Centenary* 8:462–63.

18. Lathrop, *Memories*, p. 161; Tharp, *Peabody Sisters*, p. 196.

19. *Centenary* 16:415; Porter, "Mr. John Remond of Hamilton Hall, Salem," delivered at meetings of the Association for the Study of Afro-American Life and History. I am grateful to the late Dorothy Porter Wesley for permission to examine this unpublished paper.

20. Cuba Journal I; Sophia Peabody letters 20 Dec. [1833]–2 July [1834]; Mary Peabody letters 8 Jan. 1834–31 May 1834; Sophia Peabody, 19 January 1834; Mary Peabody, 25 Mar. 1834 and 12 May 1834, all in

Berg Collection. The quotation is from Mary Peabody to Elizabeth Palmer Peabody, 8 Feb. 1834.

21. [Horatio Bridge], *Journal of an African Cruiser: Comprising Sketches of the Canaries . . . and Other Places on the West Coast of Africa. By an Officer of the United States Navy*, ed. Nathaniel Hawthorne (1845; rpt. London: Dawson of Pall Mall, 1968).

22. See, for example, Patrick Brancaccio, " 'The Black Man's Paradise': Hawthorne's Editing of the *Journal of an African Cruiser*," *New England Quarterly* 53 (1980): 23–41. *Centenary* 15:683; 16:82, 113–14, 126–27,195; *Life of Franklin Pierce*, 416–17.

23. *Centenary* 16:176, 203; Frederick T. McGill, *Channing of Concord* (New Brunswick, N.J.: Rutgers University Press, 1967), p. 103; and Mellow, *Nathaniel Hawthorne*, p. 630.

24. See Wendell P. Garrison and Francis J. Garrison, *William Lloyd Garrison: The Story of His Life Told by His Children*, 4 vols. (1885; rpt. New York, 1969), 2:1–30; Boston Female Anti-Slavery Society, *Right and Wrong in Boston* (Boston: The Society, 1836).

25. *American Monthly Magazine* 2 (1835), p. 164.

26. *American Monthly Magazine* 2 (1836), pp. 505–6.

27. Sophia Peabody to Mr. Peabody, 9 Feb. 1839; Harriet Martineau, "The Martyr Age," *London and Westminster Review* (Dec. 1838): 43; *Autobiography of Harriet Martineau*, ed. Maria W. Chapman, 3 vols. (London: Smith, Elder, & Co., 1877), 1:347–57. See William Lloyd Garrison's description of Chapman at Pennsylvania Hall and of her subsequent illness in his letters to his mother-in-law dated 19 May 1838 and to George Benson, 25 May 1838, in *The Letters of William Lloyd Garrison*, ed. Walter M. Merrill and Louis Ruchames, vol. 2 (Cambridge, Mass.: Belknap, 1971), pp. 361–68; also see Lydia Maria Child to Caroline Weston, 28 July 1838, in *Selected Letters, 1817–1880*, ed. Milton Meltzer and Patricia G. Holland (Amherst: University of Massachusetts Press, 1982), and to Louisa Loring, 3 June 1838, and to Lydia B. Child, 7 Aug. 1838, in *The Collected Correspondence of Lydia Maria Child, 1817–1880*, ed. Patricia G. Holland and Milton Meltzer (Millwood, N.Y.: Kraus-Thompson, 1979).

28. Both Walker and Drayton later lectured for the abolitionists. For Whittier's poem "The Branded Hand," see *The Complete Poetical Works of John Greenleaf Whittier* (Boston: Houghton Mifflin, 1894), p. 296. For a daguerreotype of Walker's "branded hand," see the illustrated chronology in this volume. Drayton published an account

of his ordeal in *Personal Memoir* (Boston: Bela Marsh, 1855). For the Edmondsons, see Catherine M. Hanchett, "'What Sort of People & Families': The Edmondson Sisters," *Afro-Americans in New York Life and History* 6 (July 1982): 21–38; and Harriet Beecher Stowe, *Key to Uncle Tom's Cabin* (1853; rpt. New York: Arno, 1968), pp. 306–30. For Beecher's "slave sales," see William C. Beecher and the Reverend Samuel Scoville, *A Biography of Henry Ward Beecher* (New York: C. L. Webster, 1888), pp. 292–300; and William G. McLaughlen, *The Meaning of Henry Ward Beecher* (New York: Knopf, 1970), pp. 200–201.

29. *The Autobiography of Harriet Martineau,* 2:33–35. For Mann's defense of Drayton, see Louise Tharp, *Until Victory: Horace Mann and Mary Peabody Mann* (Boston: Little Brown, 1953), pp. 224–34, and Jonathan Messerli, *Horace Mann* (New York: Knopf, 1972).

30. Hawthorne to Sophia, 26 Mar. 1840; to H. W. Longfellow, 12 Oct. 1840; and to Sophia, 12 Aug. 1841 in *Centenary* 15:428, 497, 557; also see Nathaniel Hawthorne to Sophia Peabody, 22 Aug. 1841 *Centenary* 15:562.

31. Between 1 June 1842 and 27 July 1844, *Centenary* 8:236, 237; between 27 July 1844 and 15 Mar. 1845, 8:253.

32. Cuba Journal 1. Sophia Peabody letters, 20 Dec. [1833]–2 July [1834]; Mary Peabody letters, 8 January–31 May 1834; Sophia Peabody to Elizabeth Palmer Peabody, 21 Mar. [1834], Berg Collection.

33. *Centenary* 8:10, 136.

34. See, for example, the following, all published in *Mosses from an Old Manse* (1846): "The Hall of Fantasy," *Pioneer* (Feb. 1843); "The New Adam and Eve," *Democratic Review* (Feb. 1843); "The Procession of Life," *Democratic Review* (Apr. 1843); "The Celestial Railroad," *Democratic Review* (May 1843); "The Christmas Banquet," *Democratic Review* (Jan. 1844); "The Intelligence Office," *Democratic Review* (Mar. 1844); "Earth's Holocaust," *Graham's Magazine* (May 1844); "A Select Party," *Democratic Review* (July 1844); and "The Old Manse" (1846). *Centenary* 10.

35. See "Chiefly about War-Matters," *Atlantic Monthly* (July 1862); rpt. *Centenary* 23:403–42.

36. "The Hall of Fantasy," *Centenary* 10:181.

37. Hawthorne to Elizabeth Peabody, 13 Aug. 1857, *Centenary* 18:89.

38. Hawthorne to Burchmore, 9 June 1850, *Centenary* 16:340.

39. Hawthorne to Elizabeth Peabody, 13 Aug. 1857 and 8 Oct. 1857, *Centenary* 18:89, 115.

40. Sophia Peabody Hawthorne to Elizabeth Palmer Peabody [Spring 1860], quoted in Tharp, *Peabody Sisters*, p. 288; and in Lathrop, *Memories*, p. 358.

41. *American Monthly Magazine* 2 (1836): 386, 486, 511.

42. 15 Aug. 1838, *Centenary* 8:111–12.

43. 9 Sept. [1838], *Centenary* 8:151.

44. Hawthorne to Horatio Bridge, Apr. 1844, *Centenary* 16:26.

45. "Chiefly about War-Matters," *Centenary* 23:419–20; for a condemnation of Hawthorne's racism and politics in this piece, see the *Liberator* (27 June 1862): 102.

46. 16 Nov. 1837, in *Emerson in His Journals*, ed. Joel Porte (Cambridge, Mass.: Belknap, 1982), pp. 178–79. For the responses of the northern intellectuals, see George W. Frederickson, *The Inner Civil War: Northern Intellectuals and the Crisis of the Union* (New York: Harper & Row, 1965).

47. Hawthorne to Longfellow, 24 Dec. 1842, *Centenary* 15:664.

48. Hawthorne to Longfellow, 8 May 1851, *Centenary* 16:431.

49. Critic Richard Brodhead suggests that "for Hawthorne, the political is a mode of engagement that generates plural and incompatible outlooks, each with the power, at certain moments, to compel understanding and to motivate action, and each with the power to make the others appear delusory." Again and again, he continues, Hawthorne's prose embodies paradox: the conviction that politics are delusive, that people engage in political action for reasons that they do not acknowledge, for ends that they do not envision, and, at the same time, that to be politically disengaged is to lose vitality. Brodhead also acknowledges Emerson's reluctance to entrust social reform to the reformers; see "Hawthorne and the Fate of Politics," *Essays in Literature* 11 (Spring 1984): 95–96, 102.

50. Harriet Beecher Stowe's *Uncle Tom's Cabin*, serialized in the antislavery newspaper the *National Era* from 3 June 1851 to 2 Apr. 1852, was published in two volumes in Mar. 1852.

51. The convergence of Western notions and patterns signifying diabolism and spiritual enslavement and Western patterns signifying Africans and the African slave trade are discussed in Jean Devisse, *The Image of the Black in Western Art II: From the Early Church to the "Age of Discovery" I: From the Demonic Threat to the Incarnation of*

Sainthood, and Jean Devisse and Michel Mollat, *The Image of the Black in Western Art II: From the Early Christian Era to the "Age of Discovery" II: Africans in the Christian Ordinance of the World, Fourteenth to the Sixteenth Century*. (New York: William Morrow, 1979).

52. *Centenary* 5:416–17.

53. Claude M. Simpson, Introduction to *Our Old Home*, xxv–xxviii.

54. "Nathaniel Hawthorne," *North American Review* 99 (Oct. 1864): 552.

55. "Chiefly about War-Matters," *Centenary* 23:420.

56. For the classic essay suggesting the use of this phrase, see Sidney Kaplan, "Herman Melville and the American National Sin," *Journal of Negro History* 41 (Oct. 1956): 31–38, and 42 (Jan. 1957): 11–37.

ILLUSTRATED CHRONOLOGY

Hawthorne's Life

1804: Born 4 July in Salem, Massachusetts, the second of three children of Nathaniel and Elizabeth Manning Hathorne.

1808: Father, a sea captain, dies of yellow fever at Surinam (Dutch Guiana); moves with his mother and two sisters into the Manning family home in Salem.

Historical Events

1804: Lewis and Clark expedition (1804–6); Napoleon crowns himself emperor of France; Aaron Burr kills Alexander Hamilton in a duel; Thomas Jefferson reelected president.

1807: Act of Congress prohibits African slave trade; Robert Fulton's steamboat, the *Clermont*, makes its first run on the Hudson.

Nathaniel Hawthorne. Oil on canvas by Charles Osgood, 1840. Courtesy Peabody Essex Museum, Salem, Mass.

Gallows Hill, scene of the witch hangings of 1692. Photograph by Robb Studios. Courtest Peabody Essex Museum, Salem, Mass.

1813: Injures his foot and suffers lameness for fourteen months.

1818: Moves with his family to Raymond, Maine, near Sebago Lake; hunts, fishes, and roams the wilderness.

1819: Returns to Salem and lives with the Mannings under the guardianship of his Uncle Robert Manning; attends school in Salem.

1821: Enters Bowdoin College in Brunswick, Maine, where he forms lifelong friendships with Horatio Bridge, Jonathan Cilley, and Franklin Pierce (fourteenth president of the United States).

1808: John Jacob Astor incorporates American Fur Company; James Madison elected president.

1809: Washington Irving, *Knickerbocker's History of New York*.

1811: Slave rebellion in Louisiana; Tecumseh, chief of the Shawnees, organizes confederacy of Indian tribes; William Henry Harrison defeats Indians at battle of Tippecanoe.

1812: War of 1812 (1812–15); Madison reelected president; George Gordon Byron, *Childe Harold* (1812–18).

1813: American naval forces win the battle of Lake Erie.

1825: Graduates from Bowdoin; returns to Salem and lives with his mother and sisters for the next twelve years, taking trips throughout New England and pursuing a writing career.

1828: Publishes his first novel, *Fanshawe*, anonymously at his own expense but soon burns all copies he can locate.

1830: Publishes his first story, "The Hollow of the Three Hills," in the *Salem Gazette*.

1830–39: Publishes tales and sketches anonymously in newspapers, magazines, and *The Token*, an annual gift book.

Mesmer's tub. From a print in the Bibliothèque Nationale, Paris.

1814: British burn Washington, D.C.; Treaty of Ghent ends war; Sir Walter Scott, *Waverley*.

1815: General Andrew Jackson defeats British at the battle of New Orleans; New England Federalists disband; Napoleon defeated at the battle of Waterloo; *North American Review* begins publication.

1816: James Monroe elected president.

1817: First Seminole War (1817–18); George Gordon Byron, *Manfred*.

1818: Regular transatlantic ship crossings between United States and Great Britain begin.

1819: Financial panic; first crossing of the Atlantic by a steamship; Sir Walter Scott, *Ivanhoe*; Washington Irving, *The Sketch Book* (1819–20).

1820: Congress passes Missouri Compromise; Sydney Smith, English clergyman and writer, asks, "Who reads an American book?"

1821: Mexico declares independence from Spain; Greek War for Independence begins; Santa Fe Trail opens; James Fenimore Cooper, *The Spy*.

1822: Denmark Vesey's conspiracy to lead slave uprising in South Carolina is discovered; Liberia founded by American Colonization Society.

"Instructing the Saintly Child."
Frontispiece (detail) to Graham's
Magazine (1847).

1836: Moves to Boston for eight
months to edit, with the help of his
sister Elizabeth, the *American Magazine
of Useful and Entertaining Knowledge.*

1837: Publishes *Peter Parley's Universal
History,* also written with his sister
Elizabeth; publishes *Twice-Told Tales*
under his own name, with help from
Horatio Bridge, who guarantees the
publisher against loss; his former Bow-
doin classmate Henry Wadsworth
Longfellow writes favorable review.

1838: Almost challenges John L.
O'Sullivan to a duel over Mary Sils-
bee; spends the summer in western
Massachusetts collecting material for
future writings; begins to publish in
United States and Democratic Review.

1823: Monroe Doctrine proclaimed;
James Fenimore Cooper, *The Pioneers.*

1824: Lafayette tours United States;
Lord Byron dies at Missolonghi.

1825: Erie Canal opens, connecting
Great Lakes with the Atlantic;
Charles Finney leads religious
revivals in New York state.

1826: American Society for the
Promotion of Temperance
founded; James Fenimore Cooper,
The Last of the Mohicans.

1827: *Freedom's Journal,* first
newspaper for blacks in America,
begins publication; first U.S.
passenger railroad chartered.

1828: Andrew Jackson elected presi-
dent; Noah Webster, *An American
Dictionary of the English Language*;
Susanna Rowson, *Lucy Temple.*

1830: Indian Relocation Act allows
Jackson to forcibly remove eastern
Indians to areas west of the
Mississippi; Joseph Smith, *Book of
Mormon.*

1831: Supreme Court denies right of
Cherokee tribe to sue in federal
courts; Cyrus McCormick demonstrates his reaper; fur trappers explore
the Rockies; William Lloyd Garrison
founds the antislavery newspaper
the *Liberator*; Nat Turner leads a slave
rebellion in Virginia; James Kirke
Paulding, *The Dutchman's Fireside.*

Frontispiece to Samuel G. Goodrich, Peter Parley's Winter Tales *(1829). Pierpont Morgan Library, New York. JPW 3670.*

1839: Accepts appointment as salt and coal measurer at the Boston Custom House, obtained through the help of friends in the Democratic party; becomes engaged to Sophia Peabody.

1841: Resigns from Boston Custom House; publishes *Grandfather's Chair, Famous Old People,* and *Liberty Tree*; joins Brook Farm community in April and leaves in October.

1832: Black Hawk War begins; first streetcar goes into operation in New York City; New England Anti-Slavery Society formed; Joseph Mazzini founds Young Italy movement; Jackson reelected president; Washington Irving, *The Alhambra*.

1833: American Anti-Slavery Society formed; publication of *New York Sun*, first "penny press"; Oberlin, first co-education college, opens and admits blacks; Lydia Maria Child, *An Appeal in Favor of that Class of Americans Called Africans*.

Sophia (Peabody) Hawthorne. Etching by S. A. Schoff. Courtesy Peabody Essex Museum, Salem, Mass.

Brook Farm Buildings. *By M. G. Cutter, 1910, after an 1845 drawing. Courtesy Concord Free Public Library*

1842: Publishes *Biographical Stories for Children* and second, expanded edition of *Twice-Told Tales*; 9 July marries Sophia Peabody, and they rent the "Old Manse" in Concord; becomes friends with Ralph Waldo Emerson, Henry David Thoreau, Margaret Fuller, and Ellery Channing.

1843: February, Sophia suffers a miscarriage.

1844: 3 March, daughter Una born.

1845: Edits Horatio Bridge's *Journal of an African Cruiser*; moves family back to Salem, where they reside with his mother and sisters.

1834: Opponents of Andrew Jackson form Whig party.

1835: Attempt to assassinate President Jackson fails; Samuel F. B. Morse invents the telegraph; Samuel Colt invents a pistol with a revolving cylinder.

1836: Texas proclaims independence from Mexico; battle of the Alamo; Martin Van Buren elected president; Ralph Waldo Emerson, *Nature*; Washington Irving, *Astoria*.

1837: Financial panic and beginning of prolonged economic depression; Mount Holyoke, first women's college, established; Ralph Waldo

Domestic Happiness. *Oil on canvas by Lilly Martin Spencer, 1849. Bequest of Dr. and Mrs. James Cleland, Jr. Photograph © 1993 Detroit Institute of Arts.*

"The Old Manse." Engraving from Homes of American Authors *(1853).*

1846: Appointed surveyor in the Salem Custom House; *Mosses from an Old Manse* published; 22 June, son Julian born.

1849: June, removed from surveyorship by new Whig administration; 31 July, mother dies; September, becomes fully engaged in writing "The Scarlet Letter."

1850: *The Scarlet Letter* published; moves to the "Red Cottage" in Lenox, Massachusetts; becomes friends with Herman Melville.

1851: Publishes *The House of the Seven Gables*; 20 May, daughter Rose born; moves his family to West Newton, Massachusetts.

Emerson delivers "The American Scholar" address; Jared Sparks, *Life of Washington*; William Ware, *Zenobia*.

1838: Cherokees, removed from their homelands by federal troops, begin walking the Trail of Tears; Underground Railroad established; Alexis de Tocqueville, *Democracy in America*.

1839: Louis Daguerre invents the photographic process known as daguerreotyping; American Art Union established in New York City.

1840: William Henry Harrison elected president; first issue of the *Dial* (1840–44), edited by Margaret Fuller; Edgar Allan Poe, *Tales of the Grotesque and Arabesque*.

1841: Dorothea Dix begins crusade on behalf of the insane; Brook Farm (1841–47) established at West Roxbury, Massachusetts; first covered wagon train leaves Kansas for California; the *New York Tribune*, edited by Horace Greeley, begins publication; Ralph Waldo Emerson, *Essays, First Series*.

1842: P. T. Barnum opens his American Museum; Charles Dickens begins five-month tour of United States; Henry Wadsworth Longfellow, *Ballads and Other Poems*.

Una and Julian Hawthorne. Daguerreotype, c. 1850. Courtesy Boston Athenaeum.

Nathaniel Hawthorne. Oil portrait by Cephas Giovanni Thompson, 1850. Courtesy of the Grolier Club.

1843: Charles Lane and Bronson Alcott found Fruitlands at Harvard, Massachusetts; North American Phalanx (1843–54), Fourierist community, established at Red Bank, New Jersey; William H. Prescott, *History of the Conquest of Mexico*; Charles Dickens, *A Christmas Carol*.

1844: Mormon leader Joseph Smith killed by a mob at Carthage, Illinois; Goodyear patents vulcanization process; Ralph Waldo Emerson, *Essays, Second Series*; George Lippard, *The Monks of Monk Hall*.

1845: Texas annexed; Ireland's potato crop fails, beginning mass migration to the United States; Henry Thoreau moves to Walden Pond; Margaret Fuller, *Woman in the Nineteenth Century*; Frederick Douglass, *Narrative of the Life of Frederick Douglass*; Alexandre Dumas, *The Count of Monte Cristo*.

1846: Mexican War (1846–48) begins; introduction of the cylinder press in the print industry; Herman Melville, *Typee*; Joel Tyler Headley, *Napoleon and His Marshals*.

1847: U.S. troops defeat Mexican armies; Mormons reach the Great Salt Lake; Henry Wadsworth Longfellow, *Evangeline*; Alphonse de Lamartine, *History of the Girondists*; Charlotte Brontë, *Jane Eyre*.

1852: Publishes *The Snow-Image and Other Twice-Told Tales*, *A Wonder-Book for Girls and Boys*, *The Blithedale Romance*, and *The Life of Franklin Pierce*; moves to "The Wayside" in Concord, Massachusetts, the former home of Bronson Alcott; 27 July, sister Louisa dies in a steamboat accident on the Hudson River.

1853: Appointed U.S. consul at Liverpool by President Pierce; leaves for England; *Tanglewood Tales for Girls and Boys* published.

1848: Gold discovered at Sutter's Mill in California, beginning the gold rush; Treaty of Guadalupe Hidalgo ends Mexican War; revolutions erupt throughout Europe; first women's rights convention held in Seneca Falls, New York; government troops kill thousands of workers during Bloody June Days in Paris; Whig Zachary Taylor elected president; Henry Thoreau delivers "Civil Disobedience" lecture; Karl Marx and Friedrich Engels, *Communist Manifesto*; James Russell Lowell, *The Bigelow Papers*.

Frontispiece to Nathaniel Hawthorne, A Wonder-Book for Girls and Boys *(1852). Pierpont Morgan Library, New York. PML 16664.*

"The Golden Touch." From Nathaniel Hawthorne, A Wonder-Book for Girls and Boys *(1852). Pierpont Morgan Library, New York. PML 16664.*

"Residence of Nathaniel Hawthorne, Concord, Massachusetts" ("The Wayside"). Engraving from Homes of American Authors *(1853).*

1854: Second, revised edition of *Mosses from an Old Manse* published.

1857: Resigns consulship.

1858: Travels to Italy by way of France; January to June resides in Rome; May to October lives near Florence, where he becomes friends with Robert and Elizabeth Barrett Browning.

1859: April, serious illness of daughter Una; returns to England.

1849: Astor Place riot in New York City leaves twenty-two dead; Margaret and Kate Fox in Rochester, New York, hold spirit-rapping sessions; Henry Thoreau, *A Week on the Concord and Merrimack Rivers*.

1850: Senator Daniel Webster of Massachusetts delivers speech on behalf of Compromise of 1850; Fugitive Slave Act goes into effect; Jenny Lind's tour (1850–52); Margaret Fuller dies in the shipwreck of the *Elizabeth*; Ralph Waldo Emerson, *Representative Men*; Susan Warner, *The Wide, Wide World*; Grace Greenwood, *Greenwood Leaves*.

Piaza Barberini, c. 1856–60. Photograph by Robert Macpherson. Gernsheim Collection, Harry Ransom Humanities Research Center, University of Texas at Austin.

Archangel Michael. *By Guido Reni, Courtesy Santa Maria della. Concezione, Rome.*

Faun. *By Praxiteles. Courtesy Capitoline Museum, Rome.*

Spiritualism handbill. Courtesy Rokeby Museum, Ferrisburgh, Vt.

1851: Shadrach, fugitive slave, rescued from Boston jail by mob of blacks; Herman Melville, *Moby Dick*, dedicated to Hawthorne.

1852: Democrat Franklin Pierce elected president; Herman Melville, *Pierre*; Harriet Beecher Stowe, *Uncle Tom's Cabin*.

1853: Crystal Palace Exhibition opens in New York City; Fanny Fern, *Fern Leaves from Fanny's Portfolio*.

1854: Republican party formed; Kansas-Nebraska Act passed; antislavery mob attacks courthouse in Boston in unsuccessful attempt to rescue fugitive slave Anthony Burns; Henry Thoreau, *Walden*; Maria Susanna Cummins, *The Lamplighter*.

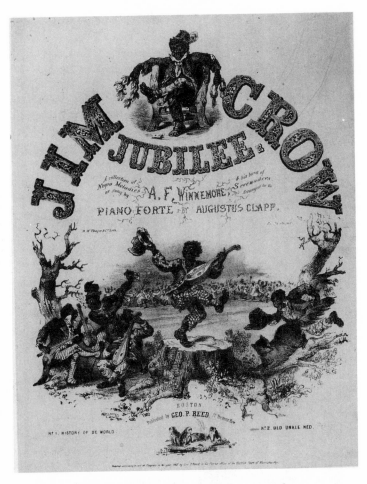

"Jim Crow" sheet music cover, 1847, Granger Collection, New York.

1860: Publishes *The Marble Faun*, produced in England under the title *Transformation* one month before the American edition appears in March; returns to the United States and the Wayside.

1855: Beginning of Bleeding Kansas; Massachusetts desegregates public schools; Henry Wadsworth Longfellow, *Song of Hiawatha*; Walt Whitman, *Leaves of Grass*.

"Georgine H. Thomas and Nurse." Undated daguerreotype. Courtesy Massachusetts Historical Society.

"The Branded Hand of Captain Jonathan Walker." Daguerreotype by Southworth and Hawes, c. 1845. Courtesy Massachusetts Historical Society.

1856: Know-Nothing movement begins; South Carolina representative Preston Brooks assaults Massachusetts senator Charles Sumner in the U.S. Senate; Ralph Waldo Emerson, *English Traits*; Herman Melville, *The Piazza Tales.*

1857: Supreme Court makes Dred Scott decision, denying rights of U.S. citizenship to Africans; financial panic.

1858: First stagecoach line runs from Missouri to Pacific coast; Lincoln-Douglas debates.

1859: John Brown leads raid on the arsenal at Harpers Ferry and is hanged for treason; the last ship to bring slaves to the United States, the *Clothilde*, arrives in Mobile Bay, Alabama; Charles Dickens, *A Tale of Two Cities*; George Eliot, *Adam Bede*; Charles Darwin, *Origin of Species.*

1860: Abraham Lincoln elected president; South Carolina secedes from the Union; South Carolina militia seizes federal arsenal at Charleston.

1861: Civil War (1861–65) begins with attack on Fort Sumter; Congress passes first income tax law as war finance measure; first battle of Bull Run; telegraph links East and West coasts; Harriet Jacobs, *Incidents in the Life of a Slave Girl*; Rebecca Harding Davis, *Life in the Iron Mills*; George Eliot, *Silas Marner.*

1862: Visits Horatio Bridge in Washington, D.C.; meets Abraham Lincoln; publishes "Chiefly about War-Matters" in the *Atlantic Monthly*.

1863: Publishes *Our Old Home*, dedicated to Franklin Pierce.

1864: 19 May, dies in his sleep at Plymouth, New Hampshire; 23 May, buried at Sleepy Hollow Cemetery in Concord, Massachusetts; four romances remain incomplete at his death: "Dr. Grimshawe's Secret," "Septimius Felton," "The Ancestral Footstep," and "The Dolliver Romance."

1862: Slavery abolished in federal territories; battles of Shiloh, Antietam, and second Bull Run; Victor Hugo, *Les Miserables*.

1863: Lincoln issues Emancipation Proclamation; New York City draft riots; battles of Chancellorsville, Gettysburg, and Chattanooga; Louisa May Alcott, *Hospital Sketches*.

1864: Sherman's march to the sea; Lincoln reelected.

"Punishing Slaves in Cuba." Photograph by C. D. Fredericks, from Harper's Weekly, *28 Nov. 1868, p. 753.*

Bibliographical Essay

Hawthorne and History

Leland S. Person

Historical studies of Hawthorne may be divided into two broad categories: those that emphasize his use of older historical settings, particularly the world of seventeenth-century Puritan New England, and those that emphasize his connections to the nineteenth-century world in which he wrote. Hawthorne knew his seventeenth-century New England history, but the trend in Hawthorne scholarship, as it is generally in American literary studies, is toward stressing the political and social context offered by the politically volatile world in which he lived. The decade of the 1990s was dominated by New Historicist analyses of Hawthorne and his writing, which place him within the context of that culture, often unflatteringly, because of what critics regard as his relatively conservative views toward questions of gender, class, and race.

Editions

The Centenary Edition of the Works of Nathaniel Hawthorne, begun in 1962 by Ohio State University Press and now complete in twenty-three volumes, contains virtually everything that Hawthorne wrote. Besides his five novels (*Fanshawe, The Scarlet Letter,*

The House of the Seven Gables, *The Blithedale Romance*, and *The Marble Faun*), three collections of tales (*Twice-Told Tales*, *Mosses from an Old Manse*, and *The Snow-Image*), and his sketches of English life, *Our Old Home*, the edition includes all of his extant letters (in six volumes), his *American Notebooks* (including a "lost" notebook rediscovered in 1976), *French and Italian Notebooks*, and *English Notebooks*, his children's tales (*True Stories from History and Biography* and *A Wonder Book and Tanglewood Tales*), the novels he left unfinished at his death (*The American Claimant* and *The Elixir of Life*), and a final volume of *Miscellaneous Prose and Verse*, which includes his 1852 campaign biography for presidential candidate Franklin Pierce.

Biographies

Hawthorne has been the subject of biographical and critical interest since his death in 1864, and the nineteenth-century reminiscences of his family members, including his son, Julian Hawthorne, daughter Rose Hawthorne Lathrop, son-in-law George Parsons Lathrop, and friends, such as Horatio Bridge and publisher James T. Fields, offer good starting places as long as readers make some allowances for bias. The most thorough and readable modern biography of Hawthorne is James R. Mellow's *Nathaniel Hawthorne in His Times* (1980). As his title suggests, Mellow is particularly sensitive to the historical and social context of Hawthorne's life, and he provides richly detailed accounts of Hawthorne's activities. Mellow's biography overshadowed Arlin Turner's *Nathaniel Hawthorne*, published in the same year, but Turner also emphasizes the connections between Hawthorne's writing and the cultural context in which he produced that writing. Since Mellow's and Turner's, biographical treatments of Hawthorne have become more pointedly focused. For example, Edwin Haviland Miller's *Salem Is My Dwelling Place* (1991) focuses on Hawthorne's personality, emotions, and family relationships. Hawthorne's early tale "The Gentle Boy" offers Miller a convenient paradigm for this Freudian analysis of Hawthorne's anxiety about his sexuality, his poverty, and attractive young women and men. Miller offers excellent analyses of Hawthorne's courtships of Mary Silsbee and Sophia Peabody and of his relationship with Herman Melville, which Miller casts in homoerotic terms.

T. Walter Herbert's *Dearest Beloved* (1993) is a psychocultural family biography and New Historicist expose of the "torments intrinsic to the domestic ideal," which dominated nineteenth-century life—and one of the most provocative views of Hawthorne and the Hawthorne marriage that we are ever likely to see. Herbert creates a family portrait "teeming with covert sexual politics," in which the Hawthornes' unresolved childhood traumas visit themselves upon their three children. Herbert keys each of four sections to one of the major romances and ingeniously interprets the conversation between life and art that such juxtaposition establishes. His best section involves *The Marble Faun*, the climactic family romance because of the psychic forces and characters that surfaced during the Hawthornes' Roman visit.

Psychologically grounded biographies like Miller's and Herbert's owe a debt to Frederick C. Crews's *The Sins of the Fathers: Hawthorne's Psychological Themes* (1966), the most significant book on Hawthorne in the 1960s. Crews wrote against earlier views of Hawthorne as a "dogmatic moralist," arguing instead that Hawthorne was a "self-divided, self-tormented man" (7), whose fiction is marked by psychological and moral ambiguity and whose plots feature a "return of the repressed" (17). He went on to argue that repressive forces in Hawthorne's psyche usually cause his plots to end in "symbolic amnesty" (24), but he emphasized Hawthorne's secret attraction to powerful forces of rebellion against restrictive paternal authority. Even though Crews subsequently questioned the reductionist tendency of the Freudian paradigm with which he worked, his psychological study of Hawthorne's fiction has had enormous influence on critics and biographers alike.

Other important biographical treatments of Hawthorne in the last twenty years of the twentieth century include Gloria C. Erlich's *Family Themes and Hawthorne's Fiction* (1984). Erlich emphasizes Hawthorne's early childhood experiences after his father's death, when his mother (Elizabeth Hathorne) moved him and his two sisters into the Manning family home, and he came under the influence of his maternal Uncle Robert Manning. She stresses three major themes: "maternal deprivation, paternal loss, and avuncular domination" (xvii). The latter influence, resulting from the Mannings' aggressively mercantile values, caused Hawthorne to doubt his literary vocation throughout his life, in Erlich's view, until he finally achieved a breakthrough with *The Scarlet Letter*. In her recent biography, *The Salem World of Nathaniel Hawthorne* (1998), Margaret B. Moore also emphasizes Hawthorne's early background, especially the conflicted legacy bequeathed him by his Salem ancestors, William Hathorne (notable for his punishment of Quakers) and John Hathorne (a judge in the Salem witchcraft trials). Moore provides the most comprehensive account we have of Hawthorne's Salem environment, his early education, and religious background. Particularly useful is her description of Salem's black population (133–44) and her assessment of Hawthorne's Democratic politics (169–98). At the other end of Hawthorne's life, Raymona E. Hull's *Nathaniel Hawthorne: The English Experience* (1980) provides expanded coverage of Hawthorne's English years, but it should be supplemented by Bryan Homer's *An American Liaison: Leamington Spa and the Hawthornes* (1998).

Criticism: Hawthorne and History

Approaching Hawthorne historically can mean many different things. Writers engage readers along a continuum of historical moments and with many different needs and purposes in mind. Jane Tompkins provoked many Hawthorne scholars in 1985, when she examined the "politics" of Hawthorne's literary reputation in *Sensational Designs*. Tompkins resituated Hawthorne *in history* by arguing that he has been aided at various times—and according to changing values—by a series of differently motivated patriarchal networks, which have promoted his writing and have prevented him from ever going out of style.

Any serious historical approach to Hawthorne needs to be informed about how his contemporaries responded to his work.

Many early reviews are conveniently available in Bertha Faust's *Hawthorne's Contemporaneous Reputation* (1968), B. Bernard Cohen's *The Recognition of Nathaniel Hawthorne* (1969), J. Donald Crowley's *Hawthorne: The Critical Heritage* (1970), and especially *Nathaniel Hawthorne: The Contemporary Reviews* (1994), edited by John L. Idol, Jr., and Buford Jones, which offers the best single collection of nineteenth-century responses to Hawthorne's work. Gary Scharnhorst's *The Critical Response to Nathaniel Hawthorne's "The Scarlet Letter"* (1992) is also especially valuable for nineteenth-century American and British reviews of Hawthorne's first major novel. Many of these reviews make it clear, as Tompkins points out, that the terms for assessing Hawthorne and his writing are historically grounded. Whereas twentieth-century readers have tended to value Hawthorne's dark psychological complexity and epistemological ambiguity, many early reviewers praised his sentimentality, domestic but spiritualized realism, and moral purity and beauty.

Other obvious questions involve Hawthorne's knowledge of history and American culture. Albeit in different ways, from the beginning, scholars have seen him as a historical writer. Hawthorne set many of his tales, as well as *The Scarlet Letter*, in seventeenth-century Massachusetts—usually in Salem or Boston—but many recent scholars suggest that even these fictional works have been inscribed with their nineteenth-century cultural context. Given Henry James's famous claim in his *Hawthorne* (1879), which appeared in Macmillan's English Men of Letters Series, that Hawthorne struggled with a paucity of American literary and historical materials, James would probably be surprised by the number of scholarly studies that connect Hawthorne directly and deeply with his nineteenth-century culture.

In arguing for the historicity of Hawthorne's nineteenth- and twentieth-century reputations, Tompkins claims that "a literary text exists only within a framework of assumptions which are historically produced" (19), and many of the historical studies that have dominated Hawthorne criticism in the 1990s seem rooted in that same assumption. Good starting places are Susan L. Mizruchi's, *The Power of Historical Knowledge* (1988) and J. Hillis Miller's *Hawthorne and History* (1991). Mizruchi limits her focus to *The House of the Seven Gables*, which she considers as "part of a cultural dialogue" on the "possibilities and limits of historical knowledge" (84). Like other New Historicists, Mizruchi emphasizes the literary text as a "vehicle of ideology," and she considers *Seven Gables* "exceptional" because it portrays the actual "process of creating an ideology" (85). That ideology is largely conservative, and for Mizruchi the novel is designed to defuse, evade, and ultimately harmonize social, political, and economic realities, particularly class conflict. Miller, too, examines a single text, "The Minister's Black Veil," and the theory of history and historical knowledge that may be inferred from it. Parson Hooper's "wearing of the veil," in Miller's view, "suspends two of the assumptions that make society possible: the assumption that a person's face is the sign of his selfhood and the accompanying presumption that this sign can in one way or another be read" (92). As Hawthorne represents it, history does not remain "safely stored up in traces, texts, memorials, records, vestiges, or material artifacts that can then later on be deciphered by future generations as the means of access to the original happening as it really happened" (113–14). In other words, there is no way to "get behind the veil"—or any other historical object of investigation—to "find out what is really going on back there." As historian, Miller's Hawthorne appears almost postmodern in his skeptical view of knowledge.

Most of the historical studies of Hawthorne in the 1990s emphasize his political and social attitudes. For whatever reason, the year 1991 featured the publication of numerous books on Hawthorne, many of them focusing on his vexed relation to his culture and its political turmoil. The most influential of these studies, Sacvan Bercovitch's *The Office of "The Scarlet Letter"* (1991), offers an excellent example of New Historicist cultural studies. Bercovitch assays Hawthorne's politics, and he seeks to "repoliticize" *The Scarlet Letter* (xvii) by examining its "profound ideological engagement" (xviii), which he considers a "prime instance" of literature as "cultural work" (xxi). Bercovitch focuses on the matter of Hester Prynne's return to Boston in the novel's epilogue. He explains that return and its political implications, particularly Hester's "conversion to the letter": erstwhile rebel, Hester becomes an "agent of the law," and the "new bond" she forms with the community "reconstitutes" her, "*as a marginal dissenter*, into an exemplum of historical continuity" (3). Bercovitch reads *The Scarlet Letter*, therefore, as a "subtle and devastating critique of radicalism" (6) that teaches us finally to "embrace gradualism and consensus" (17). Particularly influential has been Bercovitch's application of these ideas to the issue of nineteenth-century abolitionism, for he finds Hawthorne to be a purveyor of "thick propaganda" (89) in which the existence of slavery figures as a necessary evil, or stage, in America's progressive evolution (87).

Milton Stern, *Contexts for Hawthorne* (1991), and Charles Swann, *Nathaniel Hawthorne: Tradition and Revolution* (1991), cover some of the same ground, although without Bercovitch's historical particularity. Stern also finds Hawthorne in deep conflict with his culture and its politics, because he was "a representative Classicist conservative as a man and a vocational radical dissenter as a writer" (15). Stern takes for his example *The Marble Faun*, which illustrates the tension between romanticism and classicism, freedom and fate, the primitive and the social self, revolutionary radicalism and counterrevolutionary conservatism. "Hawthorne's books reveal a utopian conservatism," Stern concludes, "predicated upon a sense of history as repetitive and continuous, rather than progressive and perfectible or millennialistically discontinuous" (36). *The Marble Faun*, more than any other of his works, expresses the "fundamental conflicts" of Hawthorne's life: "American *ideological conservatism* was paradoxically a reflection of *utopian Romantic* assumptions about America; Hawthorne's Classicist *utopian conservatism* was paradoxically a *radical* contradiction of American ideological conservatism" (108). Swann believes that Hawthorne knew not only his history but his historiography, and he disagrees with Bercovitch and others who stress Hawthorne's "axis of conservatism" (4). He shows very clearly, for example, how in "Alice Doane's Appeal" and "Main-Street," Hawthorne foregrounds issues of historical truth and demonstrates the constructedness of all histories. He also makes an ingenious claim about the manuscripts Hawthorne left unfinished at his death—that they remained unfinished because historical events (especially the Civil War) threatened to destroy the world and historical setting he needed in order to finish them and because Hawthorne's skepticism about the possibility of writing a complete history made him reluctant to end his narrative.

Alide Cagidemetrio, *Fictions of the Past* (1992), on the other hand, discovers a more modern Hawthorne, more interested in "referentiality" than in "representation," who seems in the forefront of constructing a "modern historical consciousness." Hawthorne's "own symbolic method of writing history," Cagidemetrio argues, "presupposes the attitude of the archaeologist, who uncovers the palimpsestic writings of literature *and* historiography" (34). Hawthorne discards the "closure of both progressive historiography and of its literary counterpart, the classic historical novel" (47) and "enhances the subjective quality of any discourse of history" (53). To illustrate this subjective history, Cagidemetrio examines "Legends of the Province-House" and the unfinished "American Claimant" manuscripts.

In a profound and sometimes difficult study, Lauren Berlant, *The Anatomy of National Fantasy: Hawthorne, Utopia, and Everyday Life* (1991), examines Hawthorne's engagement in what she calls the "fantasy-work of national identity," and she ranges authoritatively between seventeenth- and nineteenth-century moments to explore Hawthorne's politics, particularly the representation of citizenship that may be inferred from his writing. Berlant zeroes in on the question of how "national culture becomes local—through the images, narratives, monuments, and sites that circulate through personal/collective consciousness" (5). *The Scarlet Letter* figures as prime example for its "privatization of national fantasy" (102). In contrast to Bercovitch, Berlant sees a "populist tinge" to Hawthorne's work, and she gives him more credit for critiquing and countering the "hegemonizing strategies and privileges of 'official' national identity" (7).

Several other scholarly studies examine one or more connections between Hawthorne and his nineteenth-century world. In three chapters of *American Romanticism and the Marketplace* (1985), Michael T. Gilmore brilliantly examines how "Rappaccini's Daughter," *The Scarlet Letter*, and *The House of the Seven Gables* illustrate Hawthorne's "pressing concern with the economies of authorship," especially his "difficulty in selling" his writing at a moment when literature was becoming a commodity of trade (53). The characters of Beatrice Rappaccini, Hester Prynne, and Hepzibah Pyncheon register Hawthorne's own deep anxieties about submitting himself—in literary form—to the public gaze in the marketplace. Gillian Brown also examines Hawthorne's implication in the economic sphere in *Domestic Individualism* (1990). Focusing separate chapters on *The House of the Seven Gables* and *The Blithedale Romance*, she explores the impact of the domestic cult of true womanhood on Hawthorne's conception of work. Through its angel in the house (Phoebe), she argues, *The House of the Seven Gables* unfolds a "domestic romance of transformative, invisible labor" (77) and "spiritualized" women's work, which protects women's bodies from marketplace excesses (79), both of these reflecting the "rise of American bourgeois domesticity" (93–94). Brown shifts from Marx to Freud (and fetishism) when she turns to *The Blithedale Romance*, and she focuses on Miles Coverdale's role as spectator within the context of a burgeoning nineteenth-century consumer culture. Despite Coverdale's effort to establish a "utopian consumerism" (110), she says, the novel depicts the "pitfalls of watching what nineteenth-century consumer culture creates"—the "convertibility" of viewers into objects (97). Coverdale's "strategic consumerism" (115) involves "self-protective psychic work" (117)—defense against homoerotic desire and desirability—that ends up revealing the "fetishist's bondage to his objects" (125). Richard H. Brodhead, *Cultures of Letters* (1993), also focuses on *The Blithedale Romance*, specifically, on the Veiled Lady (Priscilla) as a "figure for the disembodiment of women in nineteenth-century domesticity" (50). Hawthorne's novel explores the "cultural construction of a certain version of 'woman,'" Brodhead argues (51). As a public performer, Priscilla exemplifies women's emergence into public life, on the one hand, and a policing or disciplinary action, on the other hand, which results in their confinement to the private space of the home. Like Gilmore and Brown, Brodhead skillfully illustrates Hawthorne's attunement to cultural conflicts involving separate spheres of work, and his analysis of *Blithedale* is especially astute for the connections he makes to the newly emerging public entertainment industry (e.g., P. T. Barnum) in which Hawthorne necessarily had an authorial part.

Both Jean Fagan Yellin and Nancy Bentley explore Hawthorne's relationship to slavery and abolitionism by decoding subtexts in novels that keep such connections relatively hidden. In *Women and Sisters* (1989), as in her chapter in this volume, Yellin demonstrates Hawthorne's knowledge of the slave trade and illustrates the iconographic and discursive links between *The Scarlet Letter* and the abolitionist movement. She concludes, however, that Hawthorne rejects the liberationist discourse of anti-slavery women and "endorses patriarchal notions" (126). In *The Ethnography of Manners* (1995), Bentley explores connections between fauns and slaves in *The Marble Faun*, and through the mediating concept of primitivism, she shows how contemporaneous issues of race and race classification, which are prominent in Hawthorne's Italian novel, would have resonated with significance for American readers on the eve of the Civil War. Bentley argues finally that Hawthorne contains the "transgressions and freedoms" that he represents in his "dark" characters (Miriam and Donatello) by confining them to the Old World and to the realm of romance.

Most studies of Hawthorne and history consider American connections, but a few scholars have explored Hawthorne's interest in foreign affairs. Frederick Newberry, *Hawthorne's Divided Loyalties* (1987), analyzes Hawthorne's career-long interest in England, concluding that Hawthorne tried to recover an aesthetic inheritance that Americans lost when they achieved political independence from England. Like Michael Colacurcio (see below), Newberry claims that "Hawthorne's historiography adamantly resists a patriotic reading in any way commensurate with the democratic ideology of his time" (19). As an artist in the tradition of the English Renaissance, Hester Prynne in particular demonstrates the possibility of Old and New World compromise: democratic independence and aesthetic inheritance. In *European Revolutions and the American Literary Renaissance* (1988), Larry J. Reynolds discusses Margaret Fuller's influence on Hester Prynne's characterization and, more important, the response (a reactionary one) that the Italian revolution of 1849, as well as the English Civil War of 1642–49 and the first French Revolution of 1789, had on *The Scarlet Letter*. Luther Luedtke, *Nathaniel Hawthorne and the Romance of the Orient* (1989), also focuses on Hawthorne's knowledge of foreign culture and history—in this case, a lifelong fascination with the Orient, which developed from his extensive reading (especially in Eastern travel literature and *The Arabian Nights*). Like Reynolds, he presents a Hawthorne much more aware of non-Anglo world history and culture than most other scholars have credited him with being, but Luedtke moves the frame of Hawthorne's references considerably beyond the bounds of Western civilization, as he analyzes the Oriental subtext in some of Hawthorne's early tales and especially the orientalism of his "dark" heroines in "Rappaccini's Daughter" and the four major novels. Evan Carton, *"The Marble Faun": Hawthorne's Transformations* (1992), takes a different tack and one more common among New Historicist scholars, when he emphasizes how even a "foreign" setting can be inscribed with American political and cultural issues, such as "separate spheres" ideology and the racial tensions (inscribed in the ambiguous racial identities of Miriam and Donatello) of pre–Civil War America. In *Practicing Romance: Narrative Form and Cultural Engagement in Hawthorne's Fiction* (1992), Richard Millington reconstructs Hawthorne as a New Anthropologist. Synthesizing Freudian psychoanalysis, New Historicism, reader-response theory, and other critical methodologies, he provides a twist on an old idea: the interplay of individual and society in Hawthorne's fiction. Millington argues that the "neutral territory," which Hawthorne defines in "The Custom-House," represents a contested space in which he can perform revisionary cultural work, and he emphasizes the "disciplinary" power of Hawthorne's fiction to bridge the personal and the cultural.

Other critics explore Hawthorne's relation to particular nineteenth-century social movements. Taylor Stoehr, *Hawthorne's Mad Scientists* (1978), analyzes Hawthorne's keen interest in nineteenth-century pseudosciences—mesmerism, physiognomy, phrenology, homeopathy, associationism, spiritualism—feminism, and even prison reform, and he examines the influence of such "isms" on *The House of the Seven Gables* and *The Blithedale Romance* in particular. In a more extensive manner than he does in his chapter in this volume, Samuel Chase Coale, *Mesmerism and Hawthorne* (1998), examines the mesmerist-spiritualist "craze" in mid–nineteenth-century American culture and then relates it to Hawthorne's four major novels and selected tales. Even though Hawthorne despised mesmerism because of the way mesmerists dominated their mediums, Coale argues, "What mesmerism and spiritualism provided for Hawthorne was a reaffirmation of his own neo-Calvinist sensibility, his Puritan leanings, and his gothic imagination, underscoring his interest in the dynamics between master and slave, male and female, and mesmerist and medium" (6–7).

While the trend in Hawthorne scholarship is a New Historicist focus on how nineteenth-century political and social issues inscribe themselves on texts, there are many examples of an older historical approach to the question of Hawthorne's historical knowledge. The best recent exception to this New Historicist assumption is Michael Colacurcio's *The Province of Piety: Moral History in Hawthorne's Early Tales* (1984), which provides exhaustive, erudite analyses of selected tales (most notably, "The Gentle Boy," "The Minister's Black Veil," "Young Goodman Brown," and the four "Legends of the Province-House") in the context of their seventeenth-century and eighteenth-century settings. Colacurcio focuses on what Hawthorne knew from his readings in religious and political history, and the Hawthorne he depicts entered into richly nuanced debates with his moral historian precursors, which deconstruct their "pre-texts." Colacurcio's Hawthorne is "our first significant intellectual historian" (3), who "carried on a lifelong dialectic with the historical 'thesis' of American Puritanism" (1). Readers might usefully contrast Colacurcio's richly and deeply informed study with Roy R. Male's *Hawthorne's Tragic Vision* (1957), a good example of the classic "universalist" criticism—with its emphasis on sin and redemptive "moral growth"—upon which Colacurcio seeks to improve. One might also consult Carol Marie Bensick's *La Nouvelle Beatrice: Renaissance and Romance in "Rappaccini's Daughter"* (1985), a tour de force in the Colacurcio mode, which features a masterful analysis of the sixteenth-century Italian (Paduan) scientific background of Hawthorne's tale. Most provocative is Bensick's argument, based on solid historical evidence, that Giovanni Guasconti carries syphilis into Rappaccini's garden. Like Colacurcio, Bensick portrays a Hawthorne engaged in profound conversations with his historical sources.

Other valuable studies of Hawthorne's use of historical background materials include Michael Davitt Bell's *Hawthorne and the Historical Romance of New England* (1971), Neal Frank Doubleday's *Hawthorne's Early Tales: A Critical Study* (1972), John P. McWilliams, Jr.'s *Hawthorne, Melville, and the American Character* (1984), and George Dekker's *The American Historical Romance* (1987). Bell concerns himself less with the question of Hawthorne's historical accuracy than with the question of how he presents and interprets the past, especially within a context of more than two dozen nineteenth-century romances about Puritan New England. Reading Hawthorne less ironically than Colacurcio, Bell interests himself particularly in the way these historical romances represent a "battle between embryonic democracy and decadent authoritarianism" (8)—that is, in how they reflect nineteenth-century beliefs in an American progressivism, which had culminated in the American Revolution. Nineteenth-century romancers zeroed in on the contradiction, therefore, between the Puritans' "supposed advocacy of liberty and the actual denial of it" (13)—a theme that resonates especially in *The Scarlet Letter*. Doubleday focuses his attention closer to Hawthorne's own time by exploring the sources (both historical and literary) of his literary theory and practice, especially his use of local historical materials, which he gleaned from his voluminous reading. Unlike more recent scholars, who look for the political implications of Hawthorne's engagement with history, Doubleday assumes that history was important to Hawthorne "only as it was, or might be, literary material" (41). His source study remains valuable for placing Hawthorne's early writing within the context of other writing, both past and present.

Both McWilliams and Dekker examine linear connections among seventeenth-century, eighteenth-century, and nineteenth-century moments in American history, especially the relationship of the Puritan experiment to the American Revolution and then to the progressive movements associated with Jacksonian America. Like Lauren Berlant, McWilliams explores the concept of American national identity, or "character," which he derives from early republican rhetoric (e.g., from Crevecoeur, Tocqueville, and others). Whereas Berlant focuses on a national "imaginary," McWilliams interests himself in the way political ideals and rhetoric configure identity. Hawthorne's tales, he believes, "constitute a thorough study of New England's development" between the time of the first settlement and the aftermath of the Revolution (25), and he places these tales within the context of the "popular beliefs" that Hawthorne's readers would have brought to them (26). Grounded in political oratory and a patriotic rhetoric of consensus, those beliefs trace a straight line from "the Puritan character" (exemplified by John Winthrop) through revolutionary war filiopietism (associated with George Washington) to nineteenth-century American character. Hawthorne appears more skeptical, as he emphasizes a decline in the Puritan character beginning as early as 1640 before acknowledging a rebirth of "character" in the eighteenth century. McWilliams concentrates on how *Grandfather's Chair* and such early tales as "My Kinsman, Major Molineux" and "The Gray Champion" reflect the "march of New England civilization into progressive republicanism" (50), but he argues that Hawthorne differs from nineteenth-century orators both because he denies his readers the comfort of progressive rationalizations (about the Salem witch trials, for example) and "subtly challenges his age's assumptions about the Revolution" (80). In his survey of historical fiction in the *Waverley* tradition established by Sir Walter Scott, Dekker also examines Hawthorne's "filiopietistic reading of history," his efforts to reconcile "regional and national loyalties by highlighting those aspects of the New England past (e.g., Puritan love of 'liberty') which could be construed to foreshadow or, like seeds, contain the future nation" (129). Much like McWilliams, Dekker concludes that Hawthorne should be considered a "historical ironist" who recognized Puritan excesses (e.g., in the treatment of Ilbrahim in "The Gentle Boy" and Hester Prynne in *The Scarlet Letter*) and, despite being a "faithful

Democrat" (as he characterized himself in "The Custom-House"), recognized and exposed his own party's ideological weaknesses. The "recurrent theme" in Hawthorne's fiction, in short, is "American national survival and its human cost" (156).

Increased interest in Hawthorne's relation to his times has prompted publication of several valuable casebooks. In *Understanding "The Scarlet Letter": A Student Casebook to Issues, Sources, and Historical Documents* (1995), for example, Claudia Durst Johnson provides excerpts from seventeenth-century, nineteenth-century, and even twentieth-century documents to aid readers in developing various historical contexts for understanding the novel. In his edition of *The Blithedale Romance* (1996), William E. Cain provides a rich cultural context for understanding Hawthorne's novel by including selections of nineteenth-century works of social philosophy (especially on utopianism and women's rights).

What Frederick Crews did for those interested in Hawthorne's psychology, Nina Baym has done for those interested in Hawthorne's relation to issues of gender and sexuality. In a remarkable series of insightful essays in the early 1970s, culminating in *The Shape of Hawthorne's Career* (1976), Baym posited a romantic rather than Puritan or Christian Hawthorne, a man who secretly identified with his powerful and passionate female characters as they rebelled against patriarchal authority. In sharp contrast, in her provocative feminist study *Nathaniel Hawthorne* (1987), Louise DeSalvo considers Hawthorne complicit with those who victimize women, including Miles Coverdale in *The Blithedale Romance* and the Puritan patriarchs in *The Scarlet Letter*. DeSalvo terms the latter work a "revisionist history" (64) that "deflects attention away from the reality of Hester's utter powerlessness in the Puritan scheme" (65), and she concludes that the "universe of Hawthorne's fiction is an accurate representation of a patriarchy gone mad with misogyny"(122). Leland S. Person comes to a conclusion closer to Baym's in three chapters of *Aesthetic Headaches* (1988), as he focuses on female characters (including Hester) who refuse to be controlled by men—creating a paradigm of female empowerment and influence that can be observed in tales such as "Rappaccini's Daughter" and in each of the four major romances. Monica M. Elbert, *Encoding the Letter "A"* (1990), measures Hawthorne's representations of male and female characters against an androgynous ideal, and she concludes that Hawthorne anticipates many of the ideas of modern feminists. Male characters such as Robin Molineux, Reuben Bourne, and Goodman Brown struggle against patriarchal authority to discover and liberate their feminine or maternal selves. It is only Hester Prynne, in Elbert's view, who successfully "displaces patriarchal authority" and substitutes "creative mothering" and "creative artistry" (219–20). Whereas Elbert takes a mythopsychological approach to issues of Hawthorne and gender, Joel Pfister, *The Production of Personal Life* (1991), historicizes Hawthornian psychology by focusing on the intersection of gender and class (especially new, middle-class domestic values) in Hawthorne's fiction. In particular, he explores the question of why women in Hawthorne's fiction are "psychological targets of male monomaniacs in the home," and he concludes that Hawthorne critiqued the "sentimental construction of 'masculine' and 'feminine' roles upon which the economic and cultural ascendancy of his class relied" (8). Pfister's study exemplifies New Historicist criticism at its best, as he situates Hawthorne's writing ("The Birthmark," "Rappaccini's Daughter," and the four major romances) within a rich context of medical discourse, advice and conduct manuals, and Marxist and feminist theory. Pfister argues, for example, that in portraying Aylmer's victimization of Georgiana in "The Birthmark," Hawthorne is "operating within a discourse that biologizes cultural anxieties about creative women" (37). He considers Arthur Dimmesdale a "lubricious lad liberated from the pages of antimasturbation tracts of the 1830s and 1840s" (139). Elbert, Pfister, and Person credit Hawthorne with recognizing women's power and the constructedness of male and female gender roles, even as he critiques his male characters' failures (Miles Coverdale offers a representative example) to achieve the same liberal perspective. As Pfister puts it, Hawthorne "is a product, agent and critic of an emerging middle-class interiority" (183). Emily Miller Budick, *Engendering Romance* (1994), actually places Hawthorne at the head of a female and even matriarchal tradition of romance writing, which includes Carson McCullers, Flannery O'Connor, Toni Morrison, and Grace Paley (as well as Henry James and William Faulkner). Emphasizing consent rather than consensus, this protofeminist tradition of reliance on strong mothers, inaugurated in *The Scarlet Letter*, "has intimately to do with questions of choice and responsibility—in particular, with choosing a place within history and tradition and with assuming responsibility both for oneself and for one's progeny" (2).

One of the most compelling recent books on Hawthorne is Thomas R. Mitchell's *Hawthorne's Fuller Mystery* (1998), a tour de force that explores Hawthorne's obsession with Fuller throughout his writing career. Mitchell correlates dates and meetings, Fuller's letters and notebook entries with Hawthorne's (and often Emerson's), as he reconstructs the Hawthorne-Fuller relationship during the Old Manse years (1842–45). More interested in Fuller's emotional and psychological effect on Hawthorne than in the influence of her feminist ideas, Mitchell makes a persuasive case for Fuller's inspiration of the strong, mysterious women characters in "Rappaccini's Daughter," *The Scarlet Letter*, *The Blithedale Romance*, and *The Marble Faun*. Fuller challenged Hawthorne's conception of his own gender identity, Mitchell argues, and he considers Sophia Peabody Hawthorne and Fuller the "Strophe and Antistrophe" of Hawthorne's life and art (243). Because the connections are less expected in "Rappaccini's Daughter" and *The Scarlet Letter*, Mitchell's readings of those two narratives are truly groundbreaking in their originality.

Each of these studies takes a gynocentric approach to Hawthorne's views of women and his representation of male-female relationships. In *Manhood and the American Renaissance* (1989), David Leverenz explores Hawthorne's quarrel with contemporaneous models of manhood, which he depicts as "aggressive, insensitive, and murderously dominant" (231). Ingeniously, Leverenz analyzes Hawthorne's notorious ambiguity as a ploy, encouraging and then frustrating the reader's "will to power" (230)—unmanning him in the process. Male rivalries and a dominance-humiliation dynamic dominate Hawthorne's fiction (in "My Kinsman, Major Molineux," "Rappaccini's Daughter," and *The Scarlet Letter*, for example), culminating in the threat of homosexual rape (Coverdale by Hollingsworth) in *The Blithedale Romance*. Such questions about Hawthorne's sexual identity and especially his attitudes toward male-male relationships have most often arisen in discussion of his friendship with Herman Melville. In addition to Edwin Haviland Miller's speculations in his biographies of both Melville and Hawthorne, Monika Mueller's *This Infinite Fraternity of Feeling: Gender, Genre, and Homoerotic Crisis in Hawthorne's "The Blithedale Romance" and Melville's "Pierre"* (1996) assembles and examines both textual and extratextual evidence pointing toward the presence of homoerotic desire in Hawthorne's relationship with Melville, as well as in the novels (*The Blithedale Romance* and *Pierre*) in which each writer arguably represented their relationship.

"The history of Hawthorne's genius is in some sense a summary of all New England's history," George Parsons Lathrop wrote in his early study of Hawthorne (8), but the scholars whose work I have summarized in this essay have ranged much more widely in pursuing the author's relationship to history. Studies of Hawthorne and history show no signs of diminishing, and it seems likely that we shall see more scholarship that explores Hawthorne's connections to his nineteenth-century world in even more particularity. If Jane Tompkins's principle is correct—that "a literary text exists only within a framework of assumptions which are historically produced"—then the changing needs and assumptions of late twentieth-century and early twenty-first-century culture will produce new historically oriented angles of vision on Hawthorne. More work needs to be done on Hawthorne's sense of himself as a man, for example, and some of that work must engage questions about his sexual identification. Hawthorne's relationship to nineteenth-century utopianism offers another potential area for valuable research, and additional work can certainly be done on Hawthorne's views on racial differences. Whether or not Hawthorne's genius can reasonably be considered a summary of all of *America's* history, scholarly studies that examine Hawthorne's relationship to American culture and its history should flourish like rose bushes in the footsteps of Ann Hutchinson well into the twenty-first century.

Secondary Bibliography

Abel, Darrel. *The Moral Picturesque: Studies in Hawthorne's Fiction.* West Lafayette, Ind.: Purdue University Press, 1988.

Arac, Jonathan. "The Politics of *The Scarlet Letter,*" in *Ideology and Classic American Literature,* ed. Sacvan Bercovitch and Myra Jehlen, 247–66. New York: Cambridge University Press, 1986.

Arvin, Newton. *Hawthorne.* Boston: Little, Brown, 1929.

Baym, Nina. *"The Scarlet Letter": A Reading.* Boston: Twayne, 1986.

———. *The Shape of Hawthorne's Career.* Ithaca, N.Y.: Cornell University Press, 1976.

Becker, John E. *Hawthorne's Historical Allegory: An Examination of the American Conscience.* Port Washington, N.Y.: Kennikat, 1971.

Bell, Michael Davitt. *Hawthorne and the Historical Romance of New England.* Princeton, N.J.: Princeton University Press, 1971.

Bell, Millicent. *Hawthorne's View of the Artist.* New York: State University of New York Press, 1962.

———. *New Essays on Hawthorne's Major Tales.* New York: Cambridge University Press, 1993.

Bensick, Carol Marie. *La Nouvelle Beatrice: Renaissance and Romance in "Rappaccini's Daughter."* New Brunswick, N.J.: Rutgers University Press, 1985.

Bentley, Nancy. *The Ethnography of Manners: Hawthorne, James, Wharton.* Cambridge: Cambridge University Press, 1995.

Bercovitch, Sacvan. *The Office of "The Scarlet Letter."* Baltimore: Johns Hopkins University Press, 1991.

Berlant, Lauren. *The Anatomy of National Fantasy: Hawthorne, Utopia, and Everyday Life.* Chicago: University of Chicago Press, 1991.

Boswell, Jeanetta. *Nathaniel Hawthorne and the Critics: A Checklist of Criticism, 1900–1978.* Metuchen, N.J.: Scarecrow, 1982.

Bridge, Horatio. *Personal Recollections of Nathaniel Hawthorne.* New York: Harper, 1893.

Brodhead, Richard H. *Cultures of Letters: Scenes of Reading and Writing in Nineteenth-Century America.* Chicago: University of Chicago Press, 1993.

———. *Hawthorne, Melville, and the Novel.* Chicago: University of Chicago Press, 1976.

———. *The School of Hawthorne.* New York: Oxford University Press, 1986.

Brown, Gillian. *Domestic Individualism: Imagining Self in Nineteenth-Century America*. Berkeley: University of California Press, 1990.

Budick, Emily Miller. *Engendering Romance: Women Writers and the Hawthorne Tradition, 1850–1990*. New Haven, Conn.: Yale University Press, 1994.

Buitenhuis, Peter. *"The House of the Seven Gables": Severing Family and Colonial Ties*. Boston: Twayne, 1991.

Bunge, Nancy. *Nathaniel Hawthorne: A Study of the Short Fiction*. Boston: Twayne, 1993.

Cagidemetrio, Alide. *Fictions of the Past: Hawthorne and Melville*. Amherst: University of Massachusetts Press, 1992.

Cain, William E., ed. *The Blithedale Romance*. Boston: St. Martin's, 1996.

Cameron, Sharon. *The Corporeal Self: Allegories of the Body in Melville and Hawthorne*. Baltimore: Johns Hopkins University Press, 1981.

Cantwell, Robert. *Nathaniel Hawthorne: The American Years*. New York: Rinehart, 1948.

Carton, Evan. *"The Marble Faun": Hawthorne's Transformations*. New York: Twayne, 1992.

Clark, C. E. Frazer, Jr. *Nathaniel Hawthorne: A Descriptive Bibliography*. Pittsburgh, Pa.: University of Pittsburgh Press, 1978.

Coale, Samuel Chase. *In Hawthorne's Shadow: American Romance from Melville to Mailer*. Lexington: University Press of Kentucky, 1985.

———. *Mesmerism and Hawthorne: Mediums of American Romance*. Tuscaloosa: University of Alabama Press, 1998.

Cohen, B. Bernard, ed. *The Recognition of Nathaniel Hawthorne*. Ann Arbor: University of Michigan Press, 1969.

Colacurcio, Michael J. *The Province of Piety: Moral History in Hawthorne's Early Tales*. Cambridge, Mass.: Harvard University Press, 1984.

———, ed. *New Essays on "The Scarlet Letter."* Cambridge: Cambridge University Press, 1985.

Conway, Moncure D. *Life of Nathaniel Hawthorne*. New York: Lovell, 1890.

Crews, Frederick. *The Sins of the Fathers: Hawthorne's Psychological Themes*. New York: Oxford University Press, 1966.

Crowley, J. Donald, ed. *Hawthorne: The Critical Heritage*. New York: Barnes and Noble, 1970.

Dauber, Kenneth. *Rediscovering Hawthorne*. Princeton, N.J.: Princeton University Press, 1977.

Davidson, Edward H. *Hawthorne's Last Phase*. New Haven, Conn.: Yale University Press, 1949.

Dekker, George. *The American Historical Romance*. Cambridge: Cambridge University Press, 1987.

DeSalvo, Louise. *Nathaniel Hawthorne*. Atlantic Highlands, N.J.: Humanities Press, 1987.

Dolis, John. *The Style of Hawthorne's Gaze: Regarding Subjectivity*. Tuscaloosa: University of Alabama Press, 1993.

Donahue, Agnes McNeil. *Hawthorne: Calvin's Ironic Stepchild*. Kent, Ohio: Kent State University Press, 1985.

Doubleday, Neil Frank. *Hawthorne's Early Tales: A Critical Study*. Durham, N.C.: Duke University Press, 1972.

Dryden, Edgar A. *Nathaniel Hawthorne: The Poetics of Enchantment*. Ithaca, N.Y.: Cornell University Press, 1977.

Dunne, Michael. *Hawthorne's Narrative Strategies*. Jackson: University Press of Mississippi, 1995.

Easton, Alison. *The Making of the Hawthorne Subject*. Columbia: University of Missouri Press, 1996.

Elbert, Monica M. *Encoding the Letter "A": Gender and Authority in Hawthorne's Early Fiction*. Frankfurt, Germany: Haag & Herchen, 1990.

Elder, Marjorie J. *Nathaniel Hawthorne: Transcendental Symbolist*. Athens: Ohio University Press, 1969.

Erlich, Gloria C. *Family Themes and Hawthorne's Fiction: The Tenacious Web*. New Brunswick, N.J.: Rutgers University Press, 1984.

Faust, Bertha. *Hawthorne's Contemporaneous Reputation: A Study of Literary Opinion in America and England, 1828–1864*. New York: Octagon, 1968.

Fick, Rev. Leonard J. *The Light Beyond: A Study of Hawthorne's Theology*. Westminster, Md.: Newman, 1955.

Fields, James T. *Yesterdays with Authors*. Boston: Houghton Mifflin, 1871.

Fogle, Richard H. *Hawthorne's Fiction: The Light and the Dark*. Norman: University of Oklahoma Press, 1964.

————. *Hawthorne's Imagery: The "Proper Light and Shadow" in the Major Romances.* Norman: University of Oklahoma Press, 1969.

Gable, Harvey L., Jr. *Liquid Fire: Transcendental Mysticism in the Romances of Nathaniel Hawthorne.* New York: Peter Lang, 1998.

Gale, Robert L. *A Nathaniel Hawthorne Encyclopedia.* Boston: G. K. Hall, 1991.

Gilmore, Michael T. *American Romanticism and the Marketplace.* Chicago: University of Chicago Press, 1985.

Gollin, Rita K. *Nathaniel Hawthorne and the Truth of Dreams.* Baton Rouge: Louisiana State University Press, 1979.

Gollin, Rita K., and John L. Idol, Jr., eds. *Prophetic Pictures: Nathaniel Hawthorne's Knowledge and Uses of the Visual Arts.* Westport, Conn.: Greenwood, 1991.

Greenwald, Elissa. *Realism and the Romance: Nathaniel Hawthorne, Henry James, and American Fiction.* Ann Arbor: University of Michigan Press, 1989.

Hall, Lawrence Sargent. *Hawthorne: Critic of Society.* New Haven, Conn.: Yale University Press, 1944.

Harris, Kenneth Marc. *Hypocrisy and Self-Deception in Hawthorne's Fiction.* Charlottesville: University Press of Virginia, 1988.

Hawthorne, Julian. *Nathaniel Hawthorne and His Circle.* New York: Harper & Brothers, 1903.

————. *Nathaniel Hawthorne and His Wife: A Biography,* 2d ed. 2 vols. Boston: James Osgood, 1885.

Hawthorne, Nathaniel. *The Centenary Edition of the Works of Nathaniel Hawthorne,* ed. William Charvat et al. 23 vols. Columbus: Ohio State University Press, 1962–97.

Herbert, T. Walter. *Dearest Beloved: The Hawthornes and the Making of the Middle-Class Family.* Berkeley: University of California Press, 1993.

Hoeltje, H. H. *Inward Sky: The Mind and Heart of Nathaniel Hawthorne.* Durham, N.C.: Duke University Press, 1962.

Homer, Bryan. *An American Liaison: Leamington Spa and the Hawthornes, 1855–1864.* Rutherford, N.J.: Fairleigh Dickinson University Press, 1998.

Hull, Raymona E. *Nathaniel Hawthorne: The English Experience, 1853–1864.* Pittsburgh, Pa.: University of Pittsburgh Press, 1980.

Hutner, Gordon. *Secrets and Sympathy: Forms of Disclosure in Hawthorne's Novels*. Athens: University of Georgia Press, 1988.

Idol, John L., Jr., and Buford Jones, eds. *Nathaniel Hawthorne: The Contemporary Reviews*. New York: Cambridge University Press, 1994.

Idol, John L., Jr., and Melinda Ponder, eds. *Hawthorne and Women: Engendering and Expanding the Hawthorne Tradition*. Amherst: University of Massachusetts Press, 1999.

Jacobson, Richard J. *Hawthorne's Conception of the Creative Process*. Cambridge, Mass.: Harvard University Press, 1965.

James, Henry. *Hawthorne*. English Men of Letters Series. London: Macmillan, 1879.

Johnson, Claudia Durst. *The Productive Tension of Hawthorne's Art*. Tuscaloosa: University of Alabama Press, 1981.

———, ed. *Understanding "The Scarlet Letter": A Student Casebook to Issues, Sources, and Historical Documents*. Westport, Conn.: Greenwood, 1995.

Jones, E. Michael. *The Angel and the Machine: The Rational Psychology of Nathaniel Hawthorne*. Peru, Ill.: Sherwood Sugden, 1991.

Kesselring, Marion L. *Hawthorne's Reading, 1828–1850*. New York: New York Public Library, 1949.

Kesterson, David B., ed. *Critical Essays on Hawthorne's "The Scarlet Letter."* Boston: G. K. Hall, 1988.

Laffrado, Laura. *Hawthorne's Literature for Children*. Athens: University of Georgia Press, 1992.

Lathrop, George P. *A Study of Hawthorne*. Boston: Osgood, 1876.

Lathrop, Rose Hawthorne. *Memories of Hawthorne*. Boston: Houghton Mifflin, 1897.

Lee, A. Robert. *Nathaniel Hawthorne: New Critical Essays*. New York: Barnes and Noble, 1982.

Leverenz, David. *Manhood and the American Renaissance*. Ithaca, N.Y.: Cornell University Press, 1989.

Loggins, Vernon. *The Hawthornes: The Story of Seven Generations of an American Family*. New York: Columbia University Press, 1951.

Long, Robert Emmet. *The Great Succession: Henry James and the Legacy of Hawthorne*. Pittsburgh, Pa.: University of Pittsburgh Press, 1979.

Luedtke, Luther S. *Nathaniel Hawthorne and the Romance of the Orient*. Bloomington: Indiana University Press, 1989.

Lundblad, Jane. *Nathaniel Hawthorne and European Literary Tradition.* New York: Russell and Russell, 1965.

McCall, Dan. *Citizens of Somewhere Else: Nathaniel Hawthorne and Henry James.* Ithaca, N.Y.: Cornell University Press, 1999.

McPherson, Hugo. *Hawthorne as Myth-Maker: A Study in Imagination.* Toronto: University of Toronto Press, 1969.

McWilliams, John P., Jr. *Hawthorne, Melville, and the American Character: A Looking-Glass Business.* Cambridge: Cambridge University Press, 1984.

Male, Roy R. *Hawthorne's Tragic Vision.* Austin: University of Texas Press, 1957.

Martin, Terence. *Nathaniel Hawthorne*, rev. ed. Boston: Twayne, 1983.

Matthiessen, F. O. *American Renaissance: Art and Expression in the Age of Emerson and Whitman.* New York: Oxford University Press, 1941.

Mays, James O'Donald. *Mr. Hawthorne Goes to England: The Adventures of a Reluctant Consul.* Burley, England: New Forest Leaves, 1983.

Mellow, James R. *Nathaniel Hawthorne in His Times.* Boston: Houghton Mifflin, 1980.

Miller, Edwin Haviland. *Salem Is My Dwelling Place: A Life of Nathaniel Hawthorne.* Iowa City: University of Iowa Press, 1991.

Miller, J. Hillis. *Hawthorne and History: Defacing It.* Cambridge: Basil Blackwell, 1991.

Millington, Richard H. *Practicing Romance: Narrative Form and Cultural Engagement in Hawthorne's Fiction.* Princeton, N.J.: Princeton University Press, 1992.

Mitchell, Thomas R. *Hawthorne's Fuller Mystery.* Amherst: University of Massachusetts Press, 1998.

Mizruchi, Susan L. *The Power of Historical Knowledge: Narrating the Past in Hawthorne, James, and Dreiser.* Princeton, N.J.: Princeton University Press, 1988.

Moore, Margaret B. *The Salem World of Nathaniel Hawthorne.* Columbia: University of Missouri Press, 1998.

Moore, Thomas R. *A Thick and Darksome Veil: The Rhetoric of Hawthorne's Sketches, Prefaces, and Essays.* Boston: Northeastern University Press, 1994.

Mueller, Monika. *This Infinite Fraternity of Feeling: Gender, Genre, and*

Homoerotic Crisis in Hawthorne's "The Blithedale Romance" and Melville's "Pierre." Rutherford, N.J.: Fairleigh Dickinson University Press, 1996.

Newberry, Frederick. *Hawthorne's Divided Loyalties: England and America in His Works.* Rutherford, N.J.: Fairleigh Dickinson University Press, 1987.

Newman, Lea Bertani Vozar. *A Reader's Guide to the Short Stories of Nathaniel Hawthorne.* Boston: G. K. Hall, 1979.

Norman, Jean. *Nathaniel Hawthorne: An Approach to an Analysis of Artistic Creation,* trans. Derek Coltman. Cleveland, Ohio: Press of Case Western University, 1970.

Pearce, Roy Harvey, ed. *Hawthorne Centenary Essays.* Columbus: Ohio State University Press, 1964.

Person, Leland S. *Aesthetic Headaches: Women and a Masculine Poetics in Poe, Melville, and Hawthorne.* Athens: University of Georgia Press, 1988.

Pfister, Joel. *The Production of Personal Life: Class, Gender, and the Psychological in Hawthorne's Fiction.* Stanford, Calif.: Stanford University Press, 1991.

Ponder, Melissa M. *Hawthorne's Early Narrative Art.* Lewiston, Maine: Edwin Mellen, 1990.

Reid, Alfred S. *The Yellow Ruff and "The Scarlet Letter": A Source of Hawthorne's Novel.* Gainesville: University of Florida Press, 1955.

Reynolds, Larry J. *European Revolutions and the American Literary Renaissance.* New Haven, Conn.: Yale University Press, 1988.

Ricks, Beatrice, Joseph D. Adams, and Jack O. Hazlerig, eds. *Nathaniel Hawthorne: A Reference Bibliography, 1900–1971.* Boston: G. K. Hall, 1972.

Rosenthal, Bernard, ed. *Critical Essays on Hawthorne's "The House of the Seven Gables."* New York: G. K. Hall, 1995.

Scharnhorst, Gary, ed. *The Critical Response to Nathaniel Hawthorne's "The Scarlet Letter."* Westport, Conn.: Greenwood, 1992.

———, ed. *Nathaniel Hawthorne: An Annotated Bibliography of Commentary and Criticism before 1900.* Metuchen, N.J.: Scarecrow, 1988.

Schiff, James. *Updike's Version: Rewriting "The Scarlet Letter."* Columbia: University of Missouri Press, 1992.

Schubert, Leland. *Hawthorne the Artist: Fine-Art Devices in Fiction.* Chapel Hill: University of North Carolina Press, 1944.

Smith, Allan Gardner Lloyd. *Eve Tempted: Writing and Sexuality in Hawthorne's Fiction*. Totowa, N.J.: Barnes and Noble, 1984.

Stein, William Bysshe. *Hawthorne's Faust: A Study of the Devil Archetype*. Gainesville: University of Florida Press, 1953.

Stern, Milton R. *Contexts for Hawthorne: "The Marble Faun" and the Politics of Openness and Closure in American Literature*. Urbana: University of Illinois Press, 1991.

Stewart, Randall. *Nathaniel Hawthorne: A Biography*. New Haven, Conn.: Yale University Press, 1948.

Stoehr, Taylor. *Hawthorne's Mad Scientists: Pseudoscience and Social Science in Nineteenth-Century Life and Letters*. Hamden, Conn.: Shoe String, 1978.

Stubbs, John Caldwell. *The Pursuit of Form: A Study of Hawthorne and the Romance*. Urbana: University of Illinois Press, 1970.

Swann, Charles. *Nathaniel Hawthorne: Tradition and Revolution*. New York: Cambridge University Press, 1991.

Tharp, Louise Hall. *The Peabody Sisters of Salem*. Boston: McIntosh and Otis, 1950.

Thompson, G. R. *The Art of Authorial Presence: Hawthorne's Provincial Tales*. Durham, N.C.: Duke University Press, 1993.

Ticknor, Caroline. *Hawthorne and His Publisher*. Boston: Houghton Mifflin, 1913.

Tompkins, Jane. *Sensational Designs: The Cultural Work of American Fiction, 1790–1860*. New York: Oxford University Press, 1985.

Turner, Arlin. *Hawthorne as Editor: Selections from His Writings in the "American Magazine of Useful and Entertaining Knowledge."* Baton Rouge: Louisiana State University Press, 1941.

———. *Nathaniel Hawthorne: A Biography*. New York: Oxford University Press, 1980.

Van Doren, Mark. *Nathaniel Hawthorne: A Critical Biography*. New York: William Sloane, 1949.

von Abele, Rudolph. *The Death of the Artist: A Study of Hawthorne's Disintegration*. The Hague: Martinus Nijhoff, 1955.

von Frank, Albert J., ed. *Critical Essays on Hawthorne's Short Stories*. Boston: G. K. Hall, 1991.

Waggoner, Hyatt H. *Hawthorne: A Critical Study*, Rev. ed. Cambridge, Mass.: Harvard University Press, 1963.

———. *The Presence of Hawthorne*. Baton Rouge: Louisiana State University Press, 1979.

Weber, Alfred, Beth L. Lueck, and Dennis Berthold, eds. *Hawthorne's American Travel Sketches*. Hanover, N.H.: University Press of New England, 1989.

Wilson, James C. *The Hawthorne and Melville Friendship: An Annotated Bibliography, Biographical and Critical Essays, and Correspondence between the Two*. Jefferson, N.C.: McFarland, 1991.

Woodberry, George E. *Nathaniel Hawthorne*. 1902; rpt. New York: Chelsea House, 1980.

Yellin, Jean Fagan. *Women and Sisters: The Antislavery Feminists in American Culture*. New Haven, Conn.: Yale University Press, 1989.

Contributors

GILLIAN BROWN is professor of English at the University of Utah. She is author of *Domestic Individualism: Imagining the Self in Nineteenth-Century America* (California, 1990) and *The Consent of the Governed: The Lockean Legacy in Early American Culture* (Harvard, 2000).

SAMUEL CHASE COALE is A. Howard Meneely Professor of American Literature at Wheaton College (Mass.). His most recent books include *Mesmerism and Hawthorne: Mediums of American Romance* (Alabama, 1998) and *The Mystery of Mysteries: Cultural Differences and Designs* (Bowling Green, 2000). He is currently at work on a book about conspiracy in contemporary American fiction and culture.

RITA K. GOLLIN is Distinguished Professor of English at SUNY Geneseo. Her books include *Nathaniel Hawthorne and the Truth of Dreams* (LSU, 1979), *Portraits of Nathaniel Hawthorne: An Iconography* (Northern Illinois, 1983), *Prophetic Pictures* (with John Idol, Greenwood, 1991), and the forthcoming *Annie Adams Fields: Woman of Letters*.

LELAND S. PERSON is professor and head of the Department of English at the University of Cincinnati. He is author of *Aes-*

thetic Headaches: Women and a Masculine Poetics in Poe, Melville, and Hawthorne (Georgia, 1988) and numerous articles on nineteenth-century American authors. He is completing a study entitled *Henry James and the Suspense of Masculinity.*

LARRY J. REYNOLDS is professor of English and Thomas Franklin Mayo Professor of Liberal Arts at Texas A&M University. He is author of *European Revolutions and the American Literary Renaissance* (Yale, 1988), editor of *Woman in the Nineteenth Century* by Margaret Fuller (Norton, 1998), and coeditor of *National Imaginaries, American Identities* (Princeton, 2000).

BRENDA WINEAPPLE is Washington Irving Professor of Modern Literary and Historical Studies at Union College and codirector of the New York University Biography Seminar. Her most recent book is *Sister Brother: Gertrude and Leo Stein* (Johns Hopkins, 1997). She is currently writing a biography of Hawthorne.

JEAN FAGAN YELLIN is Distinguished Professor Emerita at Pace University. She is author of *The Intricate Knot: Black Figures in American Literature, 1776–1863* (NYU, 1972) and *Women and Sisters: the Antislavery Feminists in American Culture* (Yale, 1989) and editor of *Incidents in the Life of a Slave Girl* by Harriet Jacobs (Harvard, 1987). She is currently completing a biography of Jacobs.

Index

Page numbers in *italics* indicate illustrations.